SOUTH-EAST ASIA LANGUAGES AND LITERATURES

A SELECT GUIDE

Edited by
PATRICIA HERBERT
& ANTHONY MILNER

South-East Asia Library Group

UNIVERSITY OF
HAWAII PRESS
Honolulu

© 1989, The South East Asia Library Group

Published in North America by
University of Hawaii Press
2840 Kolowalu Street
Honolulu, Hawaii 96822

First published in the United Kingdom by
Kiscadale Publications
Whiting Bay
Arran KA27 8RH
Scotland

Library of Congress Cataloging-in-Publication Data

South-East Asia : languages and literatures, a select guide / edited
by Patricia Herbert and Anthony Milner.
    p.   cm.
   Bibliography: p.
   ISBN 0-8248-1267-0 (alk. paper) : $32.00
   1. Asia, Southeastern—Languages.   2. Southeast Asian literature-
-History and criticism.   I. Herbert, Patricia.   II. Milner, Anthony
Crothers. 1945-
PL3501.S66   1989
495—dc20   89-4839
                                                                    CIP

∞ The paper used in this publication meets the minimum requirements
of American National Standard for Information Sciences—Permanence of
Paper for Printed Library Materials
                                                   ANSI Z39.48-1984

Contents

Contributors		vi
Preface and Acknowledgements		vii
Abbreviations		ix
Map		x
Burma	Anna Allott, Patricia Herbert, John Okell	1
Thailand	P.J. Bee, I. Brown, Patricia Herbert Manas Chitakasem	23
Cambodia	Khing Hoc Dy, Mak Phoeun	49
Laos	P.-B. Lafont	67
Vietnam	Nguyen The Anh	77
Malaysia	R.A. Jones, Ibrahim bin Ismail, E.U. Kratz, A.C. Milner, N.G. Phillips	99
Indonesia	C.D. Grijns, A.J.W. Huisman, W.J. O'Malley, J.J. Ras, S. Robson, R. Roolvink, A. Teeuw	123
Philippines	Helen Cordell, A.C. Milner	153
Overseas Chinese	J.A.C. Mackie, A.C. Milner, Claudine Salmon	171

Contributors

ALLOTT, Anna	SOAS (University of London)
BEE, Peter	SOAS (University of London)
BROWN, Ian	SOAS (University of London)
CORDELL, Helen	SOAS (University of London)
GRIJNS, C.D.	Rijksuniversiteit te Leiden
HERBERT, Patricia	Oriental Collections, British Library
HOOKER, M.B.	University of Kent at Canterbury
HUISMAN, A.J.W.	Rijksuniversiteit te Leiden [retired]
IBRAHIM bin ISMAIL	University of Malaysia
JONES, Russell	SOAS (University of London) [retired]
KHING HOC DY	Musée de l'Homme, Paris
KRATZ, E.U.	SOAS (University of London)
LAFONT, Pierre-Bernard	Ecole Pratique des Hautes Etudes, IVe Section, Sorbonne
MACKIE, J.A.C.	Australian National University
MAK PHOEUN	Centre National de la Recherche Scientifique, Paris
MANAS CHITAKASEM	SOAS (University of London)
MILLER, W.G.	Australian National University
MILNER, A.C.	Australian National University
NGUYEN THE ANH	Centre National de la Recherche Scientifique, Paris
OKELL, John	SOAS (University of London)
O'MALLEY, W.J.	Australian National University
PHILLIPS, Nigel	SOAS (University of London)
RAGEAU, Christiane	Ecole Française d'Extrême-Orient, Paris
RAS, J.J.	Rijksuniversiteit te Leiden
ROBSON, S.	Rijksuniversiteit te Leiden
ROOLVINK, R.	Rijksuniversiteit te Leiden [retired]
SALMON, Claudine	Centre National de la Recherche Scientifique, Paris
TEEUW, A.	Rijksuniversiteit te Leiden

Preface and Acknowledgements

South-East Asia is an important world region comprising ten separate nation states which together encompass a vast range of languages, literatures and religions, cultural and political backgrounds. Scholars of the region no longer rely on source materials in European languages but have increasingly turned to indigenous South-East Asian materials. An ever-increasing number of publications on South-East Asia reflects the growing interest in South-East Asian studies and source materials. This *Guide* was conceived by members of the South-East Asia Library Group (a UK based group of librarians and scholars with specialist interests in the region), who felt there was a need for a concise introduction to the history, major languages, scripts, dating systems, manuscripts, printing and publishing histories, and literary genres of South-East Asia. Such information has up till now proved hard to locate and the *Guide* presents the required range of information in a single work. Not only designed for newcomers to South-East Asian studies, the *Guide* is also intended to be comprehensive enough to be of value to librarians and scholars as a quick reference source, particularly for bibliographical advice.

Within each chapter of the *Guide*, material is arranged in this order: historical introduction; dating systems; languages and scripts; manuscripts; printing and the development of the press; literature (including legal literature). Short references are given in the text and a bibliography provided at the end of each country section.

The compilation of the guide has been a protracted collective effort, with contributions from scholars and librarians at academic institutions in Britain, France, the Netherlands, South-East Asia and Australia. The editors are responsible for imposing overall as uniform a style as possible and for updating the original contributions, as well as for the translation of the original French texts on Cambodia, Laos and Vietnam and some of the Dutch sections on Indonesia. As well as the main contributors, the editors wish to thank the following for their advice, comments and assistance: David Chandler, Jennifer Cushman, Ariel Daigre, Jeremy Davidson, A. Day, A. Diller, Dennis Duncanson, Annabel Gallop, Henry Ginsburg, Arthur Godman, Judith Jacob, R.S. Karni, David Marr, Geoffrey Marrison, Virginia Matheson, Kate Milner, Nguyen Ngoc Tri, Milton Osborne, Norman Owen, Anthony Reid, M.R. Séguy, Ralph Smith, Alexandra Sun, J.L. Swellengrebel, B. Terwiel, William Wilder, Christine Wise, M. Winship, and Marasri Wongratana. Our thanks also to Barry Hooker, University of Kent, who kindly agreed to contribute notes on legal literature to some sections, and to George Miller, Australia National University, for providing considerable bibliographic assistance and information on publishing and periodicals. We are also grateful to William Frederick, Ohio University, for his help in restructuring certain sections and for first encouraging the *Guide*'s publication.

The editors also particularly wish to thank Madame Christiane Rageau, Ecole Française d'Extrême-Orient, for undertaking the task of co-ordinating and advising on the French contributions to the *Guide*. The editors regret that lack of comparable material in other sections prevented the inclusion of the French contributions by Saveng Phinith on People of the Central Indochinese Peninsula without a Written Language and by Po Dharma on Champa. We are also indebted to Dr C.D. Grijns of Rijksuniversiteit te Leiden, for organizing and co-ordinating the Dutch contributions on Indonesia. Lastly, special thanks are due to the Arts Faculty, Australian National University, for financial and typing assistance in the initial stages of the work. Illustrations are reproduced by kind permission of the British Library.

Patricia Herbert
Oriental Collections, British Library, London

Anthony Milner
Arts Faculty, Australian National University, Canberra

Abbreviations

BEFEO	Bulletin de l'Ecole Française de l'Extrême-Orient
BKI	Bijdragen van het Koninklijk Instituut voor Taal-, Land-, en Volkenkunde
BSEI	Bulletin de la Société des Etudes Indochinoises
BSOAS	Bulletin of the School of Oriental and African Studies
CEDRASEMI	Centre de Documentation et de Recherches sur l'Asie de Sud-Est et le Monde Insulindien
CNRS	Centre National de la Recherche Scientifique
CORMOSEA	Committee on Research Materials on Southeast Asia (USA)
HRAF	Human Relations Area Files
IOLR	India Office Library and Records, the British Library
ISEAS	Institute of Southeast Asian Studies, Singapore Library
JA	Journal Asiatique
JAOS	Journal of the American Oriental Society
JAS	Journal of Asian Studies
JBRS	Journal of the Burma Research Society
JMBRAS	Journal of the Malaysian Branch, Royal Asiatic Society
JSBRAS	Journal of the Straits Branch, Royal Asiatic Society
JSEAH	Journal of Southeast Asian History
JSEAS	Journal of Southeast Asian Studies
JSS	Journal of the Siam Society
KITLV	Koninklijk Instituut voor Taal-, Land-, en Volkenkunde
RIMA	Review of Indonesian and Malayan Affairs (Sydney, Dept of Indonesian and Malayan Studies, University of Sydney)
SEALG	South-East Asia Library Group
SEARMG	Southeast Asian Research Materials Group (Australia)
SELAF	Société d'Etudes Linguistiques et Anthropologiques de France
SOAS	School of Oriental and African Studies, University of London
TBG	Tijdschrift van het Bataviaasch Genootschap van Kunsten en Wetenschappen
VBG	Verhandelingen van het Bataviaasch Genootschap van Kunsten en Wetenschappen
VKITLV	Verhandelingen van het Koninklijk Instituut voor Taal-, Land-, en Volkenkunde

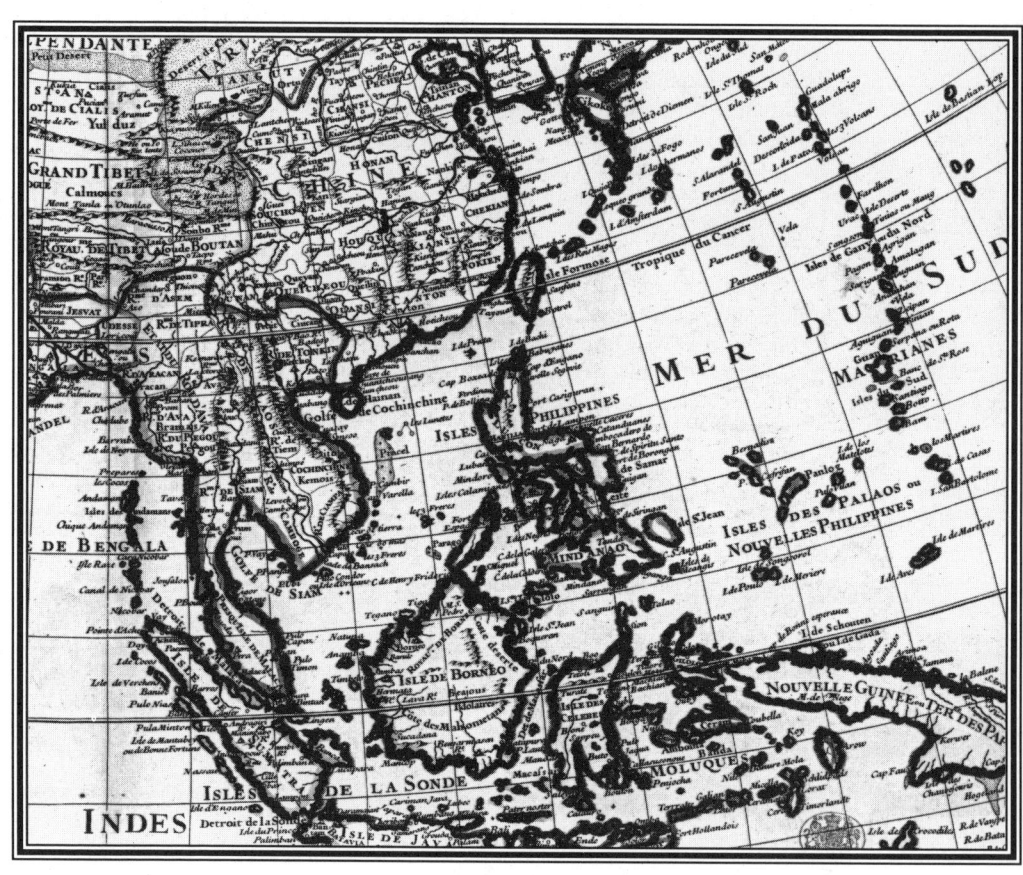

French map of China and South-East Asia, 1723

Burma

Burma, the largest country of mainland South-East Asia, is separated from neighbouring India, China and Thailand by barriers of mountain ranges. The interior divides into highland areas, inhabited by hill peoples such as the Kachin, Chin and Karen, and a lowland area running 700 miles north to south along the valleys of the Chindwin, Irrawaddy and Sittang rivers. This lowland area in turn divides naturally into a dry zone (Upper and Central Burma) and the fertile plains and deltas of Lower Burma. The dry zone, centred on the confluence of the Chindwin and Irrawaddy rivers, has been the historic heartland of the Burmans, the largest of Burma's ethno-linguistic groups, constituting about 60% of a total population of approximately 35,310,000 (1983 census).

The Burmans, migrating from the northeast, moved into the dry zone and established settlements from about the 9th century. They came into contact with, and absorbed, an early people known as the Pyu, whose ancient cities — Sriksetra (near Prome), Beik-thano (Vishnu City) and Halin — attest to the influence of Hinduism and Buddhism from India. The Burmans' southward expansion also brought them into contact with the highly-cultured Mon, an ethnically and linguistically distinct people. There were important Mon settlements in Lower Burma (classically called Ramannadesa) at Thaton and Pegu, although the real centre of Mon civilisation lay further to the east in the lower Menam valley of present-day Thailand, where the Mon kingdom of Dvaravati flourished until the 11th century. The Shan were the third group of importance in the lowlands, a Tai people who were part of a general southward migration into the Menam basin.

The main theme of Burma's history up to the 19th century was the struggle for ascendancy and for control of resources among Burmans, Mons and Shans, as a consequence of which the centre of power alternated between the Upper and Lower regions of Burma. A subsidiary theme concerns Burman efforts to annex the ancient kingdom of Arakan (centred from the early 15th century at Mrohaung) which was finally conquered in the late 18th century. Burma's other ethnic groups, being hill peoples, generally remained isolated from the territorial and dynastic struggles of the lowlands. In the mid-11th century, the early Burman settlements were consolidated under one ruler, King Anaw-rahta (1044-1077), who is regarded as the founder of the Pagan dynasty and empire. Pagan brought the Mon under its political control and in the process found itself considerably enriched by Mon cultural influence. A golden age of art and architecture followed and Theravada Buddhism became firmly established as a popular — rather than merely a court — religion, while Mahayana, Tantric and Hindu elements diminished. Thousands of great Buddhist temples were built in Pagan and its environs, hundreds of which still stand. The Mongol invasion of Pagan in 1287-1288 and the ambitions and the ambitions of Shan chiefs at this time, hastened Pagan's decline and eventual fragmentation into Mon, Burman and Shan states.

The Burmans were only gradually able to reassert their hegemony over the Mon (based at Pegu) and the Shan (based at Ava). The Taung-ngu (Toungoo) dynasty, founded in 1485, and the Kon-baung dynasty, founded in 1752, re-established through vigorous military campaigns and administrative consolidation a Burman hegemony over an area roughly equivalent to the boundaries of modern Burma. The early Taung-ngu dynasty was centred first at Taung-ngu and then at Pegu in the Lower Burma delta, but in 1635 the capital was moved to Ava in the dry zone. Upper Burma was to remain the heartland of the Burman empire (the capital changing from Ava to Amarapura to Mandalay) until 1885. In the 19th century, following bitter disputes about commercial and diplomatic relations, the British took over Burma in three stages: Arakan and Tenasserim provinces in 1826, Lower Burma in 1852 and the remaining kindom of Upper Burma in 1885. The last king of Burma, Thi-baw, was sent with his family to a long exile in India.

British Burma was ruled as a province of British India. From 1862 the principal colonial officer was a Chief Commissioner responsible to the Government of India; after 1897 rule was exercised by a Lieutenant-Governor and beginning in 1923 by a Governor and a Legislative Council with a majority of elected members in a system known as dyarchy. The Legislative Council, however, controlled only certain aspects of government and administration. Nationalist politics of the 1920s were led by the General Council of Buddhist Associations (GCBA), which had evolved from the Young Men's Buddhist Association (YMBA), but split into factions over the issue of whether to participate in or boycott the Legislative Council and whether to support or oppose separation from India. In 1937, as provided for in the Government of Burma Act of 1935, the administration of Burma was separated from that of India and a bicameral legislature was introduced. The 1930s saw the rise of the Dobama Asi-ayon (We Burmans Association) of the *thahkin* ('master') nationalists. The experience of the Japanese occupation of Burma from 1942 and the formation of the Burma Independence Army under General Aung San, ensured that at the end of the war the British would find it impossible to deny Burmese nationalist demands for independence. In accordance with the Aung San-Attlee Agreement of January 1947, elections were held in which Aung San's Anti-Fascist People's League (AFPFL) won a large majority. Before the new Constituent assembly could prepare for independence, however, Aung San and six members of the Executive were assassinated on 19th July 1947. On 4th January 1948, Burma became a fully independent state and chose not to join the British Commonwealth. The unity of the newly independent state, with U Nu as prime minister, was threatened at the outset by insurrection and, above all, by the rebellion of the Karen National Defence Organization.

The parliamentary system of government ended in 1958 when U Nu asked the head of the army, General Ne Win, to form a caretaker government. Elections were held in February 1960 and U Nu formed another government, but was overthrown by Ne Win in a coup on 2nd March 1962. Henceforth, power was invested in the military's Revolutionary Council and the country embarked on the political and economic path outlined in *The Burmese Way to Socialism* and formulated by a single political party, the Burma Socialist Programme Party (BSPP). In 1971, Ne Win and other leading military figures renounced their military rank. In 1974, a new constitution, a Council of State and a People's Assembly were introduced. In July 1988, Ne Win's resignation as chairman of the BSPP and the country's deteriorating economy led to mass demonstrations and calls for a multi-party system and free elections. On 18th

September 1988, the military under General Saw Maung resumed control of the country.

For bibliographies of Burma see **Aung Thwin** (1979), **Bernot** (1968 and 1983) and **Trager** (1973). For a bibliography of theses on Burma, see **Shulman** (1986). For a general compendium of information, see **Bunge** (1983). On ethnic groups, **LeBar** (1964) still offers broadest coverage. On religion, **Spiro** (1970) is a standard work. Useful general histories are **Harvey** (1967), **Htin Aung** (1967) and the introduction to **Trager** and **Koenig** (1979). On early Burma and Pagan, see **Luce** (1969-70) and **Aung Thwin** (1985). On the 16th to 18th centuries, **Lieberman** (1984) is indispensable. On the early nationalist period, **Moscotti** is helpful, though by no means complete. For a general introduction to modern Burma, see **Cady** (1960) and **Steinberg** (1982). On the post-1962 period, see **Silverstein** (1977) and the more cursory **Steinberg** (1981). **Taylor** (1987) puts contemporary Burma in historical perspective and provides the most up-to-date information.

Dating Systems

All government and administrative matters, including national political holidays, are regulated by the Christian era and the Gregorian calendar. The Christian era is known in Burmese as *hkarit hnit* or 'Christian year'. Religious and cultural festivals are regulated by the Burmese era (BE), now known as *myan-ma thet-gayit* or *myan-ma hnit* and sometimes called *kaw-za thet-gayit*, which is counted from 638 AD. The Buddhist era (*tha-thana thet-gayit*) dates from 544 BC, the traditional date of the Buddha's attainment of *nirvana*. Manuscripts and older texts in general use the Buddhist era and/or the Burmese era. Modern printed books mostly give an imprint in the Christian era, although some presses, such as the Hanthwaddy Press, still give the year of publication according to all three systems. For example:

Buddhist	*Tha-thana* 2524
Burmese	*Kaw-za* 1342
Christian	May 1980

As the starting dates on the Burmese era and the Christian calendar years do not coincide, two figures are needed to convert BE dates to AD dates: for BE dates in the months *Tagu* to *Nadaw*, add 638; for BE dates in the months *Pyatho* and *Tabo-dwe*, add 639. To convert Buddhist era dates to AD dates: for Buddhist era dates in the months *Tagu* to *Kahson*, subtract 543; for Buddhist era dates in the months *Kahson* to *Tabaung*, subtract 544. Old Mon and Old Burmese inscriptions give, in addition to the Burmese era date, a year name from the 12 year cycles. Unlike the Cambodians, Lao and Thai, the Burmese did not use animal names for the months but followed the Sanskrit practice of calling the years by the names of the months.

The Burmese calendar is a lunar one. As the mean lunation is a little over 29 days, Burmese months contain alternately 29 and 30 days. To make up the remainder, approximately seven intercalary months are required in 19 years. The intercalary month always has 30 days, is inserted between *Wa-zo* and *Wa-gaung* and is called 'second *wa-zo*'.

On the old Burma calendar, see **Luce** (1969-70, vol 2); on the modern Burmese lunar calendar, see **Irwin** (1909).

Languages

Several hundred languages and dialects are spoken by the indigenous population of Burma. These can be classified into four large language families:

Tai: the Shan language and its relatives, spoken mainly in the Shan states.
Austro-asiatic: Mon, spoken in the Mon State, around Moulmein; Palaung, Wa and others, spoken in parts of the Shan states.
Malay-Polynesian: Salon and Moken, spoken in the islands of the Mergui Archipelago.
Sino-Tibetan: the largest and most important language family, which consists largely of the Tibeto-Burman group of languages divided into a) the Burmese-Lolo subgroup of Burmese and its close relatives Maru, Lashi, Atsi and others, spoken throughout the central plains, and Lolo, with its relatives Akha, Lahu, Lisu and others, spoken in parts of the Kachin and the Shan states; b) the Kuki-Naga subgroup of Chin and its dialects, spoken along the Assam border; c) the Kachin subgroup of Kachin (also called Jingpaw) and its dialects, spoken in the Kachin State. Outside the Tibeto-Burman group is Karen, of which the two best-known varieties are Sgaw and Pwo, spoken in the Karen and Kayah States and in parts of the Irrawaddy delta.

Besides the indigenous languages, different varieties of Chinese and South Asian languages are spoken in Burma. English, while not the mother tongue of any significant portion of the population, is widely studied as a second language and is used for a few publications. Since 1985 English has been used for all university teaching. Burmese, of course, is the medium of instruction in schools and is the language of government, so the number of persons speaking Burmese is considerably larger than for those for whom it is not the mother tongue.

The latest available and reliable figures indicating what proportions of Burma's people speak which language are contained in the 1931 census. These indicate that Burmese is spoken by 67% of the population, Karen by 9%, Indic languages by 7%, Kachin by 3%, Mon and Chin by 2% each and Palaung by 1%. Censuses were also held in 1973 and 1983, but no figures for language speakers are yet available.

On different languages, see the appropriate sections and map in **LeBar** (1964). Studies on the Sino-Tibetan languages are listed in **Shafer** (1957 and 1963) and on the Tibeto-Burman languages in **Hale** (1982). For Karen dialects, see **Jones** (1961); for Tiddim Chin, **Henderson** (1965); for Lahu, **Bradley** (1979) and **Matisoff** (1973); and for Lisu, **Roop** (1970). **Huffman** (1986) is a comprehensive listing of all languages and linguistic studies.

Burmese Language

The earliest dated examples of written Burmese are from the early 12th century. Most are from the old capital at Pagan and consist largely of records incised on stone slabs. There are also, however, fragments of Burmese of this period written in ink on palm leaf and on plastered walls. This phase of the language is known as Old Burmese. Though there are some striking differences between Old Burmese and contemporary Burmese, it is remarkable how little the language has changed in structure and vocabulary over the centuries.

Some writers refer to Middle Burmese, covering the period from perhaps 1500 to 1700, and to modern Burmese, from about 1700 on. These terms, however, are less relevant to the structure and vocabulary of the language than to its orthography, which has undergone some changes. From an early date, perhaps the 16th century, certain pairs of sounds which were distinct in Old Burmese merged with each other. This gave rise to confusion over the spelling of words containing merged sounds. From the 18th century onwards, scholars compiled spelling books, listing words and their alternative spellings. The latest, *Myan-ma sa-lon-baung that-pon kyan,* was prepared by scholars at the request of the Burmese government and in 1978 became the basis of the official orthography.

Burmese differs markedly from Western European languages in a number of ways. It has no agreement, for example, either with gender or number; words are formed by compounding rather than derivation; the Burmese equivalent of prepositions follow the word they modify rather than precede it; verbs are always placed at the end of a sentence; relative clauses always precede their head and classifiers or numeratives are used extensively.

External influence on Burmese has come mainly from Pali and English. Pali, the language of Theravada Buddhism, was known to the Burmese since before our first records of the language and Pali loan words are found from the earliest times. The obvious need for loans was in the field of religion (for example, words for *nirvana, karma,* monk, hell), but Pali also yielded terms in other areas (for example, garden, mind, method) and, interestingly enough, continues to do so today (for example, words for entomology, science, spacecraft, department, professor, president). Pali has also influenced the structure of Burmese in some respects, a result of the centuries-old tradition of making literal translations (*nissaya*) from Pali into Burmese.

Influence from English was inevitable during British rule. Loan words are found in the predictable fields (car, telephone, radio, plug, committee, cadre, coupon). There are also some loans from Sanskrit (mostly early, in the fields of Buddhism, philosophy and grammar), from the Chinese (in the fields of games and food) and from Indic languages (in the fields of food, administration and shipping). Loans fom Mon are long-standing and are not nowadays generally perceived as loans by native speakers. They cover a wide range of fields, including flora and fauna, administration, textiles, foods, boats, crafts, architecture and music.

In contrast to the languages of the ethnic minorities, Burmese is remarkably uniform throughout the area in which it is spoken. There are a few vocabulary differences between Mandalay and Rangoon and between these and other regions, but pronounciation is virtually indistinguishable from region to region.

Recognized dialects are Arakanese (famous for preserving an 'r' sound which standard Burmese has almost completely lost), Tavoyan, In-tha (on In-lei Lake in the Shan states), Yaw (around Gan-gaw) and one or two others. The difference between dialect and standard varies according to the dialect.

A language variation that is more important for foreigners than difference of dialect is one usually referred to as a difference of style, that is, the difference between written (literary or formal) Burmese on the one hand and spoken (colloquial or informal) Burmese on the other. The distinction lies largely in the choice of words. Certain items are restricted to the written style and others to the spoken. Despite the labels 'written' and 'spoken', it is possible to write 'spoken' Burmese and to speak, or at least, read aloud, 'written' Burmese. Spoken Burmese is used for everyday conversation and is written in informal letters and in the dialogue passages of novels. Written Burmese is used for reading news bulletins on the radio (but not for television and other broadcast materials) and for writing formal letters and comments, the narrative portions of novels and virtually all serious books and journalism. The distinction between the two styles is not now wholly clear. Uses that would once have been regarded as strictly colloquial are increasingly being used and accepted in what is ostensibly literary Burmese, and since about the the mid-1960s there has been an effort on the part of some writers to have the written style abandoned altogether in favour of the spoken style. But opposition to this move is still strong for, to the orthodox, material on serious matters written about in the colloquial style lacks gravity, authority and dignity.

On loan words in general, see **Tin Htway** (1978) and for those from Pali and Mon, **Hla Pe** (1961 and 1967); on *nissaya* Burmese, see **Okell** (1967). Much information on dialects is contained in **Taylor** (1921). **Minn Latt** (1966) discusses the question of styles. Major dictionaries are: Burmese-Burmese, **U Wun** (1952-64) [unfinished], **Myan-ma-za aphwe** (1979-80); Burmese-English, **Judson** (1966), **Stewart** (1941-81) [unfinished]); English-Burmese, **Judson** (1956), **Ba Han** (1951-66); Burmese-German, **Esche** (1976a); Burmese-French, **Bernot** (1978-[in progress]); Burmese-Russian, **Minina** and **Kyaw Zaw** (1976); Russian-Burmese, **Novikov** and **Kolobkov** (1966); Chinese-Burmese, **Chen Yi-Sein** (1970); Burmese-Japanese, **Harada** and **Ono** (1979); Burmese-English-Pali, **Hok Sein** (1978). Among the teaching materials in English are: on script, **Roop** (1972); on spoken language, **Ballard** (1961), **Cornyn** and **Roop** (1968), **Defense Language Institute** (1963-64), **Okell** (1969) and **Stewart** (1955); on grammar, **Okell** (1969) and on the literary language, **Bridges** (1906), **Judson** (1951), and **Lonsdale** (1899). Two useful but by now rather outdated readers with glossaries are **Cornyn** (1957) and **Cornyn** and **Musgrave** (1958).

Script

From the 12th century, when Burmese was first written down, it used the Mon script which seems to have been derived from the Grantha alphabet of the Pallavas of South India. The Mon had to adapt the same script in some respects to suit the phonology of their language and the Burmese made further additions, for example, adding symbols to mark lexical tones. In the present form of the script, most of the letters take the shape of circles or parts of circles. The alphabet follows the standard Indic pattern, with consonants listed in

Detail from a 19th century Life of the Buddha manuscript.

ordered groups beginning with the velars (k kh g gh n) and continuing through the palatals, cerebrals, dentals, labials and so on. In use, the initial consonant forms the nucleus of each syllable and vowels are written as attachments above, below or after the consonant.

There are two schools of thought about Burmese romanization. One favours a system for those for whom the written word is of greatest importance and the other a system for those who are primarily concerned with the sounds of the words. The former uses a transliteration, which represents each symbol of the Burmese script by one or two roman letters, entirely disregarding the pronounciation. The latter uses a transcription which systematically represents each Burmese sound by one or more roman letter, irrespective of the spelling. In 1981 the United States Library of Congress adopted a transliteration system for its cataloguing.

On Burmese script, see **Roop** (1972) and on different romanizations, see **Okell** (1971).

Manuscripts

There are two main types of Burmese manuscripts: those written on palm leaves (*pei-za*) and those written on paper, folded concertina fashion, to make a folding book (*parabaik*). It is not known exactly when the use of such manuscripts began, but they date from at least the Pagan period and continued in use well into the 20th century in Buddhist monasteries.

A palm leaf was prepared for use as a writing surface in the same way as in Ceylon and ancient India. The text was incised on the prepared leaf with a metal stylus; the surface was then rubbed with lampblack and the surplus wiped off, leaving the incised characters standing out clearly. The leaves were usually also rubbed with crude oil as a preservative. The ends and sides of the leaves were often gilded or partially gilded and lacquered red or occasionally black. The traditional system of foliation of palm leaf manuscripts used a fixed order or combination of consonants and vowels in sets of twelve (*in-ga*), written on the reverse side of the palm leaves. If the manuscript was long enough to exhaust all 33 consonants (more than 33 x 12 or 396), the foliation was started over again with consonant clusters in place of single consonants. Two holes were pierced in the leaves, through which to insert bamboo pins to hold the stacked leaves securely together. Not many manuscripts have survived with their bamboo pins intact and it is common for the leaves to have been later strung together with a cord. Most manuscripts have two wooden cover boards, which may be plain or decorated. Sometimes manuscripts also come with a cloth wrapper and a narrow ribbon which may have a donor's formula woven into it. In the earliest palm leaf manuscripts the text is more commonly written in ink rather than incised. In general, palm leaf manuscripts were used for religious, grammatical, literary, historical, legal and other important texts. Half-length leaves stitched together were commonly used for horoscopes (*za-ta*). Mention should be made of an especially decorative form of Burmese manuscript which is larger in dimension (on the average, 54 x 9 cm, with 6 lines of text per side) than ordinary palm leaf manuscripts (which are roughly 49 x 5 cm with 8-12 lines per page). These larger manuscripts are known as *Kammavaca* (*kamawa-za*), collections of extracts from Pali texts used at the ordination of Buddhist monks and certain other ceremonies of the Buddhist order. *Kammavaca* texts are also found written on metal sheets, gilded and lacquered over, and on ivory.

Folding books (*parabaik*) were made of paper, coloured either black or natural cream. Some inscriptions mention *parabaik* made of metals or of leather, but these are exceedingly rare. Black paper parabaik were mostly used as notebooks and for some administrative records, the text being written on them in white soapstone or steatite and sometimes in gilded letters. Cream paper *parabaik* were written upon in ink and used for a variety of purposes, above all for painted illustrations, in which case the paper was usually first given a yellow background. Common subjects were scenes from the life of the Buddha and from the *Jataka* stories of the Buddha's previous lives, court scenes and astrological texts. The covers of folding books were sometimes decorated with raised patterns and gilding.

There are collections of Burmese manuscripts (including those in some of the minority languages of Burma, such as Mon and Shan) in many libraries in the West, as well as in Burma. The largest collections in the United Kingdom are those of the British Library and, for Shan, of Cambridge University Library. Burmese manuscript collections in Germany are also extensive. In Rangoon, the Universities' Central Library, the National Library and the Library of the Department of Religious Affairs have large collections. In Mandalay, the National Library and Museum and the Ba-gaya monastery library are important. There are, as yet, no published catalogues of these holdings in Burma.

On the preparation of manuscripts, see **Gaur** (1978). For further details and Burmese terminology for different types of manuscripts, **U Wun** (1950) and **Quigly** (1956) are helpful. **Pearson** (1971) provides a general guide to Burmese manuscript collections in the West. **Bechert**'s catalogue (1979) of some of the German collections sets a high standard and should be consulted for its introductory sections and bibliography on Burmese literature and manuscripts; see also **Braun** (1985).

Printing and Development of the Press

The first book to be printed in Burmese characters was the *Alphabetum Barmanum* [sic], printed in Rome in 1776 by the Press of the Propaganda de Fide. The Serampore Mission, founded by William Carey, began preparing a font of Burmese characters in 1807 and in 1810 printed for the Fort William College John Leyden's *A comparative vocabulary of the Barma, Melayu and Thai languages* with entries in Burmese script and Jawi. Felix Carey's *A grammar of the Burman language* appeared in 1814 and Burmese translations of the Gospels a year later. In 1816 the Serampore Mission sent a second printing press to Burma (the first, sent to the Burmese court in 1813, sank in the Irrawaddy) and with the arrival in Rangoon of a trained printer, George Hough, the printing of Burmese language books in Burma commenced. There are no surviving copies of the Christian tracts and catechism, first printed by the American Baptist Mission with their Press, but Adoniram Judson's translation of the Gospel of St Matthew, printed in 1817, is still extant. After the first Anglo-Burmese War and the British acquisition of Arakan and Tenasserim, missionary work increased and printing presses multiplied. In 1837 a Karen Mission Press was established in Tavoy and in 1855 it merged with the Moulmein Mission Press, which had been started in 1843. The Tavoy and Moulmein Missions pioneered translation and printing of the Bible in Sgaw and Pwo Karen and in Mon.

Until 1870 the American Baptist Mission Press was responsible for nearly all book printing in Burma, publishing not only translations of Christian material, but also school textbooks and standard Burmese works needed by government officials for their study of Burmese. But in about 1868, a press called the Burma Herald Press (*Myan-ma than-daw-zin pon-hneik-taik*) began publishing a newspaper in Rangoon. By 1870, it also published books, at first law texts, then moral tracts and by the mid-1870s, large numbers of popular dramas (*pya-zat*) in very cheap editions. Other Burmese presses started up and the government also began to print inexpensive editions of the Burmese classics. In 1886 Philip Ripley established the Hanthawaddy Press, using only a small hand-press. A larger press was put into service in 1897 and the Hanthawaddy Press soon became the leading publisher of Burmese classics and Buddhist texts, retaining this position to recent times.

The government-subsidized Burma Translation Society was established in 1947 with the aim of translating modern scientific and technical books into Burmese as rapidly as possible. The society also established the first Burmese encyclopaedia, *Myan-ma swe-zon kyan* (in 15 volumes, completed in 1976 and with an annual supplement thereafter). In 1963 the Society was incorporated into the Sarpay Beikman (Palace of Literature), a government publishing house charged with improving and enriching the general knowlege of all Burmese. Among the many privately-owned presses and publishing houses that have emerged since World War Two, one of the most important is the Pagan Press, founded in August 1962. It has published many works on Marxism and socialism as well as new writings and reprints of outstanding prewar books. The first newspapers to see print in Burma were in English, beginning with the *Maulmain Chronicle* in 1840. The first Burmese language newspaper, *Myan-ma than-daw-zin* (Burma Herald) began appearing in Rangoon in 1868-70. Its founder, a Sino-Burman named Ahi, moved in 1874 to Mandalay where, under the patronage of King Min-don, he produced the *Yadana-bon nei-pyei-daw thadin-za* (Mandalay Gazette). Most Burmese newspapers published before 1914 carried mainly local news, particularly of commercial affairs. They appeared once or twice weekly and were not yet vehicles for political comment or protest. Two papers which later developed along these lines and came to play an important part in the Burmese nationalist movement were *Thu-riya* (Sun), founded in 1911 and *Myan-ma Alin* (New Light of Burma), founded in 1914. During the 1920s and 1930s, daily newspapers, weeklies and magazines supporting a wide diversity of political and religious viewpoints appeared. They frequently included short stories and serialized novels in order to boost their circulation. During the 1950s and early 1960s the personal columns written by authors such as Zawana, Thein Hpei Myint, Aung Bala and Tet To were a feature of the daily press and keenly followed by the reading public.

Before the advent of the military government in 1962, Burma had more than thirty daily papers: three English language, six Chinese, a few Indian and about eighteen Burmese language papers, of which five appeared in Mandalay and three (bi-weeklies) in Moulmein. In October 1963 the government started an official daily paper, *Lok-tha pyei-thu nei-zin*, followed by an English language counterpart, *The Working People's Daily* in 1964. Only six daily papers, all government owned, are presently published in Burma. They are the *Guardian*, *The Working People's Daily*, *Lok-tha pyei-thu nei-zin*, *Kyei-mon*, *Bo-tahtaung* and *Myan-ma Alin*. There is a single official news agency, News Agency Burma (NAB), which handles all internal and foreign news. Hence, the dailies do not differ greatly in the news they carry, but only in their style and emphasis. Burma has a single broadcasting service, BBS, under the direction of the Ministry of Information. Colour television transmission began in late 1980.

Early printing developments are treated in **Phinney** (1917), **Tin Htway** (1972) and **Wright** (1910). For the press in the 1960s and 70s, see **Blackburn** (1982).

Literature

The earliest extant Burmese writings are the stone inscriptions of the Pagan and Ava periods of the 12th to 14th centuries. Most of these are prose writings recording acts of merit performed by devout Buddhist monarchs and lay persons. Poetic works must also have been written in this early period, since the earliest surviving non-inscriptional work which can be reliably dated (1455 AD) is the *Yahkaing min-thami ei-gyin* ('Cradle song of the Princess of Arakan'), which shows a high degree of sophistication.

From the mid-15th century, verse was the main vehicle for imaginative literature in Burma. Prose was reserved for subjects of a practical nature such as law, grammar, historical chronicles and interpretations of the Pali scriptures. Until the 18th century almost all Burmese verse forms were composed in four syllable lines linked by climbing rhymes and grouped into stanzas of some thirty or so lines. This style of verse is known as *lei-lon tabaik,* or 'four words one foot'. This Burmese poetry was intended for use at the royal court or by high dignitaries; both its outlook and its form were conservative. Before about 1550 there were two types of poetry. The first was written by ministers or courtiers with the aim of extolling the king's lineage and achievements (*maw-gun* and *ei-gyin*, about which more below). The second was written on religious themes by monks acting as the king's religious preceptors. Generally derived from the *Jataka* stories or from episodes in the life of the Buddha, these longish poems are known as *pyo*. The two most famous monk-poets of the period are Shin Rat-hta-tha-ra (1468-1530) and Shin Thi-lawun-tha (1453-1518) who wrote *maw-gun* as well as *pyo*.

The *yadu*, a shorter verse form of three interlinked stanzas, dominated the literary scene during the early Taung-ngu period, when the rulers of the new dynasty were expanding eastward into Thai territory and westward into Arakan. *Yadu* could be inspired by a mood, a place, or an incident, and were often addressed to a wife or sweetheart. The courtiers and soldiers of the conquering monarchs wrote not only of their kings' glory but also of their own personal emotions. Two of the best-known authors of these *yadu*, a form more suited than the elaborate *pyo* and *ei-gyin* to the active soldier, were Nawadei I (1545-1600) and Prince Nat-shin-naung (1578-1619).

The first half of the 18th century is marked by a single outstanding author, the minister Padei-tha-ya-za, who broke with tradition in several ways. He wrote successful *pyo* on non-religious subjects, such as the arrival of Thai envoys at the Burmese court and on the Fairy Princess Manohari, in *Thu-za pyo*. Possibly under Thai influence, he also wrote the first Burmese drama,*Mani-ket zat daw-gyi* and the first classical songs. His short poems (*tya-bwe*) about the joys of ordinary village life were also the first of their kind.

Considerable literary activity followed the foundation of a new dynasty by King Alaung-hpaya in 1752. Not only were the four classical verse forms composed with new vigour, but there occurred a proliferation of new free forms of verse, especially of songs, some of which were borrowed from Thailand after the Burmese sack of Ayutthaya in 1767. Among these new forms are the *tei-dat*, a kind of sonnet, the *lei-gyo* (four section) and *dwei-gyo* (two section) songs, and the *baw-le*, a form of lament. In addition to these literary songs there were other 'musical' songs, each of which had its own tune. The most prolific writer of these was the minister U Sa (1766-1853).

Beginning in the early 19th century there was a general movement toward liberalization, as shown in the appearance of humour and satire, first in a type of long narrative poem known as *yagan*, and then, from the 1840s, in dramas called *pya-zat* ('shown story'). A *yagan* usually retold a *Jataka* or other well-known story with the addition of comic asides and satirical attacks on fellow writers and ladies of the court. The best known *yagan* is the *Ya-ma Yagan* (Yagan about Rama), written about 1780 by U To. Styles of writing also became freer, and many works were composed in a mixed style which had the rhymes of verse but the varied phrase-lengths and cadences of prose. These included the *yagan* mentioned above; the romances of court life or *nan-dwin zat-daw-gyi* (*wut-htu*) ('within the palace drama [story]'), such as *I-Naung* by U Sa, and later those by the Princess of Hlaing; the literary epistles, or *myit-taza* (see below), especially those of the famous poet and playwright U Pon-nya; and finally the plays, or *pya-zat*. The earlier plays by U Pon-nya and U Kyin U were intended for performance before the king and provincial governors. By the 1870s these gave way to plays for more popular audiences, the texts of which could be printed cheaply and in large numbers as a result of the establishment of vernacular printing presses. These plays, which continued to appear well into the 20th century, mark the beginning of popular literature in Burma, and were only slowly displaced in the years after 1904 by novels of the Western type.

Apart from the stone inscriptions, prose writing began under the direct influence of the Pali scriptures and maintained this character until the end of the 19th century, when the arrival of printing and contact with European literature radically altered its function. Prose became a vehicle for story telling in the second half of the 18th century when the monk U Aw-ba-tha (fl.1752-87) translated eight of the ten greater *Jataka*. Soon after, all 537 minor *Jataka* were translated by the Nyaung-gan Hsaya-daw.

Burmese historical writings before the 20th century, and other sources of historical information of the same time, were written both in verse and prose. They fall into nine distinct categories:

1. **Kyauk-sa**: ('stone-writing') the stone inscriptions of the Pagan and Ava periods, from the second half of the 11th century until the 13th century. Mainly records of the foundation of pagodas, dedication of land and slaves, and important royal events. The inscription by Prince Rajakumar of 1113, also known as the Mya-zei-di Inscription, has become famous as the Rosetta Stone of Burma. Its four faces include the earliest dated Burmese inscription together with the same text in Pyu, Mon and Pali.
2. **Ayei-daw-bon**: a royal biography or prose memoir of an individual ruler and his military campaigns. The earliest and best known is an account of the Mon king of Pegu, Rajadhiraj (1385-1423), written by Binya Dala in the late 16th century.
3. **Maw-gun** and **ei-gyin**: longish poems dating from the 15th century. The former were written to commemorate a notable event, while the latter took the form of elaborate verses extolling the achievements of the reigning monarch and his ancestors, presented as a cradle song for a young prince.
4. **Thamaing**: accounts of the foundation of pagodas and monasteries and local histories of towns and districts.
5. **Sit-tan**: records of inquiry; especially local returns submitted by minor

officials in the rural areas of Burma in response to crown directives requesting information on particular matters.

6. **Ya-zawin**: the Pali *rajavamsa* or 'genealogy of kings', royal chronicles which focus on the rulers and their successions, court activities, wars, and, especially, acts of Buddhist patronage. There were also religious chronicles compiled in the 19th century, giving an account of the history of Buddhism and of its establishment in Burma.

7. **Damathat**: the Sanskrit *dharmasastra*, or customary law texts, partly based on Indian originals. Early Pali versions are recorded and are known in Mon. The extant *damathat* literature mostly dates from the 17th century; it deals with Burmese sovereignty and state prescriptions in sufficient depth and breadth to make it obvious that a sophisticated legal system existed. The *damathat* literature is supplemented by the more utilitarian *hpyat-hton* ('decisions').

8. **Shauk-hton**: 'decisions' or 'submissions', collections of brief accounts of famous legendary or historical cases or events, retold in simple narrative style to serve as precedents or guides to action for rulers. An extensive compilation, the *Mani-yadana-bon kyan* (Precious jewel examples), also called the *Min Ya-za shauk-hton*, was made in 1781.

9. **Myit-taza**: literally 'letters of loving kindness'. For example, *Kyi-gan shin-gyi myit-taza,* a collection of letters written before the first Anglo-Burmese War, throws much light on economic and social changes of the time.

Of these different forms, the *ya-zawin*, which comprise the bulk of true historical writings, can, with the most justification, be termed chronicles. Certain conventions were observed in Burmese chronicle writing. Legendary accounts of the origin of the world and of the foundation of dynasties and cities served to legitimate a new monarchy and were therefore imbued with the received ideas of their time on cosmology and kingship. An element of moral guidance and an affirmation of Buddhist precepts were also present, chroniclers expressly stating that one of their aims was to give guidance to rulers and their ministers.

Chronicles are known to have been written since at least the 15th century. Very few of the early chronicles have come down to us, however, and those which have survived merely present lists of kings and their lineages, and are limited in their coverage to a particular court or period. The first chronicler to attempt to give a continuous history of Burma by consulting local chronicles, *thamaing,* and other such sources, was U Kala, who in approximately 1724 produced the *Maha ya-zawin-gyi* (Great Chronicle). This was written in 21 sections and covered Burmese history down to 1711. By the late 18th century, other chronicles attempting to check traditional accounts against such evidence as inscriptions, most notably the work of the Twin-thin taik-wun, had appeared. From 1829 to 1832 a committee of scholars appointed by King Ba-gyi-daw compiled an official chronicle, named after the palace hall where the scholars met, the *Hman-nan ya-zawin-daw-gyi* (Glass Palace Chronicle). This work was compiled in 38 sections covering Burmese history to 1821. Sections 1-21 (up to 1751, the end of the Taung-ngu period) were published for the first time (in 3 volumes) in 1908-09; an English translation of the early section saw print in 1923. A continuation of the Glass Palace Chronicle in 10 sections, covering the period to 1854, was compiled by a committee, appointed by King Mindon, between 1867-9. Entitled the *Du-ti-ya maha ya-zawin-daw-gyi* (Second Great Chronicle), it was published for the first time in 1899. A further continuation up to 1885 and the end of Burmese independence was written by U Tin of Mandalay. It was published in 1905 together with the portions of the Glass Palace Chronicle covering the years 1752-1821, and with the whole of the Second Great Chronicle, in one volume of 1,670 pages under the title *Kon-baung-zet maha ya-zawin-daw-qyi,* (History of the Kon-baung dynasty). Later editions in slightly revised form have been published, the most recent appearing in 1967 in 3 volumes.

In the 20th century several different forms of historical writing took root. The nationalist author Thahkin Ko-daw Hmaing (U Lun) wrote a new chronicle for the national college established after the university boycott and student strikes of 1920. Hmaw-bi Hsaya wrote *Pazat ya-zawin,* the distinguishing feature of which was its reliance on oral traditions. New terms came into use for different types of writing: *ya-zawin* as a general term for history has largely been replaced by *thamaing,* earlier used only for pagoda histories; *ayei-daw-bon* has been extended to cover the meaning of 'incident, affair, struggle, campaign', as in *lut-lat-yei ayei-daw-bon,* the struggle for independence (as distinct from *taw-hlan-yei,* often used in the sense of 'revolution'); *ti-ga* (*tika* in Pali), a commentary on a Buddhist text, has been used in several titles by Thahkin Ko-daw Hmaing to describe a new type of work which, presented as memoirs in the style of a religious commentary given by a respected monk to his disciples, comments on the current affairs of the 1920s and 1930s (for example, *Boycot ti-ga* and *Galon ti-ga*); *at-htok-pat-ti* (Pali, *atthupatti* or 'explanation') is used

Ngwei-ta-yi magazine UnionDay issue, February 1969

in the sense of biography; and *hmat-tan* is used to mean 'records, notes, account'.

The first widely-read Burmese novel, entitled *Maung Yin Maung Ma Me Ma*, appeared in 1904. It was written by James Hla Gyaw, a government translator who was inspired by *The Count of Monte Carlo*. His work set a new fashion and the *ka-la-paw wut-thu* or modern novel (as distinct from *hpaya-haw wut-thu* or 'story told by Buddha') became firmly established with the reading public. By 1920 large numbers of adapted and original novels had appeared. Foreign works were most often chosen for their love or adventure interest, as in the works of Rider Haggard, Conan Doyle and Mrs. H. Wood, but the best original novels of the period continued to be characterized by traditional didacticism and an ornate mixed prose-verse style. Of the latter type, two novels by U Lat stand out: *Sabe-bin* (1912) and *Shwei-pyi-zo* (1914). These works show a new awareness of current social problems and the awakening spirit of nationalism. So also do the historical novels of U Maung Gyi and the brilliant satire of Thahkin Ko-daw Hmaing's *ti-ga* or 'commentaries'.

A writer with considerable influence in the prewar era was P.Mo-nin (1883-1940), who wrote some of the first truly modern novels and short stories concerned with the individual. He also adapted Western books on sociology and psychology, and his works helped introduce modern concepts to the public. Maha Hswei (1900-1953) and the first woman novelist, Dagon Hkin Hkin Lei (1904-1983), both wrote numerous novels and short stories in the 1930s and 1940s, many of which reflected, often rather sentimentally, the hardships of peasant life and the growing dissatisfaction with colonial rule.

By the turn of the century national consciousness had spread. The Buddhist revival had also gained strength, assisted by the teachings of the Le-di Hsayadaw. The Burma Research Society, founded in 1910 by J.S. Furnivall, had helped to foster the Burman's pride in his own literary and cultural heritage. A movement to establish national schools through which Burmese might acquire a complete education began in 1920, and in the following decade the first graduates in Burmese from the University of Rangoon had begun to develop a new style of writing — shorter sentences, clear and unelaborate prose — in a literary movement known as *Hkit-san*,('testing the age'). Zaw-gyi and Min Thu-wun set poetry on its modern path, freed from its conventional forms and themes. Theik-pan Maung Wa created a new genre of writing with humorous, unsentimental sketches of peasant life entitled *Hkit-san pon-byin* (Experimental Tales) — imitated by many authors from the 1940s onwards, most notably Maung Htin, Man Tin, Aung So and Aung Thein.

The end of the war and the attainment of independence in 1948 gave a tremendous impetus to the novel and, particularly, the short story. Numerous translations were made from European fiction, including, for the first time, Russian works. As already noted, beginning in 1947, the Burma Translation Society encouraged good writing and awarded prizes for literary achievement. Monthly literary magazines continued to be the most vital link between authors and the reading public. In the 1920s and 1930s the leading magazines had been *Dagon* and *Gan-da law-ka* (The world of books), but after the war *Shu-mawa*, *Thwei-thauk,* and *Mya-wadi* consistently outsold their competitors. These magazines are important because they publish general articles, cartoons, several short stories and many poems every month, as well as a considerable number of novels, memoirs and autobiographies in serial form. Publication in one of the leading magazines is the best way for a young author to gain recognition. The 1980s has seen a big increase in the publication of monthly magazines.

The most important short story writers include Yan Aung, Zei-ya, Maung Htin, Man Tin, Min Shin, Htin Lin, Maung Tha-ya and, above all, Thaw-da Hswei. Leading left-wing writers are Thein Hpei Myin (1914-1978), already well known before the war for his controversial novel *Tet Hpon-gyi* (Modern monk), Dagon Ta-Ya and Bamaw Tin Aung; all three spent periods in prison. Also imprisoned (1963-66) was the most talented and outspoken woman writer Gya-ne-gyaw Ma Ma Lei (1917-1982); the younger female author Hkin Hnin Yu writes rather poignant stories full of vivid imagery. Shwei U Daung (1888-1974) is remembered by many Burmans for his skilful and understanding adaptations of numerous classics of Western literature, from Sherlock Holmes to Sholokov's *And quiet flows the Don*. The writer and journalist Lu-du U Hla collected and published in the 1960s and 1970s some fifty books of folk tales from all the peoples of Burma.. The foremost literary critic since the 1930s is the poet, translator and scholar U Thein Han (Zaw-gyi).

On the *sit-tan*, see **Trager** and **Koenig** (1979). **Tet Htoot** (1961) discusses the chronicle tradition. For an English translation of the *Mani-yadana-bon-kyan*, see **Bagshawe** (1981); and of the *Kyi-gan shin-gyi myit-taza*, **Htin Aung** (1968). Legal literature is surveyed in **Okudaira** (1986) who provides an extensive bibliography; see also **Gledhill** (1970). On the development of drama and popular literature, **Hla Pe** (1952) and **Htin Aung** (1937) may be used as a guide. On the rise of popular literature, see also **Hla Pe** (1968) and **Aung San Suu Kyi** (1987). **Allott** (1981) discusses the important role played by the government in promoting and controlling literary expression. On short stories and for bibliographic references to literary works, see **Allott** (1982). Two volumes of translations of Lu-du U Hla's collections of folk tales have been made, in Russian, **Deopik** (1976) and in German, **Esche** (1976b); another collection in English was made by **Htin Aung** (1948).

Bibliography

Allott, A.
1981 "Prose writing and publishing in Burma: government policy and popular practice." In Tham Seong Chee, ed. *Essays on literature and society in South East Asia*. Singapore: Singapore University Press, pp. 1-35.
1982 "The short story in Burma: with special reference to its social and political significance." In J. H. C. S. Davidson and H. Cordell, eds. *The short story in South East Asia*. London: School of Oriental and African Studies, pp. 101-138.

Aung San Suu Kyi.
1987 "Socio-political currents in Burmese literature 1910-1940." In Burma Research Group, ed. *Burma and Japan: basic studies on their cultural and social structure*. Tokyo: Tokyo University of Foreign Studies, pp. 65-83.

Aung Thwin, M.
1979 *Southeast Asian research tools: Burma.* Honolulu: University of Hawaii. (Southeast Asia Paper, No. 16, part III).
1985 *Pagan: the origins of modern Burma.* Honolulu: University of Hawaii Press.

Ba Han
1951-1966 *The university English-Burmese dictionary.* Rangoon: Hanthawaddy Press.

Bagshawe, L. E. (trans.)
1981 *The Maniyadanabon of Shin Sandalinka.* Ithaca, N.Y.: Cornell University Southeast Asia Program. (Data Paper No. 115).

Ballard, E.
1961 *Lessons in spoken Burmese.* Rangoon: Burma Baptist Convention.

Bechert, E., Khin Khin Su and Tin Tin Myint
1979 *Burmese manuscripts, part I.* Wiesbaden: Franz Steiner Verlag. (Verzeichnis der Orientalischen Handschriften in Deutschland, Band XXIII,I).

Bernot, D.
1968 *Bibliography birmane: années 1950-60.* Paris: CEDRASEMI.
1978 - *Dictionnaire birman-français.* Paris: SELAF.
1983 *Bibliographie birmane: années 1960-70.* 2 vols. Paris: CRNS.

Blackburn, P.
1982 "Burma." In J.A. Lent, ed. *Newspapers in Asia: contemporary trends and problems.* Hong Kong: Heinemann Asia, pp. 177-192.

Bradley, D.
1979 *Lahu dialects.* Canberra: Australian National University. (Oriental Monographs, No. 23).

Braun, H. and Tin Tin Myint
1985 *Burmese manuscripts, part 2.* Wiesbaden: Franz Steiner Verlag. (Verzeichnis der Orientalischen Handschriften in Deutschland, Band XXIII, 2).

Bridges, J. E.
1906 *The Burmese manual.* London: Luzac; Rangoon: British Burma Press.

Bunge, F. M. (ed.)
1983 *Burma, a country study.* Washington D.C.: US Government Printing Office.

Cady, John F.
1960 *A history of modern Burma.* Ithaca, N.Y.: Cornell University Press.

Chen Yi-sein
1970 *Mu-fan Mien-hua ta-tz'u-tien.* Tokyo: Toyo Bunko. (First edition, Peking and Hong Kong, 1962).

Cornyn, W. S.
1957 *Burmese chrestomathy.* Washington D.C.: American Council of Learned Societies.

Cornyn, W. S. and J. K. Musgrave
1958 *Burmese glossary.* Washington D.C.: American Council of Learned Societies.

Cornyn, W. S. and D. H. Roop
1968 *Beginning Burmese.* New Haven: Yale University Press.

Defense Language Institute
1963-64 *Burmese basic course.* 5 vols. Monterey, Cal.: US Defense Language Institute.

Deopik, D. V. (ed.)
1976 *Skazki naradov: Birmy.* Moscow Izdatel'stvo Nauka.

Esche, A.
1976a *Wörterbuch Burmesisch-Deutsch.* Leipzig: VEB Verlag.
1976b *Märchen der Völker Burmas.* Leipzig: Insel-Verlag.

Gaur, A.
1978 *Writing materials of the East.* London: British Library Reference Division.

Gledhill, A.
1970 *Burma (Introduction bibliographique à l'histoire du droit et à l'ethnologie juridique).* Ed. J. Gibissien, Section E/7. Brussels: Editions de l'histoire de sociologie, Universitaire de Bruxelles.

Hale, A.
1982 *Research on Tibeto-Burman languages.* Berlin: Mouton. (Trends in Linguistics: State of the Art Reports, No. 14).

Harada, M. and T. Ono
1979 *Myan-ma-Gyapan abi-dan: Birumago jiten.* Tokyo: Nihon Biruma Bunka Kyokai.

Harvey, G. E.
1967 *History of Burma.* London: Frank Cass. (First Edition 1925).

Henderson, E.
1965 *Tiddim Chin: a descriptive analysis of two texts.* London: Oxford University Press. (London Oriental Series, No. 15).

Hla Pe
1952 *Konmara pyazat, an example of popular Burmese drama in the nineteenth century*. London: Luzac.
1961 "Some adapted Pali loan words in Burmese." *JBRS Fiftieth Anniversary Publication* 1:71-100.
1967 "A tentative list of Mon loan words in Burmese." *JBRS* 50: 71-94.
1968 "The rise of popular literature in Burma." *JBRS* 51, 2: 123-144.

Hok Sein
1978 *The universal Burmese-English-Pali dictionary*. Rangoon: Myit-zu-thaka.

Htin Aung
1937 *Burmese drama, a study with translations of Burmese plays*. London: Oxford University Press. (reprint edition, Westport: Greenwood, 1978).
1948 *Burmese folk tales*. Calcutta; New York: Oxford University Press.
1967 *A history of Burma*. New York: Columbia University Press.
1968 *Epistles written on the eve of the Anglo-Burmese War*. The Hague: M. Nijhoff.

Huffman, F. E.
1986 *Bibliography and index of mainland Southeast Asian languages and linguistics*. New Haven; London: Yale University Press.

Irwin, A. M. B.
1909 *The Burmese and Arakanese calendars*. Rangoon: Hanthawaddy Press.

Jones, R. B.
1961 *Karen linguistic studies*. Berkeley; Los Angeles: University of California Press.(University of California Studies in Linguistics No. 25).

Judson, A.
1951 *A grammar of the Burmese language*. Rangoon: Baptist Board of Publications. (Reprint edition).
1956 *Judson's English and Burmese dictionary*. Rangoon: Baptist Board of Publication. (Ninth edition).
1966 *Burmese-English dictionary*. Rangoon: Baptist Board of Publication. (First edition, 1826; last revised edition 1926).

LeBar, F. M., G. C. Hickey and J. K. Musgrave
1964 *Ethnic groups of mainland Southeast Asia*. New Haven: HRAF Press.

Lieberman, V. B.
1984 *Burmese administrative cycles: anarchy and conquest c. 1580-1760*. Princeton: Princeton University Press.

Lonsdale, A. W.
1899 *Burmese grammar and grammatical exercises*. Rangoon: British Burma Press.

Luce, G. H. and Pe Maung Tin (trans.)
1923 *The Glass Palace chronicle of the kings of Burma.* London: Oxford University Press. (Reprint Edition, Rangoon: Burma Research Society, 1960).

Luce, G. H.
1969-70 *Old Burma-early Pagan.* 3 vols. New York: J. J. Augustin, for Artibus Asiae.

Matisoff, J. A.
1973 *The grammar of Lahu.* Berkeley: University of California Press. (University of California Publications in Linguistics, No. 75).

Minina, G. F. and U Kyaw Zaw
1976 *Birmansko-Russkii slovar.* Russkii iazyk.

Minn Latt
1966 *Modernization of Burmese.* Prague: Oriental Institute. (Dissertationes Orientales, No. 11).

Moscotti, A. D.
1974 *British policy and the nationalist movement in Burma, 1917-1937.* Honolulu: University Press of Hawaii. (Asian Studies at Hawaii, No. 11).

Myan-ma-za Aphwe
1978-80 *Myan-ma abi-dan akyin-gyok (Concise Burmese dictionary).* Rangoon: Myan-ma-za Aphwe.

Novikov, N. N. and V. P. Kolobkov
1966 *Russko-Birmanskii slovar.* Moscow: Sovetskaia Entsiklopediia.

Okell, J.
1967 "Nissaya Burmese, a case of systematic adaptation to a foreign grammar and syntax ." *JBRS* 50, 1:95-123.
1969 *A reference grammar of colloquial Burmese.* 2 vols. London: Oxford University Press.
1971 *A guide to the romanization of Burmese.* London: Royal Asiatic Society. (James G. Forlong Fund, Vol. 27).

Okudaira R.
1986 *The Burmese dhammathat.* In M. B. Hooker, ed. *Laws of South-East Asia. Vol.1: The pre-modern texts,* Singapore: Butterworth, pp. 23-142; bibliography, pp. 500-508.

Pearson, J. D.
1971 *Oriental manuscripts in Europe and North America: a survey.* Zug: Inter Documentation Company.

Phinney, F. D.
1917 *The American Baptist Mission Press: historical, descriptive, 1816-1916.* Rangoon: American Baptist Mission Press.

Quigly, E. P.
1956 *Some observations on libraries, manuscripts and books of Burma.* London: Probsthain.

Roop, D. H.
1970 *A grammar of the Lisu language.* Ph.D. dissertation, Yale University.
1972 *An introduction to the Burmese writing system.* New Haven: Yale University Press.

Shafer, R. (ed.)
1957-63 *Bibliography of Sino-Tibetan languages.* 2 vols. Wiesbaden: Harrassowitz.

Shulman, F. J.
1986 *Burma: an annotated bibliographical guide to international doctoral dissertation research, 1898-1985.* Lanham; New York: University Press of America, for the Asia Program, The Wilson Center.

Silverstein, J.
1977 *Burma, military rule and the politics of stagnation.* Ithaca, N.Y.; London: Cornell University Press.

Spiro, M. E.
1970 *Buddhism and society: a great tradition and its Burmese vicissitudes.* New York: Harper and Row.

Steinberg, D. I.
1981 *Burma's road toward development: growth and ideology under military rule.* Boulder, Colorado: Westview Press.
1982 *Burma: a socialist nation of Southeast Asia.* Boulder, Colorado: Westview Press.

Stewart, J. A.
1955 *Manual of colloquial Burmese.* London: Luzac.

Stewart, J. A., et al.
1941-81 *A Burmese-English dictionary.* Parts 1-6 (covering the letter "a"). Rangoon; London: School of Oriental and African Studies.

Taylor, L. F.
1921 "The dialects of Burmese." *JBRS* 11:89-97.

Taylor, R. H.
1987 *The state in Burma.* London: C. Hurst.

Tet Htoot, U.
1961 "The nature of the Burmese chronicles." In D. G. E. Hall, ed. *Historians of South East Asia*. London: Oxford University Press, pp.50-62.

Tin Htway
1972 "The role of literature in nation building." In B. Grossmann, ed. *Southeast Asia in the modern world*. Wiesbaden: Harrasowitz, pp. 35-60.
1978 "Burmese word borrowing and word making." In A. Dhammotharan, ed. *Word borrowing and word making in modern Asian languages*. Wiesbaden: Franz Steiner Verlag.

Trager, F. N.
1973 *Burma: a selected and annotated bibliography*. Revised edition. New Haven: HRAF Press.

Trager, F. N. and W. J. Koenig
1979 *Burmese sit-tans 1764-1826: records of rural life and administration*. Tucson: University of Arizona Press. (Association for Asian Studies Monographs, No. 36).

Wright, A.. (ed.)
1910 *Twentieth century impressions of Burma, its history, people, commerce, industries and resources*. London: Lloyd's Greater Britain Publishing Company.

Wun, U.
1950 "Notes on Burmese manuscript books." *JBRS* 33, 2: 224-229.
1952-64 *Tet-gatho Myan-ma abi-dan (University Burmese dictionary)*. Parts 1-5 (covering the letters 'ka' to 'cha'). Rangoon: Government Printing.

Thailand

Thailand geographically divides into four natural regions: the North with Chiangmai as its capital; the Northeast; the economic and political heartland made up of the Chaophraya river (Menam) basin and central plain where the capital, Bangkok, is located; and the South (Peninsular Thailand). The Thais constitute the dominant group in a population of over 52,000,000 (1986).

The earliest history of the Thai is the source of controversy and debate. The Thai may have begun to move into the Chaophraya basin as early as the 7th century AD, from an area between Chiangmai and the mountains of Yunnan. Migration was slow and continuous; not until the 11th or 12th century did the Thai become a prominent group and begin to swamp the existing inhabitants, the Mon and Khmer. By the 13th century, the Thai were in a position to assume control of the Chaophraya basin through the establishment of a number of autonomous states. The first of these, the kingdom of Sukhothai, was founded in 1238.

Under King Ramkhamhaeng (c. 1275-c.1298), Sukhothai's authority extended down the valley of the Chaophraya and into the Malay peninsula. Religious, cultural and commercial relations were established with Sri Lanka, northern India and China. In the early 14th century, Sukhothai's power declined rapidly. From the resulting fragmentation of political power, one man, Uthong, was able to establish a new capital at Ayutthaya and to become King Ramathibodi in 1351 AD. The new kingdom of Ayutthaya sought to dominate the Chaophraya basin. By the middle of the 15th century the Khmers to the east had been forced to abandon Angkor and Sukhothai had been effectively integrated into the Ayutthaya kingdom. Ayutthaya underwent a number of major internal administrative and legal reforms, particularly during the reign of Trailok (1448-1488) whose innovations were to remain the foundation of Thai administration, legal practice and social organization until the end of the 19th century. The structure of government was centralized and reorganized on a departmental basis; the *Kot Monthianban* ('palace law') of 1450 codified and clarified existing administrative custom and law; the *sakdina* system by which the status of the different classes of people and the amount of land each was entitled to hold was reformed and firmly regulated by Trailok. Trailok's reign was also notable for its religious vitality and literary achievements.

In the 16th century Ayutthaya came under threat from a resurgent Burma, reunified under Kings Tabin-shwei-hti (1531-1550) and Bayin-naung (1550-1581). After being subjugated by the Burmese, King Naresuan was able to defeat them at the end of the century and by the early 1600s Thailand's independence was again secured. However, the struggle between Thailand and Burma for domination of Buddhist South-East Asia continued into the early 19th century. In the 17th century, Thailand began to encourage trade relations with the European powers. Ayutthaya's foreign entanglements became increasingly complex during the reign of King Narai (1657-1688) who sought to counterbalance the powerful Dutch presence by encouraging diplomatic and commercial relations with France. A Greek adventurer, Constantine Phaulkon, who had rapidly risen in Narai's court to the powerful position of Superintendent of Foreign Trade, conspired with the French to give them major interests in the Thai kingdom. Phaulkon over-reached himself and was executed in June 1688. The anti-European sentiment generated within Thailand by the Phaulkon episode was to remain a dominant element in Thai policy and administration until the middle of the 19th century.

The rise of a new Burmese dynasty founded by Alaung-hpaya in the mid-18th century was followed by a resumption of hostilities with Thailand. In 1767, Ayutthaya, after a long and fierce resistance and siege, fell to the Burmese who plundered the city. The Thai recovery was swift, and within a few years Thai authority was restored over Cambodia, Laos and Chiangmai under the leadership of Taksin who established a new capital at Thonburi. However, Taksin's severe rule and pretensions provoked a major internal revolt. Taksin resigned and his principal general took over power. In 1782, with his elevation as Rama I, a new capital and dynasty was established across the river in Bangkok. The reign of Rama I (1782-1809) saw the end of the Burmese threat, and major administrative, religious, legal and literary achievements. In the following two reigns, Thailand's contacts with the Western world were revived on a limited scale, and a treaty was signed in 1826 with Henry Burney of the East India Company. The Bowring Treaty of commerce and friendship signed with Britain in 1855 (and further treaties signed subsequently with other powers) opened Thailand to virtually unrestricted foreign commerce and to full diplomatic and cultural contact with the outside world. The reign of Mongkut (1851-1868) and of Chulalongkon (1868-1910) witnessed major changes in the economic, social and administrative structure of the Thai kingdom. Thailand's foreign trade expanded rapidly and by the early 20th century the kingdom was a major world producer of rice and teak. Slavery (a relatively unoppressive institution in traditional Thailand) was gradually abolished and the structure of both central and provincial government underwent major reform along western lines. Skilful diplomacy, internal reform and judicious if difficult abandonment of control over peripheral territory helped Thailand to avoid the fate of her neighbours and emerge as the only state in South-East Asia not to come under colonial rule.

Kings Wachirawut (1920-1925) and Prachathipok (1925-1935) lacked the political foresight and decisiveness of Mongkut and Chulalongkon. Moreover, the bureaucratic and social reforms initiated by Chulalongkon had, by the 1920s and 1930s, produced a substantial non-royal elite who felt increasingly frustrated by absolute rule. The collapse of economic activity which occurred at the end of the 1920s increased these strains on the political and administrative system, and on 24 June 1932 the absolute monarchy was brought to an end by a bloodless coup, undertaken by a coalition of government officials, military officers and radical students recently returned from abroad. Thailand has since 1932 been a constitutional monarchy (Prachathipok, 1925-1935; Anan,1935-1946; Phumiphon, 1946-) with a governing elite that has, on the whole, been dominated by the military. There have been periods of civilian rule but the inherently superior organization of the armed forces has meant that these interludes have been relatively brief.

For bibliographies, see **Hart** (1977), **Keyes** (1979), and **Watts** (1986); the articles in **Ayal** (1978) provide a survey and bibliographies on the state of Thai studies. A general handbook is **Bunge** (1981). For an introduction to modern

Thailand, see **Keyes** (1987). On Thai Buddhism, see **Ishii** (1986a). The best history is **Wyatt** (1982) which also gives bibliographic guidance; in addition, on early history, see **Charnvit Kasetsiri** (1976) and the bibliography by **Mabbett** (1977); for Thailand from the mid-18th century, see **Ingram** (1971) and **Terwiel** (1983). On modern Thai politics, see **Elliot** (1978), **Girling** (1981) and **Thak Chaloemtiarana** (1979) and, for the mid-1970s period, **Morell** and **Chai-anan Samudvanij** (1981).

Dating Systems

Throughout Thai history several dating systems have been in use. In 1911 one era, the *Phutthasakkarat* (or 'Buddhist era' - BE) was adopted as the official Thai era. Other eras continued in use, however, until 1932 when use of the *Phuttasakkarat* era became general.

The different eras and figures for conversion to the Christian era are as follows: *Phuttasakkarat* (Buddhist era) — for the Ayutthaya period (to 2324 BE), subtract 544; for the Bangkok period (from 2325 BE), subtract 543; *Chunlasakkarat* (Minor era) — add 638; *Mahasakkarat* (Major era) — add 78; *Ratanakosinsok* — add 1781.

In religious texts, the use of the *Phutthasakkarat* (Buddhist era) was common; the *Chunlasakkarat* was most used in manuscripts. During the first five reigns of the Chakri dynasty (i.e. 1782-1910) the *Ratanakosin* era is found used in manuscripts and book imprints.

Language

Thai belongs to the Tai language family which also includes Shan in Burma, Ahom in Assam, Tho and Nung in Vietnam, Zhvang (Chuang) in southern China, Lao and other languages and dialects (see sections below on language families and dialects). Thai is spoken by the great majority of the population of Thailand.

It is a tonal language. Every syllable that receives normal stress possesses a definite pitch level (high, mid or low) or pitch contour (rising or falling). Thai has conventionally been regarded as mono-syllabic, but Thai vocabulary has always had recourse to compounding whereby the compound functions as one polysyllabic word. For example, *phi su'a* (butterfly) is compounded from two Thai words both meaning 'ghost' or 'spirit'. Another source of polysyllabic words in Thai is borrowing from other languages. A large proportion of the standard Thai vocabulary — especially for Buddhist, court, literary and technical matters — consists of loan words from Khmer, Sanskrit, Pali, Mon, Javanese, Chinese (mainly Swatow) and English. Thai technical vocabulary abounds in coined words. For example, the word for postal services in Thai is *praisani,* a coinage from a Sanskrit gerundive meaning 'that which is to be despatched'. Compounds following the Thai pattern are also plentiful. For example: *khipanawut* (guided missile) is from Pali terms meaning 'throwing weapons' and *dao thiam* (satellite) is from two Thai words for 'star' and 'fake'. Thai also has a number of words formed by prefixation (e.g. *prap* 'to make level' and *krap* 'to prostrate oneself' from *rap,* 'flat') or by infixation (e.g. *tamruat* 'police' from *truat* 'to check'). Most of these kinds of words are borrowings from Khmer.

In Thai there are no endings, agreements or affixes to mark grammatical functions or relationships and the meaning depends on word class and word order in sentences. There are no marked singulars or plurals in nouns, no marked tenses in verbs, no definite or indefinite articles and meaning usually depends on the context. There are some words that, incidental to another role, can serve as word order markers. Many of these words, by joining with a set of words found at the end of sentences, can convey whether the speaker/writer is concerned with questions, suggestions, doubts, commands, etc. They can also indicate the social relationship of the speaker/writer with the person addressed or referred to. Social relationships are also indicated in Thai by choice of vocabulary. In addition, Thai has a specialised vocabulary of the royal court called *rachasap* (from Sanskrit *rajasabda*) used for addressing and referring to royalty; similarly, lay people use a specialized vocabulary for speaking to and about monks. In common with most other Southeast Asian languages, Thai uses numeral classifiers.

Spelling is rather complicated due to the survival of much original spelling in loanwords. For example, all words borrowed from Sanskrit are still spelt as in Sanskrit, although the Thai pronunciation reflects very little of this spelling. In old Thai, spelling was rather variable, but with the advent of printing, spellings have been standardized. Since 1934 the Royal Institute (*Ratchabanditsathan*) has, together with advisory committees from universities and learned bodies, functioned as the national authority in orthography and lexicography. Its first monolingual Thai dictionary was published in 1950, incorporating much that first appeared in the Government Siamese Dictionary (*Pathanukrom*) of 1925.

There are four main dialect divisions of Thai: Central Thai, including the Bangkok region, which provides the 'received pronunciation' for schools, radio and television etc; Southern Thai — dialects spoken in peninsular Thailand; Northern Thai (an area sometimes referred to as Lannathai) — the Yuan or Kam-mu'ang dialects; North-East Thai — the Isan dialects (virtually identical with Lao). Tone variations in local speech communities are considerable and form important criteria for the study of dialects. Other dialect differences — between consonants or vowels — are easier to account for and usually less circumscribed than tone variations.

On language, see **Anuman Rajadhon** (1961) and **Brown** (1965) who also covers dialects. For linguistic studies, loan words, etc., see the articles in **Gedney** (1987), **Gething** (1976), **Harris** and **Chamberlain** (1975) and **Therapan L Thongkum** (1979) and the comprehensive bibliography in **Huffman** (1986). Major dictionaries are: Thai-Thai, **Manit Manicharoen** (1977), **Royal Institute** (1980); Thai-English, **Haas** (1964), **McFarland** (1944); English-Thai, **Prae Pittaya** (1966), **So Sethaputra** (1978). Among the teaching materials are: language courses, **Anthony** (1973), **Brown** (1967-69 and 1980), **Yates** and **Tryon** (1970); on script, **Anthony** (1979), **Brown** (1979), **Haas** (1956), **Kuo** (1979); on grammar, **Kuo** (1982), **Noss** (1964). **Udom Warotamasikkhadit** (1972); readers, **Dellinger** (1980), **Gething** and **Bilmes** (1977), **Jones** (1968-69 and 1970).

Tai Language Family

There are two basic schools of thought regarding the relationship of the Tai language family to other language families. One school, while considering Tai as a unique family, is nevertheless reluctant to see Tai as utterly divorced from the great Sino-Tibetan language family with some members of which, particularly Chinese, it is close and has shared typological features (tones, monosyllables). A more recent theory (propounded by Benedict) maintains that Tai and Austronesian (languages such as Malay, Javanese, Tagalog, etc. as well as Cham in central Vietnam) are linked by word correspondences that have been accepted by many linguists despite the obvious present divergence in typological evidence. Many scholars, particularly Gedney, vigorously oppose Benedict's theories. The Lao language also belongs to the Tai language family. The term Lao is often applied outside Laos to, among others, the dialects of Northern Thailand and to the dialects of Northeast Thailand. The spelling 'Tai' is found in the names of quite specific dialects, for example, the White Red and Black Tai of North Vietnam. Linguists have been at great pains to reconstruct a parent pronunciation which they call Proto-Tai from which all these dialects developed.

Non-Thai Languages

Chinese speaking communities have been established in Thailand for generations. The Chinese form influential minorities in the rice lands and in the towns, and Chinese also live in the village alongside, or within, Thai communities. Indian communities (speaking a variety of Indian languages) are less significant in number. Malay speakers outnumber monolingual Thai speakers in the southernmost Thai provinces of Yala, Pattani, Satun and Narathiwat, and are found generally throughout rural southern Thailand. The Central region of Thailand has dwindling numbers of Mon-speaking people. The Northeast has well-established communities, speaking Mon-Khmer dialects like Kui or Suai and Surin Khmer. Until recently, this region (above all Nakhon Phanom province) had considerable numbers of Vietnamese refugees, but many have now been repatriated. There are also Cambodian refugee settlements along the border with Cambodia. In the Western border area of North Thailand, there is a thriving Karen minority.

Other non-Thai languages are spoken by two geographically distinct groups: deep forest dwellers and mountain peoples, both until very recent times hardly in contact with Thai culture at all. Examples of forest dwellers are the negrito Sakai-Semang in the South, and the so-called *phi-tong-lu'ang* (spirits of the yellow leaves), the Yumbri or Mla-bri in the North. Among the mountain peoples are the Hmong or Miao, the Yao, the Akha, the Li-su and the Lahu or Mu-soe.

On ethnic minorities and their languages, see **Kunstadter** (1967), **LeBar** (1964) and **Schrock** (1970); also **Bernatzik** (1958), **Geddes** (1976) and **Young** (1962). On the Chinese in Thailand, see **Skinner** (1957). On Austro-Thai, see **Benedict** (1975); for a bibliography of Mon-Khmer and Tai linguistics, see **Shorto** (1963); **C.I.E.L.** (1977) provides a bibliography of Tai language studies. **Huffman** (1986) is the most up-to-date bibliography covering all linguistic studies.

South-East Asia

Script

The first evidence of a Thai script is the inscription dated 1292 AD of King Ramkhamhaeng of Sukhothai who, in the inscription, is credited with achieving the reduction of the Thai language to a written form in 1283 AD. In recent years some scholars (for example, Vickery and Piriya Krairiksh) have questioned the authenticity of this inscription. Its script showed a clear debt to the Khmer script and also to the Mon script (and ultimately to south Indian scripts), but also displayed three original features: initial vowels were not written as separate symbols but with a separate 'zero' consonant symbol; consonant clusters were written separately, one after the other along the line, instead of one on top of the other or in a merged form (as, for example, Khmer); and all vowel signs were written before the consonant rather than above, below or after it. This feature was the only one to last. The 1292 AD inscription had two tone markers, but in time five tone markers became necessary. It should be noted that one mark does not mean one tone: the combination of a particular tone marker with a particular consonant group and syllable type determines the tone in Thai.

The Thai script underwent several modifications, but by about 1600 it had achieved its final form. Difficulties in reading old manuscripts and inscriptions are more likely to arise from the spelling in early texts rather than from the script forms. The present alphabet has 44 letters. Words are written and printed without spacing. Thai script has a variety of artistic styles, and is often boldly and fancifully adapted in the advertising media.

Three other scripts in Thailand deserve mention: firstly, *Khom* (old Khmer or Cambodian) script which is virtually identical with the Cambodian *mul* script (see Cambodia section). It was formerly used throughout Central Thailand for all Pali texts written mainly on palm-leaf manuscripts but also on folding books. Secondly, Northern Thai script which is referred to as *Tham* (from Pali *Dhamma*) script because of the predominence of Buddhist manuscripts over secular manuscripts written in this script. It uses tone marks and employs subscript consonants not only in initial clusters but also in syllable final position. It has clear affinities, through Shan, with Burmese script. Another name for it is Lanna script, from the name for the old Chiangmai kingdom of Northern Thailand. Finally, there is Northeastern Thai script which is best considered as a branch of the Lao script (see Laos chapter). These three scripts are now rarely used.

There are two approaches to romanizing Thai: transliteration whereby the actual spelling is represented by symbols, and transcription which records the sounds of Thai. As the spelling of many Thai words is often Indic in origin, the transliteration bears little resemblance to the sounds of spoken Thai. Transliteration is now generally regarded as useful only for texts with a high proportion of loan words from Sanskrit and Pali and when it may be important to trace the etymology of words. The most widely accepted transcription is the General System of the Royal Institute. This system, with some modification, is used by the Library of Congress in America, and by the British Library and many other libraries.

On early script, see **Burnay** and **Coedès** (1927) and on modern script, see **Haas** (1956).

Manuscripts

In Thailand, as in Burma, there are basically two types of manuscripts, palm leaf (*nangsu'bailan*), and paper folding books (*samut thai* and *samut dam*). The method of preparing manuscripts and their format is very similar to those of Burma. A special script, *khom,* is used in Thai manuscripts for writing texts (predominently religious) in the Pali language. Many manuscripts come from the North and Northeast regions of Thailand and are written in the scripts of these regions. Subjects commonly depicted in illustrated Thai folding books include astrology, cosmology, massage and the Phra Malai story. As well as in Thai libraries (particularly the National Library) and private collections, several foreign libraries have significant Thai manuscript collections.

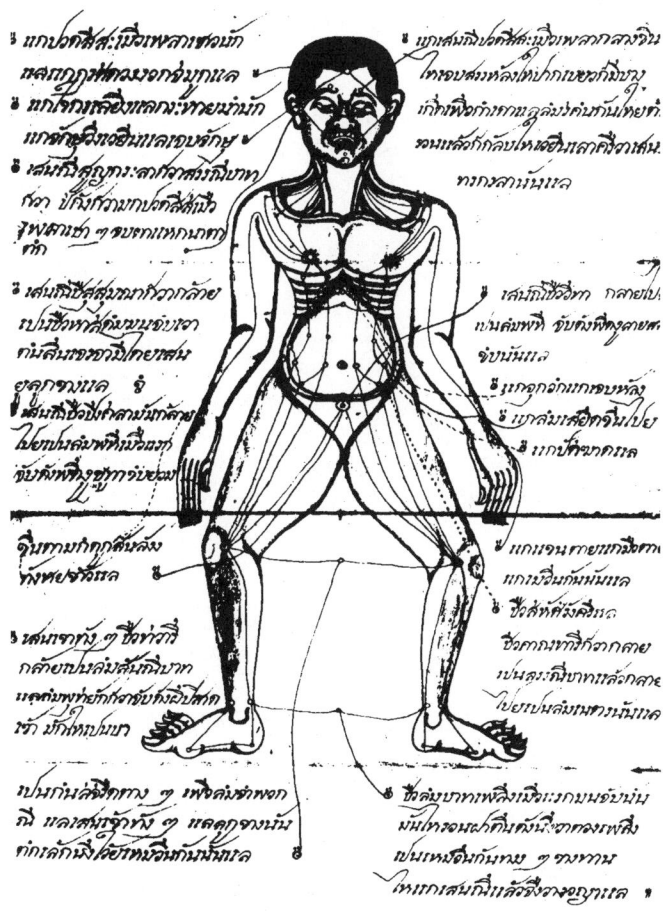

Thai massage treatise
Detail from a mid-19th century Thai MS

On the making of palm leaf manuscripts, see **Schuyler** (1908) and **Velder** (1961). There are few published catalogues of Thai manuscripts; for German collections, see **Wenk** (1963 and 1968); on illustrated manuscripts, see **Wenk** (1965).

Printing and Development of the Press

Although both the French Catholic priests in the late 17th century and the American Baptist missionaries in Burma in the early 19th century were interested in printing Christian texts in Thai, the only evidence to come to light is a catechism (in romanization) of 1796. The first surviving printing of Thai script was James Low's *A grammar of the Thai or Siamese language*, printed in Calcutta by the Baptist Mission Press in 1828. American missionaries introduced the first press to Thailand from Singapore (where some gospels in Thai were printed in the 1820s-1830s) and printed Christian tracts in Thai in 1836.

The Thai monarchy quickly recognised the potential of printing and as early as 1839 a royal decree was printed. In 1858 the first Thai official gazette (*Ratchakitchanubeksa*) was published by the newly founded Government Printing Press (*Rong Akson Phimphakan*). Between 1858 and 1868 nineteen issues of the official gazette were issued, all under the personal supervision of the king. *Ratchakitchanubeksa* then lapsed, but was revived in 1874 and continues to this day.

The first periodicals and newspapers to appear in Thailand were published by American missionaries. From 1844 to 1845 Dan Beach Bradley published the monthly *Bangkok Recorder* (in Thai). He also published an 1842 almanac in Thai. Another missionary, Chandler, published in English from 1847 the *Bangkok Calendar*. The *Bangkok Recorder* resumed publication between 1864-1867, this time published in Thai, though later with an English edition also. In the 1860s several other English newspapers appeared of which the *Bangkok Daily Advertiser* (1868-1878) and the *Siam Weekly Advertiser* (1868-1885) published by another missionary, Samuel Smith, were the most long-lived. Smith also produced (from 1869 to 1874) a quarterly English language journal, the *Siam Repository*, and from 1882 to 1885 he published a Thai weekly newspaper, *Chotmaihet Sayamsamai*.

Production of newspapers and magazines increased rapidly. In the course of Chulalongkon's reign (1868-1910), 17 newspapers and 42 journals were published, and Thais replaced foreigners as owners and editors of publishing ventures. Members of the Thai royal family predominated, but two commoners who became distinguished editors and achieved some notoriety were K. S. R. Kulap and Thianwan. The first Thai language magazine, *Darunowat* (published 1874-75) was edited by a young royal prince and another prince started the first paper to be published by a Thai; this paper was called *Court* or *Court-Khao Ratchakan* and was published from 1875 to 1876. In the 1880s and 1890s, the Wachirayan Library published *Wachirayan wiset*, originally reporting only court news but soon widening in scope to include literary and cultural topics.

Two short-lived magazines which had great influence on the development of modern Thai literature at the beginning of the 20th century were *Lak witthaya* (1901-03) and *Thawi Panya* (1904-07). The Siam Society, founded in 1904 by a group of Thai and foreign scholars, set high scholarly standards in its two publications, *Journal of the Siam Society* and the *Natural History Bulletin* which continue to this day.

Publishing continued to expand during the reign of Wachirawut (Rama VI: 1910-25). Altogether 22 daily newspapers and 127 journals were published in this period. The King himself published many of his own literary works in *Dusit Samit*, a weekly newspaper begun in December 1918 as the publication for the King's experimental city of democracy, Dusit Thani. Freedom of the press was considerable and Thai newspapers of this period also experimented with new formats and items (tabloid size, pictures to accompany news, headlines on front pages, cartoons) as well as continuing to include a lot of fiction. *Sayam Rat*, established in 1920, was noted for its translations of Chinese novels. Thailand's first daily Chinese newspaper, *Chino-Sayam Warasap*, was published from 1907-1923 with items in both Chinese and Thai.

The 1932 Revolution was a turning point for the Thai press which had done much to prepare for the change from absolute to constitutional monarchy, but which found itself after the Revolution more strictly censored than it had been before. Between June 1932 and October 1933, 28 newspapers were suspended. In the post-World War II period, the leading newspapers were *Sayam Rat, Deli niu* (established late 1940s), *Thairat* (established late 1950s), *Prachathipatai* (started 1933). A flourishing regional press also developed. The English and Chinese language newspapers are almost all owned by foreigners. The political upheavals of the 1970s closed down many newspapers and magazines.

Mention should also be made of cremation volumes which are unique to Thailand. These consist of a collection of works, texts and articles published in honour of a deceased person and distributed at their cremation. This practice started in the early 1900s and has given rise to and preserved a wealth of literary, historical and other source materials.

On early printing and publications, see **Duverdier** (1980) and **Reynolds** (1973). **Asia Library Services** (1977) gives a profile of Thai newspapers; see also **Boonrak Boonyaketmala** (1982) and, for the period 1973-76, **Lent** (1977).

Literature

The inscriptions of the Sukhothai period (1257-1376), particularly King Ramkhamhaeng's inscription of 1292, give information on Sukhothai's history, religion, kings and government in a simple prose narrative style. This prose writing with its choice of similar sounding words to form a pleasing rhythmic effect reflects a poetical influence. The *Suphasit Phraruang* (also called *Banyat Phraruang*) — 'Maxims of King Ruang' — composed, possibly by the king himself, in Ramkhamhaeng's reign, is the earliest example of Thai poetry of the didactic genre known as *suphasit*. The prototype of *suphasit* poetry is considered to be the Pali metrical work *Lōkaniti* ('Guidance to mankind'), whilst the style is influenced by canonical Buddhist texts, in particular by the *gatha* (verses) of the *Jatakas* and by the *Dhammapada*. There are several recensions of the *Suphasit Phraruang*, but the best known is the 19th century text engraved on marble slabs at Wat Pho in Bangkok, which includes 160 moral instructions and sayings in a verse form called *rai* (see below). The

Suphasit Phraruang influenced much later poetry, for example, *Phali Son Nong* (Phali teaches the young), Kritsana Son Nong (Queen Kritsana's advice to her sister) and *Suphasit Son Ying* (Advice to women).

An important Thai prose work of the period is the *Traiphum Phraruang* (Three Worlds Cosmography of Phraruang), reputedly compiled from Pali canonical texts and commentaries by King Litthai (Lidaiya or Mahadhammaraja I) in 1345. It contains the Thai Buddhist world view, presenting the three worlds in the order of the hells, the earth and the heavens and giving also a description of ideal kingship in terms of a *cakravartin* (universal monarch). Over the centuries, the text has been preserved and elaborated upon. After the destruction of Ayutthaya in 1767, in the reign of King Taksin a new illustrated copy of the work was commissioned in 1776 and a more extensive version compiled in 1778; in 1783, King Rama I commissioned a new compilation, called *Trailok winitchai*, based on a re-examination of the Pali sources. Parts of the *Traiphum* texts have found expression not only in later literary works but also in paintings of the three worlds on temple walls.

In the Ayutthaya period (1350-1767), the monarchy was influenced by Khmer concepts of divine right and gradually adopted complex Brahmanic ceremonies, elaborate court language and etiquette. Versification became popular at the royal court and much patronage was given to poets, writers, musicians and dancers. Both Buddhist and Brahmanic influence strongly affected the vocabulary, versification, imagery and themes of literary works of this period. Poetry predominated and was the medium of expression for dramatic works, epic romances, narrative and travel descriptions, boat songs and for religious literature and moral instructions. Prose was used for historical, official and legal texts.

The tonal nature of the Thai language has ensured that rhyme plays an important part in Thai poetry. Five types of verse form developed in this period and are still in use today. They are: *chan, kap, khlong, klon* and *rai* (each having numerous subclassifications). Each type of verse form has complex and rigorous prosodic rules regulating the number of syllables per line and the rhyming pattern. *Chan* (Sanskrit *chanda*) and *kap* (Sanskrit *kavya*) are of Indian origin. The *chan* verse form is the most difficult because the Thai language has only a limited number of short syllable words which are necessary to maintain the particular metrical rhythm of this form. In 1842, Prince Paramanuchit, using the Pali metrical work *Vuttodaya* as a basis, created 58 subtypes of *chan* consisting of two main groups *Varnavritti* (measured by number of syllables) and *Matravritti* (measured by syllable length). The result was that, though perfected, *chan* verse became more difficult to compose. The *khlong, klon* and *rai* verse forms are all believed to be indigenous Thai forms, the *rai* form being the simplest. Thai scholars treat the literature of the Ayutthaya period chronologically and divide it into three main periods: King Trailok's reign (1448-1488) during which a type of poem called *lilit*, composed by combining the *rai* and *khlong* verse forms, was predominant; the period commencing with King Narai's reign (1656-1688) in which the *chan* and *khlong* forms predominated; and the period of King Boromakot (1733-1758) in which the *klon* form became most popular. The oldest poem in the *lilit* form is the *Lilit Ongkan Chaeng Nam*. It provides the text for recitation at the ceremony of drinking the oath waters of allegiance performed from the beginning of the

Ayutthaya period. Archaic both in style and vocabulary, the poem refers to many Hindu gods and characters from the *Ramayana*. The *Lilit Yuan phai*, composed around 1475 by an unknown author, is a panegyric on King Trailok's victory over the Yuan, the northern kingdom, and narrates events from 1431-66, closing with an epic battle scene. It has some 294 verses in the four line *khlong* form and two passages in *rai* form. The date and authorship of another poem, the *Lilit Phra Lo* are in dispute, but the poem is acknowledged to be a masterpiece in which human passions are strongly and erotically expressed.

The literary genre known as *khamluang* (royal version) also emerged during this period. These are poetic works often based on the last great *Jataka*, the *Vessantara Jataka*. The *Mahachat khamluang*, recounting the *Vessantara Jataka*, was composed by scholars at Trailok's court and it was considered important for the story to be recited regularly to preserve Buddhist lore. The *Mahachat khamluang* is divided into thirteen chapters (*kanda*) and includes all one thousand of the Pali *gatha*, each being followed by a Thai paraphrase written in *rai* verse form (but with some inserts in *chan*, *kap* and *khlong* verse forms also). Another and improved version called the *Kap Mahachat* was composed in *rai* verse form during the reign of Songtham (1602-1628). Many versions of the *Vessantara Jataka* exist, including regional versions, and they are still recited at temple ceremonies, usually at the beginning of the Buddhist Lent.

Culture and literature flourished during the reign of King Narai (1656-1688) and the literary genre known as *nirat* reached perfection in this period. *Nirat* are long, reflective and lyrical poems written in *khlong* verse form. In *nirat* poetry, the poet, who is usually away on a journey or in exile, expresses his longing for his beloved and how the scenery and incidents encountered on his journey remind him of the happy times when he was with his love. The *nirat* genre has continued to this day, adapting to modern circumstances and often relating journeys abroad. Possibly the earliest *nirat* is the *Khlong Thawathotsamat* in which no place names are mentioned, and the theme is the poet's longing throughout the year and the changes and ceremonies of each month. Other *nirat* poems are the *Khlong nirat Hariphunchai*, written by Sithep about a journey from Chiangmai to Lamphun and *Khlong Kamsuan Siprat*, written by the great poet Siprat, on his journey into exile at Nakhonsithamarat in southern Thailand. Written with consummate skill to express the poet's longing for his beloved and for Ayutthaya city, *Khlong Kamsuan Siprat* is the acknowledged masterpiece of the *nirat* genre, and has influenced many subsequent poems.

The Indian *Ramayana* (known in its Thai version as *Ramakian*) was an important inspirational source for Thai literature. King Narai, for example, used episodes from the *Ramayana* in his *suphasit* poems, *Khlong Phali son nong* (Phali teaches his younger brother), *Khlong Thotsarot son Phra Ram* (Thotsarot teaches Rama) and *Khlong Ratchasawat* (the ideal king). But the greatest influence of the *Ramayana* and other Indian sources was on Thai dramatic poetry texts composed for stage performances of *nang* (shadow-play), *khon* (masked drama) and *lakhon* (dance-drama). An extract from the *Ramayana* thought to have been written especially for *khon* performance was the *Rachaphilap khamchan*.

In the Ayutthaya period, dramatic poetry was mostly written in *chan* verse form. Important court poets such as Phramaharatchakhru and Siprat produced

Buddhist monks. Detail from a 19th century Phra Malai MS

dramatic poetry drawing on various sources. Phramaharatchakhru wrote *Suakho khamchan* based on the *Pannasa Jatakas* (the extra-canonical cycle of Chiangmai origin) and began another work, *Samuthakhot Khamchan* which was based on the Samuthakhot *Jataka* of the *Pannasa* cycle. The poem *Samuthakhot Khamchan* was completed only in the 19th century by Prince Paramanuchit. The dramatic poem *Anirut khamchan* is generally ascribed to Siprat. Traditionally the *Visnu Purana* has been regarded as the prototype for the *Anirut khamchan*, but a recent study (by Maneepin) considers the *Harivamsa* to be a more likely source. A later poem, *Bunnowat khamchan*, by Phra Mahanak marks a development in the *khamchan* form. Instead of telling a story, it gives a description of the Buddha's footprint, the only association with drama being a description of dramatic performances seen by the poet. The first text on the writing of poetry was written by a royal astrologer, Phra Horathibodi, during King Narai's reign. It gave vocabulary for poetic composition and quotations from well known literary works to illustrate various types of poems and verse forms. Chronicle writing also started in this period. The earliest chronicle is the *Phongsawadan chabap luang Prasoet* ('the chronicle discovered by Luang Prasoet').

In the late Ayutthaya period, *klon* verse became popular and was used in the composition of both dramatic poetry (displacing *chan* form) and narrative poetry. A court grammarian, Luang Sipricha, wrote the first known manual on *klon* prosody, *Siriwibunkiti*, which laid down rather contrived varieties of *klon* called *klon konlabot*. During the reign of Boromakot (1733-1758) two *klon* forms in particular were popular: *klon phleng yao* (love epistles) and *klon bot lakhon* (dance-drama texts in *klon*).

Dance-drama (*lakhon*) is known to have been performed in the 17th century, but no early texts have survived. The classical dance dramas *Dalang* and *Inao*, which are derived from the Javanese *Panji* story cycle, date from this period. More and more stories, particularly drawing on the *Jatakas*, were written for performance and *lakhon* dance-drama developed three different forms. These were: *lakhon chatri*, an early form, performing the *Sudhana Jataka*, still popular in the south and known there as *nora*; *lakhon nok* ('outside court *Lakhon*') which was relatively informal and was performed exclusively in the palaces of minor royalty and nobles. Its sources include *Jatakas* and many folk stories now known collectively as *bot lakhon khrang krung kao* (dance-drama texts of the old capital); and *lakhon nai* ('inside dance-drama') which were performances by women in the royal court of episodes from the *Ramakian* (and possibly from *Inao*).

In the late Ayutthaya period, court poets continued to make use of *chan*, *kap*, *khlong* and *rai* verse forms for the composition of such established genres as *nirat*, *khamluang* and *khamchan* works. Two notable *khamluang* works were composed by Prince Thammathibet (who is better known as Chao Fa Kung). *Nanthopananthasut khamluang*, in *rai* verse form, tells how the Buddha's disciple, Phra Mokkhala, reduced the angry Naga (serpent) King to a state of tranquillity and an understanding of the Buddha's teachings. *Phra Malai khamluang*, in *klon* verse form, is the story of a monk, *Phra Malai*, who attained a state of purification and emancipation and visited the heavens and hells. The story of Phra Malai's travels was a favourite subject for illustration in manuscripts. Chao Fa Kung is best known, however, for his works using a verse technique called *kap ho khlong*, in which *kap* and *khlong* stanzas are used in alternate succession to depict the same idea. The poem *Nirat phrabat* is an extended and refined treatment of the temporal element in *nirat* poetry. *Nirat thansok* and *nirat than thongdaeng* are more superficial but demonstrate great mastery of punning and knowledge of Thai flora and fauna.

As a result of the Burmese destruction of Ayutthaya in 1767, many Thai literary works have been lost to posterity. Literary activity at the new capital, Thonburi, was limited but King Taksin himself wrote four episodes of the *Ramakian* in *klon* verse form and ordered the compilation of a new *Traiphum* ('three worlds') text and a prose chronicle. Phraya Mahanuphap wrote the first *nirat* poem about a journey to a foreign country, based on his experience as a member of a Thai embassy to China in 1781. His poem *Nirat Kwangtung* (later renamed *Nirat Phraya Mahanuphap pai muang Chin*), written in *klon* verse, contained very little of the conventional *nirat* theme of love and longing and concentrated much more on a description of the actual journey.

South-East Asia

After the establishment of Bangkok as the new capital in 1782, Rama I set about reconstructing the Thai kingdom and reviving Thai literature. More traditional literary works were produced during the first three reigns than at any other period and a high standard of prose writing was established by such important works as the Buddhist cosmology *Trailok winitchai* (1783), the law code *Kotmai tra sam duang* (1805) and revised versions (in 1793 and 1850) of the Ayutthaya chronicles, *Phra ratcha phongsawadan*. New emphasis is detectable in these works. For example, in the *Trailok winitchai*, the origins of king and government, which in the *Traiphum* version appeared at the end, are now placed prominently at the beginning, the centre of the world is shifted from Mount Meru to the seat of the lord Buddha (*Phutthabanlang*) and the Boddhisattva quality of kingship is emphasized.

During the reign of Rama I, the first prose fiction was written by a court poet, Chao Phraya Phra Khlang (personal name Hon). His works, *Sam kok*, an adaptation of the Chinese historical romance of the three kingdoms, and *Rachathirat*, an adaptation of a Mon text, are still regarded as models of Thai prose style. Rama I began what is known as *Phra Ratchaniphon* ('royal writing'), a term applied to a king's own work and to literary works written with royal direction or collaboration. The *Krom Alak* (Royal Scribes' Department) formed a circle of illustrious poets and scholars to compose works at court. Many dramatic poems, all in *klon* verse form, fall into the *Phra Ratchaniphon* category. They include the first (and only) full versions of the *Ramakian*, of *Dalang*, of *Inao* and *Unarut* (based on the Ayutthaya period poem *Anirut Khamchan*). King Rama I's *Ramakian* incorporated many Thai legends and customs and it has been the basis for all subsequent *Ramakian* versions (except for one by Rama VI which was based on an English translation of the Sanskrit original).

During the reign of Rama II (1809-1824), *Lakhon nai* was perfected and the *Ramakian* and *Inao* texts were carefully revised for dramatic performance. A popular epic romance (some 20,000 lines long), called *Khun Chang khun Phaen,* was also composed at this time. It was based on a story long known and sung as *Sepha* recitation by country bards in central Thailand. Passages from it were read at court during tonsure ceremonies for the royal children. A master of *klon* verse was Sunthon Phu (c.1786-c.1855) who rose to fame as court poet under Rama II but fell into disgrace under Rama III. His most famous work was a 30,000 line epic romance, *Phra Aphaimani*. He also wrote many *nirat* poems with autobiographical and innovative elements. His work made *nirat* poetry very popular and inspired such later poets as Nai Mi and Mom Rachothai. Conventional *nirat* poetry in *khlong* verse continued to be written and noteworthy works include *Nirat Narin* by Narinthibet and two poems by Phraya Trang.

The revival and rewriting of Thai classical literature reached a peak during the reign of Rama III when Prince Paramanuchit not only revised chronicle texts, but completed the *Samutthakhot khamchan* and composed a *lilit* poem, *Taleng Phai*, recounting King Naresuan's 16th century victory over the Burmese. In the course of the 19th century, as the Thai reading public increased, prose writing came to predominate, although poetry, particularly dramatic poetry, remained popular.

In the reign of Rama V, three types of *Lakhon* (dance-drama) were created: *Lakhon Rong, Lakhon Du'kdamban* and *Lakhon Phanthang*. Performers continued to sing their parts but also began to speak dialogue passages in poetic prose. Many new songs and lines were written for these *lakhon,* including a poem, *Ngo Pa,* by Rama V. *Khon* (masked drama) also changed. Many songs written by Prince Narit for *Lakhon Du'kdamban* were used also for *khon* performances instead of using the old *Ramakian* text. Rama VI (1910-25) made many innovations. He translated several plays of Shakespeare for performance in Thai and wrote long poems, *Phranon Khamluang* and *Sakuntala,* based on English translations of Sanskrit texts, and a poem, *Mathanaphatha,* in which he experimented with the difficult *chan* verse form. As crown prince he had started a literary club, many of whose young noble and official members rose to prominence in the 1920s and 1930s. For instance, Prince Phitthayalongkon (1876-1945) wrote *Kanok Nakhon* (adapted from an English translation of a Sanskrit work) and *Sam Krung,* a long epic about Ayutthaya, Thonburi and Bangkok. Chit Burathat (1892-1942) wrote in strict *chan* verse form the poem *Samakhiphet khamchan* which had the theme of national unity.

The 1932 revolution brought about a change in literary themes and style. Composition of traditional genres declined. *Chan* verse form came to be reserved for writing royal eulogies and commemorative works. Chao Phraya Thammasak Montri or Khru Thep (1877-1943), initiated the use of verse as a medium for political and social commentary. In 1950, M. R. Khu'krit Pramot began using the *sakawa* type of *klon* in his newspaper *Sayam Rat,* for expressing editorial opinion and commentary, and other newspapers have copied this practice. A strong critic under the Phibun and Sarit regimes was the poet Chit Phumisak who, writing under the pen name Kawi Kanmuang, made use of various verse forms including popular oral verses. His work had a strong influence upon students and intellectuals at the time of the 1973 uprising. An outstanding contemporary poet is Angkhan Kanlayanaphong whose first published work appeared in 1960. Angkhan shocked and dismayed many literary traditionalists by his use of unusual imagery, paradoxical metaphors and expressionist and provoking symbolism. In his famous poem, *Wak Thale The Sai Chan* (Scoop up the sea), the gods come down to earth and enjoy eating faeces, whereas earthworms rise to the heavens and make love to *apsaras* (angels). Recurrent themes in his poetry are concern for man and his environment, the ugliness of materialism and the beauty of spiritual concerns. Collected editions of his poems are *Lamnam Phukradung, Suan Kaeo* and *Kawiniphon khong Angkhan.* Another important contemporary poet is Nawarat Phongphaibun whose poem *Athit thung Chan* described the October 1973 uprising, although he is popularly respected and known for his more conventional poem, *Chak Ma Chom Muang.*

Between 1973 and 1976, publishers became less cautious about publishing politically sensitive materials. Many young poets began to use poetry as an effective means of criticising the government and society. These poets, with different degrees of radicalism, include Khanchai Bunpan, Suchit Wongthet, Rawi Domphrachan, Wat Wanlayangkun, Witthayakon Chiangkun and Khomthuan Khanthanu.

Modern Thai prose literature is generally dated from the introduction of printing techniques, journalism and modern education consequent upon the policy of Mongkut (Rama IV) of opening up Thailand to the West. An American missionary, D. B. Bradley, began publishing Thai literary works including Mom

Rachothai's *Ruam Chotmaihet ru'ang thut thai pai Prathet Angkrit mu'a pho so 2400* (Records of the Siamese Embassy to England in 1857-1858), *Chindamani*, a text on writing poetry (1861), *Kotmai tra sam duang* (1863), *Sam kok* (1865) and *Rachathirat* (1880). Bradley also introduced the concept of copyright when in 1862 he bought the rights to Mom Rachothai's *Nirat London*. Another missionary, Smith, began a publishing house in 1865 and published such works as *Khun chang Khun Phaen* and *Phra Aphaimani*, as well as two English journals and one Thai journal. In 1858 the Thai government began publishing the *Ratchakitchanubeksa*, or Royal Gazette, which became the official means of informing the public of decrees, laws and news. Its prose style marks the beginning of modern critical prose writing. Non-fictional prose writing also developed through the writing of chronicles. In King Mongkut's reign, a revised version of the chronicles covering the period from Sukhothai to the first reign of the Bangkok period was compiled. It is known as the *Phra Ratchaphongsawadan Phra Ratchahatlekha* (Royal autograph edition). The chronicle emphasized kingship as an institution, as distinct from the king's person. Thai scholars have a high regard for the literary and historical prose style of this chronicle. The writing of prose received much impetus through the works of Mongkut's children who wrote memoirs, travel descriptions, letters, scholarly essays, biographies and addresses. The works of Chulalongkon (Rama V) include *Phra Ratchaphithi Sipsong Duan* (Royal ceremonies of the twelve months of the year) and *Klai Ban* (Far from home), an account of a journey to Europe in 1907. Prince Wachirayanwarorot in 1915 wrote the first Thai autobiography, *Phra Prawat Trat Lao*. Another autobiography, *Khwam Songcham* (Memoirs) was written by Prince Damrong who also wrote an account of the wars between Thailand and Burma (*Thai rop Phama*), biographies and many articles on history and archaeology and whose voluminous correspondence with Prince Narit was published under the title, *San Somdet*.

The writing of fiction can be dated to the appearance of 1874 of *Darunowat* (Advice to young men), the first Thai journal published by Thais. Satirical short stories such as *Nithan Patyuban* (A tale of the present time), *Khwam Fan* (the dream), and *Nai Rak kap Nai Ru'ang* (Mr Rak and Mr Ru'ang) were first published in this journal. An influential bi-weekly journal, *Wachirayan wiset*, later printed many short stories known collectively as *Nithan Wachirayan*. Some of these stories were adaptations and translations from Western sources. *Khwam Phayabat* by Mae Wan (a pseudonym) was a translation of Marie Corelli's *Vendetta* and its appearance started a new trend in Thai literature. It was first published in Prince Phitthaya's magazine *Lak Witthaya* (Plagiarism) in 1900. This magazine introduced the term *Nam Pakka*— 'pen name' — and encouraged the translation and adaptation of many works by such writers as Corelli, Conan Doyle, Alexander Dumas, Rider Haggard and Guy de Maupassant. The Thai reading public developed a taste for these new detective and mystery stories and romances with a Cinderella type theme, and the popularity of such old forms as the *Ru'ang Pralom Lok* (Mundane stories) in the *Bot Lakhon nok* tradition (which told of the adventures and romances of princes and princesses) declined sharply. When *Lak Witthaya* ceased publication in 1904, Crown Prince Wachirawut started a journal called *Thawi Panya* (Increasing Wisdom) in which his adaptations of Sherlock Holmes detective stories were published. A collected edition of these stories, *Nithan Nai Thong In*, was also published. Another successful work was *Chotmai Changwang Ram*, an adaptation of Lorimer's *Letters from a self-made merchant to his son*, made by Prince Phitthaya (writing under the pen-name of N. M. S.). From 1928 onwards, Thai writers began to write novels that were closer to realism. *Luk Phuchai* by Siburapha, *Lakhon haeng Chiwit* and *Phiu Lu'ang Phiu Khao* by Akatdamkoeng and *Sattru khong Chao Lon* by Dokmai Sot depicted social values and conflicts as well as human and family relations. In 1929 the *Suphapburut* (Gentlemen) Group was formed by such writers as Siburapha, Malai Chuphinit, Chot Phraephan and Sot Kuramarohit to seek recognition and financial security. After the 1932 revolution, more short stories and novels were written and both the short story and the novel have become firmly established as a genre and a vehicle for criticism. Today there are more than 15 weekly and monthly journals that publish short stories in every issue. The political upheavals of the last few decades have both inspired and affected writers. Important modern writers include Siburapha, Dokmai Sot, Akatdamkoeng, Ko Surangkhanang, Malai Chuphinit, Sirat Sathapanawat, Manat Chanyong, Sot Kuramarohit, Nimitmongkhon, Itsara Amantakun, Yot Watcharasathian, Suwat Woradilok, Seni Sawaphong, Khu'krit Pramot and Lao Kham Hom.

Legal Literature

The *Kot Monthianban* (Palace or Palatine Laws) of 1450 set out the basis of bureaucratic polity in the Ayutthaya period. After the destruction of Ayutthaya, Rama I, as part of the general reconstruction work of the kingdom, in 1805 ordered the compilation of the *Pramuan Kotmai Ratchakan thi nung* ('Law of the Three Seals'). In this, a connection was made between royal orders (*Rajasattham*) and the absolute legal concepts embodied in *Thammasat* (law texts derived from the Indian *dhammasastra*).

For an English and French translation of the Ramkhamhaeng inscription, see **Coedès** (1965); research in inscriptions is given in **Coedès** (1918, 1923, 1924, 1929) and in the series of articles by **Griswold** and **Prasert na Nagara** (1968-) of which no. 9 (1971) is a new translation of the Ramkhaemhaeng inscription taking into account more recent research and also providing background information on its discovery and previous translations; **Ishii** (1977) provides a glossary of Sukhothai inscriptions. For a French translation of the *Traiphum Phraruang*, see **Coedès** and **Archaimbault** (1973), while **Reynolds** (1982) gives an English translation; on the significance of these texts, see also **Reynolds** (1976). On the *Ramakian*, see **Bofman** (1984). For a French translation and comments on the epic poem *Khun chang khun Phaen*, see **Sibunruang** (1960). For comments and a translation of *Suphasit Phraruang*, see **Gerini** (1904); on *Phali son nong*, see **Wenk** (1980); on the *Lilit Phra Lo*, see **Dhani Nivat** (1953); for an English translation of *Lilit Yuan Phai*, see **Griswold** and **Prasert na Nagara** (1976). On poetry of the *nirat* genre, see **Manas Chitakasem** (1972) and **Schweisguth** (1950 and 1951); on works in *chan* verse, especially *Anirut khamchan*, see **Rosenberg** (1976), also **Maneepin Phromsuthirak** (1979) and **Wenk** (1962). **Wenk** (1986) provides an introduction to Sunthon Phu, who is discussed in more detail in **Wenk** (1985). **Cooke** (1980) discusses the *khlong* verse form; and for *Lakhon nora*, see

Nicholas (1924). For a detailed discussion and interpretation of Thai poetical forms, see **Wenk** (1982, 1985, 1987). On 20th century poetry, see **Mosel** (1961), and on literary developments in general, see **Srisurang Poolthupya** (1979). The origins of the novel are discussed in **Wibha Senanan** (1975). On short stories, see **Manas Chitakasem** (1982) and **Smyth** (1987). On modern Thai literature and authors, see **Mattani Rutnin** (1978), **Peltier** (1974), and **Srisurang Poolthupya** (1981). For a discussion of contemporary literature and an anthology in translation, see **Phillips** (1987). On the Thai chronicles and development of Thai historical writing, see **Charnvit Kasetsiri** (1979) and **Wyatt** (1975) which has an extensive bibliography. **Wood** (1925) gives a translation of the *Phongsawadan chabap luang Prasoet*. For a translation of some Thai folk tales, see **Le May** (1958). On Thai legal literature and for a bibliography, see **Ishii** (1986b).

Bibliography

Anthony, E. M., et al.
1973 *Foundations of Thai.* 2 vols. Ann Arbor: University of Michigan Press. (4th printing).

Anthony E. M.
1979 *A programmed course in reading Thai syllables.* Honolulu: University of Hawaii. (Southeast Asia Papers, No. 12). (1st published 1962, University of Michigan).

Anuman Rajadhon, Phraya
1954 *Thai language.* Bangkok: National Culture Institute. (Thailand Culture Series No. 17).
1961 *The nature and development of the Thai language.* Bangkok: Fine Arts Dept.

Asia Library Services
1977 *A guide to research materials on Thailand and Laos.* Auburn, N.Y.: Asia Library Services.

Ayal, E. B. (ed.)
1978 *The study of Thailand: analyses of knowledge, approaches and prospects in anthropology, art history, economics, history and political science.* Athens, Ohio: Ohio University Centre for International Studies. (Papers in International Studies, Southeast Asia Series, No. 54).

Benedict, P. K.
1975 *Austro-Thai: language and culture, with a glossary of roots.* New Haven: HRAF Press.

Bernatzik, H. A.
1958 *The spirits of the yellow leaves.* London: R. Hale. (Translated into English by E. W. Dickes from *Die Geister der Gelben Blätter*, Munich: 1938).

Bofman, T. H.
1984 *The poetics of the Ramakian.* DeKalb: Northern Illinois University, Center for Southeast Asian Studies.

Boonrak Boonyaketmala
1982 "Thailand." In J. A. Lent, ed. *Newspapers in Asia: contemporary problems and trends.* Hong Kong: Heinemann Asia, pp. 334-362.

Brown, J. M.
1965 *From ancient Thai to modern dialects.* Bangkok: Social Science Association Press of Thailand.(Reprinted 1985).
1967-69 *AUA Language Center Thai course.* 3 vols. Bangkok: AUA Language Center.
1979 *AUA Language Center Thai course: reading and writing.* 2 vols. Bangkok: AUA Language Center.
1980 *AUA Thai language course.* Bangkok: AUA Language Center.

Bunge, F. M. (ed.)
1981 *Thailand: a country study.* Washington D.C.: U.S. Govt. Printing. (American University, Foreign Area Studies, Area Handbook Series).

Burney, J. and G. Coedès
1927 "The origins of the Sukhodaya script." *JSS* 21, 2: 87-102.

Charnvit Kasetsiri
1976 *The rise of Ayudhya: a history of Siam in the fourteenth and fifteenth centuries.* Kuala Lumpur: Oxford University Press.
1979 "Thai historiography from ancient times to the modern period." In A. J. S. Reid and D. G. Marr, eds. *Perceptions of the past in Southeast Asia.* Kuala Lumpur: Heinemann, pp. 156-170.

C.I.E.L. (Central Institute of the English Language)
1977 *Bibliography of Tai language studies.* Bangkok: Indigenous Languages of Thailand Research Project, C.I.E.L., Office of State Universities.

Coedès, G.
1918 "Notes critiques sur l'inscription de Rama Khamhaeng." *JSS* 12: 1-27.
1923 "Nouvelles notes critiques sur l'inscription de Rama Khamhaeng." *JSS* 17:113-120.
1924 *Recueil des inscriptions du Siam. Première partie: Inscriptions de Sukhodaya.* Bangkok: Vajiranana National Library.
1929 *Recueil des inscriptions du Siam. Deuxième partie: Inscriptions de Dvaravati, de Crivijaya et de Lavo.* Bangkok: Bangkok Times Press.

Coedès, G. (ed.)
1965 *L'inscription du roi Rama Gamhen de Sukhodaya* (1292 AD). (French & English translations of the inscription). Bangkok: Siam Society.

Coedès, G. and C. Archaimbault
1973 *Les trois mondes, Traibhumi Brah R'van (Traibhumikatha)*. Paris: EFEO. (Publications de l'EFEO, 89).

Cooke, J. R.
1980 "The Thai Khlong poem: description and examples." *JAOS* 100:421-438.

Dellinger, D. W.
1980 *First year Thai programmed reader*. Rev. edn. DeKalb: Northern Illinois University, Center for Southeast Asian Studies.

Dhani Nivat, Prince.
1953 "The date and authorship of the romance of Phra Lo." *JSS* 41, 2:179-182.

Duverdier, G.
1980 "La transmission de l'imprimerie en Thailande: du catechisme de 1796 aux impressions bouddhiques sur feuilles de latanier." *BEFEO* 68:209-259.

Elliot, D.
1978 *Thailand: origins of military rule*. London: Zed Press.

Geddes, W. R.
1976 *Migrants of the mountains: the cultural ecology of the Blue Miao of Thailand*. Oxford: Clarendon Press.

Gedney, W. J.
1987 *Selected papers on comparative Tai studies*. Edited by R. J. Bickner, et al. Ann Arbor: University of Michigan, Center for South and Southeast Asian Studies. (Michigan Papers No. 29).

Gerini, G. E.
1904 "On Siamese proverbs and idiomatic expressions." *JSS* 1:11-168.

Gething, T. (ed.)
1976 *Tai linguistics in honor of Fang-Kuei Li*. Bangkok: Chulalongkorn University Press.

Gething, T. W. and P. T. Bilmes
1977 *Thai basic reader*. Honolulu: University of Hawaii.

Girling, J.
1981 *Thailand, society and politics*. London; Ithaca, N.Y.: Cornell University Press.

Griswold, A. B. and Prasert na Nagara
1968- "Epigraphic and historical studies." *JSS*. A series of articles commencing in vol. 56.

1976 "A fifteenth century Siamese historical poem." In C. D. Cowan and O. W. Wolters, eds. *Southeast Asian history and historiography: essays presented to D. G. E. Hall*. Ithaca, N.Y.: London: Cornell University Press, pp. 123-163.

Haas, M. R.
1954 *Thai reader*. Washington D.C.: American Council of Learned Societies. Program in Oriental Languages, Publication Series A, Texts 1.
1954 *The Thai system of writing*. Washington D.C.: American Council of Learned Societies. Program in Oriental Languages, Publication Series B, Aids No. 5. (Reprinted 1980, Ithaca, N.Y., Spoken Languages Series).

Haas, M. R. et al.
1964 *Thai-English student's dictionary*. Stanford: Stanford University Press.

Harris, J. G. and J. R. Chamberlain
1975 *Studies in Tai linguistics in honor of William J. Gedney*. Bangkok: Central Institute of English Language, Office of State Universities.

Hart, D. V.
1977 *Thailand: an annotated bibliography of bibliographies*. DeKalb: Northern Illinois University. (Center for Southeast Asian Studies, Occasional Paper No. 5).

Huffman, R. E.
1986 *Bibliography and index of mainland Southeast Asian languages and linguistics*. New Haven; London: Yale University Press.

Ingram, J. C.
1971 *Economic changes in Thailand 1850-1970*. Stanford: Stanford University Press.

Ishii, Y., et al.
1977 *A glossarial index of the Sukhothai inscriptions*. Kyoto: Center for Southeast Asian Studies, Kyoto University Press.

Ishii, Y.
1986a *Sangha, state and society: Thai Buddhism in history*. Kyoto: Center for Southeast Asian Studies, Kyoto University.
1986b "The Thai thammasat (with a note on the Lao thammasat)." In M. B. Hooker, ed. *Laws of South-East Asia, Vol 1: The pre-modern texts*. Singapore: Butterworth, pp. 143-203; bibliography, pp. 509-517.

Jones, R. B., et al.
1968-69 *Thai cultural reader*. 2 vols. Ithaca, N.Y.: Cornell University, Southeast Asia Program.

Jones, R. B. and R. C. Mendiones
1970 *Introduction to Thai literature*. Ithaca, N.Y.: Cornell University, Southeast Asia Program.

Keyes, C. F.
1979 *Southeast Asian research tools: Thailand*. Honolulu: University of Hawaii. (Southeast Asia Paper, No. 16, part VI).
1987 *Thailand: Buddhist kingdom as modern nation state*. London: Westview Press.

Kunstadter, P.
1967 *Southeast Asian tribes, minorities and nations*. Princeton: Princeton University Press.

Kuo, W.
1979 *A workbook for writing Thai*. Berkeley: University of California, Center for South and Southeast Asian Studies.
1982 *Teaching grammar of Thai*. Berkeley: University of California, Center for South and Southeast Asian Studies.

LeBar, F. M., G. C. Hickey and J. K. Musgrave
1964 *Ethnic groups of mainland Southeast Asia*. New Haven: HRAF Press.

Le May, R.
1958 *Siamese tales old and new*. London: Arthur Probsthain.

Lent, J. A.
1977 "The burnt out candle: Thailand's brief experience with press freedom 1973-1976." In *A guide to research materials on Thailand and Laos*. Auburn, N.Y.: Asia Library Services, pp. 1-10.

McFarland, G. B.
1944 *Thai-English dictionary*. Stanford: Stanford University Press; London: Oxford University Press.

Mabbett, I. (ed.)
1977 *Early Thai history: a select bibliography*. Clayton: Center of Southeast Asia Studies: Monash University. (Papers on SE Asia, No. 11).

Manas Chitakasem
1972 "The emergence and development of the Nirat genre in Thai poetry." *JSS* 60: 135-168.
1982 "The development of political and social consciousness in Thai short stories." In J. H. C. S. Davidson and H. Cordell, eds. *The short story in South East Asia: aspects of a genre*. London: SOAS, pp. 63-100.

Maneepin Phromsuthirak
1979 "Thai interpolations in the story of Aniruddha." *JSS* 67: 45-53.

Manit Manitcharoen
1977 *Phochananukrom thai: sombun-thansamai thisut.* 6th ed. Bangkok: Ruam Sasana.

Mattani Rutnin
1978 *Modern Thai literature: the process of modernization and the transformation of values.* Tokyo: Centre for East Asian Cultural Studies, 17.

Morell, D. and Chai-anan Samudvanij
1981 *Thailand: reform, reaction and revolution.* Cambridge, Mass.: Oelgeschlager, Gunn and Hain.

Mosel, J. N.
1961 *Trends and structure in contemporary Thai poetry.* Ithaca, N.Y.: Cornell University Press.

Nicholas, R.
"Le Lakhon Nora ou Chatri et les origines du théâtre traditionnel siamois." *JSS* 18:85-110.

Noss, R. B.
1964 *Thai reference grammar.* Washington, D.C.: Foreign Service Institute, Dept of State.

Peltier, A-R.
1974 "Le roman contemporain thailandais." In P. B. Lafont and D. Lombard, eds. *Littératures contemporaines de l'Asie du Sud-est.* Paris: L' Asiathèque, pp. 73-86. (Colloque du XXIXe Congrès International des Orientalistes).

Phillips, H. P., et al.
1987 *Modern Thai literature, with an ethnographic interpretation.* Honolulu: University of Hawaii Press.

Prae Pittaya
1966 *Modern standard English-Thai dictionary.* Bangkok: Prae Pittaya. (Revised edition).

Reynolds, C. J.
1973 "The case of K. S. R. Kulap: a challenge to royal historical writing in late nineteenth-century Thailand." *JSS* 61, 2:63-91.
1976 "Buddhist cosmography in Thai history, with special reference to nineteenth-century culture change." *JAS* 35, 2: 203-220.

Reynolds, F. E.
1982 *Three worlds according to King Ruang: a Thai Buddhist cosmology.* Berkeley: University of California. (Berkeley Buddhist Studies, 4).

Rosenburg, K.
1976 *Die epischen chan-Dichtungen in der Literatur Thailands.* Hamburg: Gesellschaft für Natur-und Völkerkunde Ostasiens. (Mitteilungen, Band 67).

Royal Institute
1980 *Photchananukrom chabap ratchabanditsathan [Dictionary of the Royal Institute].* Bangkok: Aksorn Charoen Dasna Press (Revision of 1st 1950 edn.).

Schrock, J. L., et al.
1970 *Minority groups in Thailand.* Washington D.C.: US Govt. Printing Office.

Schuyler, M., Jr.
1908 "Notes on the making of palm leaf manuscripts in Siam." *JAOS* 29:281-283.

Schweisguth, P.
1950 "Les 'Nirat' ou poèmes d'adieu de la littérature siamoise." *JSS* 38 1:67-78.
1951 *Etude sur la littérature siamoise.* Paris: Imprimerie Nationale.

Shorto, H. L., J. M. Jacob and E. H. S. Simmonds
1963 *Bibliographies of Mon-Khmer and Tai linguistics.* London: Oxford University Press.

Sibunruang, J. K.
1960 *Khun Cheng, Khun Phen: la femme le héros et le vilain, poème populaire thai.* Paris: Presses Universitaires de France. (Annales du Musée Guimet, Bibliothèque d'Etudes, Vol. 65).

Skinner, G. W.
1957 *Chinese society in Thailand: an analytical history.* Ithaca, N.Y.: Cornell University Press.

Smyth, D.
1987 "The later short stories of Siburapha." In J. C. H. S. Davidson, ed. *Lai su Thai: essays in honour of E. H. S. Simmonds.* London: School of Oriental and African Studies, pp. 98-115.

So Sethaputra
1978 *New model English-Thai dictionary.* 3rd edn. 2 vols. Bangkok: Thai Wattana Panich.

Srisurang Poolthupya
1979 *Thai intellectual and literary world.* Bangkok: Research Institute Thammasat University.
1981 "Social change as seen in modern Thai literature." In Tham Seong Chee, ed. *Literature and society in Southeast Asia.* Singapore: Singapore University Press, pp. 206-215.

Terwiel, B. J.
1983 *A history of modern Thailand 1767-1942.* St Lucia: University of Queensland Press.

Thak Chaloemtiarana
1979 *Thailand: the politics of despotic paternalism.* Bangkok: Social Science Association of Thailand: Thai Khadi Institute, Thammasat University.

Therapan L. Thongkum
1979 *Studies in Tai and Mon-Khmer phonetics and phonology in honour of Eugenie J. A. Henderson.* Bangkok: Chulalongkorn University Press.

Udom Warotamasikkhadit
1972 *Thai syntax: an outline.* The Hague: Mouton.

Velder, C.
1961 "Die Palmblatt-Manuskript-Kultur Thailands." *Nachrichten der Gesellschaft für Natur-und Völkerkunde Ostasiens* 89/90:110-114.

Watts, M.
1986 *Thailand.* Oxford: Clio Press. (World Bibliographical Series vol. 65).

Wenk, K.
1962 *Das Lieben und Werk des Si Prat im Speigel der Thailändischen Literaturforschung.* Hamburg: Institüt für Asienkunde. (Thailand Studien, Band 11).
1963,1968 *Thai Handschriften.* 2 vols. Wiesbaden: Franz Steiner Verlag. (Verzeichnis der Orientalischen Handschriften in Deutschland, Band IX, 1 and 2).
1965 *Thailändische Miniaturmalerein, nach einer Handschrift der Indischen Kunstabteilung der Staatlichen Museen Berlin.* Wiesbaden: Franz Steiner Verlag.
1980 *Phali teaches the young: a literary and sociological analysis of the Thai poem Phali son nong.* Honolulu: University of Hawaii. (Southeast Asian Studies Working Paper, No 18). (Translation of the original German, Hamburg 1977).
1982 *Studien zu Literatur der Thai: Band 1: Texte und Interpretatione.* Hamburg: Gesellschaft für Natur-und Völkerkunde Ostasiens. (Mitteilungen der Gesellschaft für Natur-und Völkerkunde Ostasiens, Band 89).
1985 *Studien zu Literatur der Thai: Band 2: Texte und Interpretatione von und zu Sunthon Phu.* Hamburg: Gesellschaft für Natur-und Völkerkunde Ostasiens. (Mitteilungen, Band 94).
1986 "Some remarks about the life and works of Sunthon Phu." *JSS* 74: 169-198.
1987 *Studien zu Literatur der Thai: Band 3: Texte und Interpretationen zur Literatur des 19. Jahrhunderts.* Hamburg: Gesellschaft für Natur-und Völkerkunde Ostasiens. (Mitteilungen, Band 107).

Wibha Senanan
1975   *The genesis of the novel in Thailand.* Bangkok: Thai Watana Panich.

Wood, W. A. R.
1925   "The 'Phongsawadan' of Luang Prasot." *JSS* 19:153-157.

Wyatt, D. K.
1975   "Chronicle traditions in Thai historiography." In C. D. Cowan and O. W. Wolters, eds. *Southeast Asian history and historiography: essays presented to D. G. E. Hall.* Ithaca; London: Cornell University Press, pp. 107-123.
1982   *Thailand: a short history.* New Haven; London: Yale University Press.

Yates, W. G. and Absorn Tryon
1970   *Thai basic course.* 2 vols. Washington D.C.: U.S. Govt. Printing Office. (Foreign Service Institute Basic Course Series).

Young, G.
1962   *The hill tribes of Northern Thailand.* 2nd edition. Bangkok: Siam Society.

Cambodia

Bordered by Thailand, Laos and Vietnam, modern Cambodia consists predominantly of a vast plain containing the huge Tonlé Sap, a lake drained to the southeast by the Mekong and Bassac rivers. The plain, its agriculture dependent on the flooding of the rivers and of the lake itself, is the most populous region of Cambodia; it is surrounded by sparsely populated low mountain ranges (the Cardomom Mountains, Elephant Range and Dangrek Range) and plateaus.

In the 1970s, Cambodia was engulfed by political and military conflict. The population, estimated to be 7,200,000 in 1984, was greatly diminished during the period of Khmer Rouge rule, though the exact number is a subject of much debate. The Cambodians or Khmers, who inhabit central Cambodia, make up about 85% of the population. There are also large settlements of Cambodians in Thailand (mainly in the frontier areas near the Cambodian border) and in Vietnam (in the western provinces of what was formerly French Cochinchina, where they are known by the Cambodians as Khmer Krom). Other ethnic groups within Cambodia are the Khmer Loeu ('upland Khmer'), a tribal minority of about 70,000 (in 1970), mainly inhabiting the northeastern plateaus; the Pear and the Saoch, located in the south; the Kuoy and the Samrê, located in the north; the Khmer Islam, Muslims of Cham and Malay descent who are estimated to number about 185,000 in 1984; the Chinese, who numbered about 300,000 to 450,000 in 1970 and are settled in the towns; and the Vietnamese, slightly less numerous (in 1970) than the Chinese, who are established for the most part close to the frontier with Vietnam and along the Mekong. The number of Vietnamese has since 1979 temporarily greatly increased with the Vietnamese military presence in Cambodia.

Indianized states existed in the Cambodian region from the earliest years of the Christian era. Chinese texts speak of a state called Funan, and subsequently of one named Chenla. After a period of disunity in the 8th century, Cambodia was to a certain extent united under Jayavarman II (802-834), and Yasovarman I (889-910), who founded the great city of Angkor. For five centuries Angkor was the capital of Cambodia and a succession of kings built there a complex of great temples and reservoir systems. The reign of Jayavarman VII (1181-1218?) was particularly notable for the grandeur and scale of its building programme and public works. During the 14th and 15th centuries, Angkor came increasingly under threat from the Thai kingdom of Ayutthaya. Angkor was abandoned and the capital moved, first to Srey Santhor and then to Phnom Penh. In the following centuries Cambodia had to defend herself against both Thai and Vietnamese expansion until 1863, when the French assumed control and established a protectorate. Cambodia regained her independence in 1953. Following the overthrow of Prince Sihanouk in March 1970, the nation was plunged into civil war. The fighting did not end with the establishment of the communist government of the Khmer Rouge in 1975 or with the Vietnamese intervention of 1979.

The religion of Cambodia has from the 14th century been predominantly Theravada Buddhist. The Cambodian Buddhist clergy is divided into two groups; the Mahanikay order, which includes the majority of monks and monasteries in Cambodia, and the Dhammayuttikanikay order, which was introduced from Thailand in 1855. The main difference between the two orders lies in their manner of observing monastic discipline and in their pronunciation of the Pali texts. Recent events have noticeably affected Buddhism and the position of the clergy in Cambodia. Side by side with Buddhist beliefs, Cambodians also believe in ancestor spirits and territorial spirits (*anak ta*), in somewhat ambivalent beings called *arakh* and in *devata*, celestial beings who are generally benevolent.

On the different peoples of Cambodia, see **LeBar** (1964). For the Khmer Islam, see **Cabaton** (1927); the Vietnamese community, **Khy Phanra** (1975 and 1976) and **Pouvatchy (**1975 and 1986); the Cham, **Po Dharma** (1981 and 1982); the Chinese, **Wilmott** (1967 and 1970). A classic study of the Cambodian peasant is **Delvert** (1961). Much scholarly work has been done on the religion, archaeology, history and art and architecture of pre-modern Cambodia. On early Brahmanic religion, see **Bhattacharya** (1961); on Buddhism specifically, **Bizot** (1976, 1979, and 1981), **Lêclère** (1975), and **Porée-Maspero** (1958); on spirit cults, **Porée-Maspero** (1954,1962-69). On early history, see **Briggs** (1951), **Coedès** (1962 and 1964 or, in English, 1969 and 1975), **Giteau** (1974) and **Malleret** (1959-63). For references on inscriptions, see the literature section below. There is a large literature on Angkor, but a good introduction is provided by **Giteau** (1976) and for detailed study there is *Le Temple d'Angkor Vat* (1929-32), **Dumarçay** (1967), **Groslier** (1973), and **Nafilyan** (1969). For post-Angkorian history see **Chandler** (1975), **Groslier** (1958), and **Vickery** (1977); on the French period, **Forest** (1980) and **Osborne** (1969); for the post-independence years, see **Kiernan** and **Chantou Boua** (1982), **Kiernan** (1985), **Osborne** (1973), and **Preschez** (1961); for the period after 1975, see **Chandler** and **Kiernan** (1983). **Ponchaud** (1977), and **Vickery** (1984 and 1986). An excellent general history of Cambodia is **Chandler** (1983). A handbook is **Whitaker** (1973), and for a general bibliographical guide see **Keyes** (1979).

Dating Systems

Cambodians use several eras for determining and expressing dates: the Buddhist era, used above all by monks and in Buddhist texts, beginning with the Buddha's attainment of nirvana in (according to the Sinhalese tradition) 544 BC; the Saka era ('great era'), used in the inscriptions of Angkor and also in more recent texts, beginning 17th March 79 AD; the Culla era ('small era'). which begins on 22nd March 639 AD; and the Christian era.

The Cambodian calendar is lunar-solar, taking account, simultaneously, of the positions of the moon and the sun. In place of names, numbers are used in old texts to indicate the days of the week. The months are similarly cited either by their numerical order or by name. The months are lunar and last alternately 29 and 30 days. The gap between the solar year of 365 days and the lunar year of 354 days is made up by adding, every three or four years, an intercalary month of 30 days, called Dutiyasadh, placed after the eighth month, which is then called Pathamasadh. The use of animal year names and cycles to designate years dates from the Angkor period and is first found in an inscription of 992 AD; the practice was also commented upon by the 13th century Chinese traveller, Chou Ta-Kuan.

On the Cambodian calendar, see **Faraut** (1910).

Language

The Cambodian or Khmer language belongs to the Mon-Khmer family, different branches of which are found from Vietnam to the frontiers of India. The first written evidence of the Cambodian language is on stone inscriptions from the 7th century. Over the course of centuries, Khmer has been continuously enriched by Indian, Thai and European influences. Until the end of the Angkor period, Sanskrit was the language of the elite, but it never fully supplanted Khmer, which was used alongside it in inscriptions. From the 14th century onwards, with the spread of Theravda Buddhism in Cambodia, many words were borrowed from Pali. Khmer has also received much from Thai, but Thai words are themselves often originally old Khmer absorbed into early Thai and since lost from the Khmer vocabulary. In the 20th century, words to express new ideas and concepts in many fields had to be invented. The Buddhist Institute in Phnom Penh was responsible for creating much new vocabulary based on Pali, while many other words were derived from European languages, especially French.

Khmer does not have tones. Though often considered to be a monosyllabic language, it nevertheless possesses many words formed by prefixation, infixation, reduplication and compound formation, and has adopted many polysyllabic words of foreign origin. Khmer has no special indication of gender or number. Generally speaking, for living creatures the masculine or feminine is indicated by a word denoting the sex; the plural is likewise indicated by auxiliary words. The position of words in a sentence, together with intonation and pause determines their grammatical function.

Dictionaries: Khmer-Khmer, **Vacananukram Khmaer** (5th ed. 1967- 68); Khmer-French, **Guesdon** (1930); Khmer-English, **Headley** (1977), **Huffman** and **Im Proum** (1977a) and **Jacob** (1974); English-Khmer, **Huffman** and **Im Proum** (1978); French-Khmer, **Tep-Yok** and **Thao-Kun** (1962-64). The bibliography in **Huffman** (1978) gives a listing of dictionaries and lexicons. Teaching materials: **Cambefort** (1950), **Huffman** (1970b, 1972, and 1977b), **Jacob** (1968), **Lewitz [Pou]** (1968). On specific aspects of grammar, see **Maspero** (1915), **Midoux** (1973-74), **Henderson** (1952), and **Huffman** (1967). On aspects of vocabulary, see **Lewitz [Pou]** (1967), and on foreign vocabulary, see **Jacob** (1986b). For the language of the Khmer Loeu, see articles in **Mon-Khmer Studies** (1964-1979). **Huffman** (1986) lists everything published on Khmer language and linguistics.

Script

In ancient Cambodia there was an elegant script, used only for inscriptions, and a more commonly used cursive script, found mostly on bronzes but also on stone. These two types of script were, it appears, precursors of the two scripts in modern use, *mul* (meaning 'round'), which is used to write Pali texts, and for book and newspaper titles and headings; and *crien* (meaning 'sloping'), the ordinary Khmer script. The most ancient written texts still extant are those inscribed on stone slabs and pillars, on lintels and doorways of temples and on statues of bronze or precious metals. The oldest dated inscription in Khmer is from Saka 533 (611 AD). The earliest inscriptions are in Sanskrit and/or Khmer, but from the 14th century onward, inscriptions were written only in Pali and Khmer, in a script that does not differ substantially from that in modern use.

The Khmer language is written from left to right with no separation between words. In the past, the spelling of words was free and as a consequence there is a lack of consistency in spelling even within a single text. Spelling was standardized, however, by the Buddhist Institute's publication in two volumes of a Khmer dictionary (*Vacananukram Khmaer* [1939-43]). The spelling laid down in this dictionary is taught in schools. Words of Sanskrit and Pali origin are spelt out in full (that is, including the characters which are not sounded in Khmer pronunciation) and the final semi-vowel, r, found in ancient texts but pronounced in modern times only in certain regions of the country, has been restored to the spelling.

The ordinary Khmer writing system (*crien*) has 33 consonant syllables. These are classed according to their point of articulation in five groups, a system derived from the Indic alphabet. Consonants form two vocalic series and the pronunciation of a vowel symbol in combination with an initial consonant is determined by the series to which the consonant belongs. Eight independent vowel signs (that is, those which can be used without the support of a consonant symbol) are in common use. There are also four independent syllabic signs, the value of each corresponding to the combination of a consonant sign with a vowel sign. Two consonants can also be associated to form a combination known as a double consonant; these cannot, however, be written one after the other: the second of the consonants is written below the first and called a subscript consonant. When the double consonants are of different vocalic series, there are rules to determine the dominant vocalic series and pronunciation in combination with vowels. There are ten diacritical signs which are used to modify the value of consonant and vowel signs. Khmer also has ten numerals.

Lewitz's transliteration of Khmer (**Lewitz [Pou]** 1969) has been widely adopted in France for library cataloguing and scholarly references. A modified form of this transliteration by Huffman and Bonsack is used by the Library of Congress and by most other American and United Kingdom libraries; it has been published in *Library of Congress Cataloguing Service Bulletin* 120 (Winter, 1977), pp. 19-21.

For general discussion of the Khmer writing system, see **Huffman** (1970a), and for more on transliteration into a romanized system, **Huffman** (1974) and **Lewitz [Pou]** 1969). A transcription system reproducing the pronunciation, rather than the spelling, of modern Khmer is given in **Huffman** (1978).

Manuscripts

The majority of Cambodian manuscripts are made of palm leaf, which has been used for this purpose since Angkorian times. Palm trees grow abundantly in the forests and along the waterways in the north. The leaves are treated and incised in a fashion similar to the methods used in Burma, Thailand and Laos. The dimensions of a Cambodian palm leaf manuscript are generally either 35 x 5

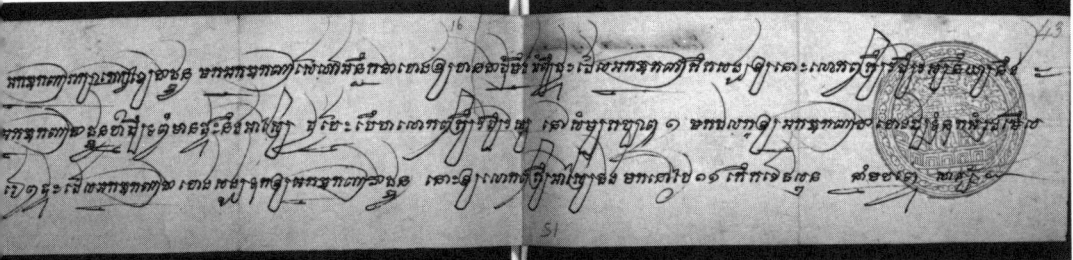

Cambodian travel document issued to Henri Mouhot and party 1859-60

cm or 60 x 6 cm, with an average of five lines of text per side.

Paper manuscripts in folding book form were also used in Cambodia. Before the introduction of European paper, the Cambodians made paper from the bark of the mulberry and from the *snay* shrub, cut in small pieces, mixed with rice chaff or straw, then boiled in a water and lime mixture until pulpy. The pulp was then spread out thinly on a cloth and laid in the sun to dry. The paper produced in this way was yellowish-white in colour, but this was then generally painted black. Sticks of steatite were used for writing on black paper and charcoal for light-coloured paper. For more permanent writing, a kind of metal pen filled with Chinese ink or with *gamboge*, an orange-colored gum resin, was used. Manuscripts were for the most part kept in monasteries; those of Phnom Penh and Battambang had particularly valuable and ancient collections. The Buddhist Institute in Phnom Penh also had a good collection of 1,647 manuscripts (as of 1975). Other manuscripts, especially literary texts, resided in private collections. In Paris, the Bibliothèque Nationale and the Ecole Française d'Extrême-Orient have important collections of Cambodian manuscripts.

On the preparation of manuscripts, see **Groslier** (1921). For details of the Bibliothèque Nationale's collections, see **Au Chhieng** (1953) and **BEFEO** (1902); for information on manuscripts in Berne, see **Régamey** (1948).

Printing and Development of the Press

In France, at the end of the 19th century, Abbé J. Guesdon designed a set of Khmer type and published (with Plon-Nourrit) several Cambodian literary texts as well as Christian material. By the beginning of the 20th century, three Khmer-French dictionaries had been printed (in Paris, Avignon and Hong Kong). But in Cambodia itself, the establishment of printing presses and of printing in Khmer characters was a late development. The official French colonial press established in Vietnam in 1862 gave some coverage to Cambodian affairs in its *Bulletin official de l'expedition de Cochinchine*. A publication devoted solely to Cambodia was not created until 1884, when the *Bulletin officiel du Cambodge* was published in Saigon. The first official publications to be printed in Cambodia were the *Annuaire illustré du Cambodge* (from 1890 onwards) and the *Bulletin de la chambre mixte du commerce et d'agriculture* (from 1897).

Printing in its early stages was used only by the French colonial administration, by the royal palace (whose first publication was a 1903 program for the inauguration of the Preah Keo pagoda), by institutions such as the Ecole

Française d'Extrême-Orient (EFEO, founded in 1901) and by Christian missions. The first literary text to be printed in Khmer characters (*Rioen pantam ta mas*) was published in Phnom Penh in 1908 by Adhémard Leclère. In 1911, *Rajakic Rajakar/Recueil des actes du gouvernement cambodgien,* an official journal in Khmer that was modelled on French official publications, appeared for the first time. Publishing in Khmer was at first rather limited; traditionalist monks in particular were opposed to printing, and religious texts could only be published with the permission of the heads of the two Buddhist orders and of the council of Ministers. In the 1920s, modernist monks such as the Venerables Chuon Nath and Huot Tath, with the help of Louis Finot, the director of the EFEO, obtained permission to edit and publish all kinds of texts. Periodical publications started to appear: a bilingual journal for teachers, *Bulletin élémentaire franco-khmer,* appeared in 1925. *Kambuja Suriya* was started in 1926 with the aim of maintaining the traditional culture of Cambodia; it printed many folk tales in the 1930s and 1940s, and developed into an influential literary journal publishing modern Cambodian novels. The review *Sruk Khmaer* commenced in 1927, *Sasanakiccanukron/Rapport mensuel sur les affaires religieuses* in 1931 and *Ratri thnai Sau(r)* in 1935. Finally, the first political journal, *Nagaravatt* appeared in 1936.

The first newspaper produced in Cambodia was *Le Petit Cambodgien,* lithographed in 1899-1900 from a handwritten text. Printed newspapers appeared about a decade later when the *Impartial de Phnom Penh* and the *Opinion du Cambodge* were published, but newspaper publishing was not firmly established until the appearance of *Echo du Cambodge* in 1922 and of a new *Impartial de Phnom Penh* in 1925.

Following the crisis of World War II, the attainment of independence in 1953 and the establishment of Khmer as the official national language, there was considerable expansion in publishing official and institutional bulletins, such as *Dassanavatti samrap gru panrien/Revue de l'Instituteur Khmer* (1957?) and *Annales de la Faculté de droit de Phnom Penh* (1960); newspapers and periodicals representing the government view, such as the Khmer daily *Kambuja,* the monthly *Cambodge d'aujourd'hui* (1955) and the weekly *Réalités cambodgiennes* (1956); and those representing opposition groups, such as the Democratic Party's *Prajadhipateyy* and the Communists' *Prajajan* and *Observateur* (1960). There was also a very small number of independent, privately-owned papers such as *Matubhumi.* Gradually a pro-government press came to dominate the scene. From about 1956, the weekly *Anak Jatiniyam* expressed the government viewpoint in Khmer, as did the political review *Sangkum* (1965), the information journal *Kambuja* (1965) and its cultural supplement *Etudes cambodgiennes* (1965).

Although the private press, publishing chiefly in Khmer, also expanded at this time, it began to encounter difficulties as the political situation deteriorated. Following the suppression of September 1967, censorship and control of the press were placed under the Ministry of Information. Only government publications and one nationalized daily paper — in Khmer, Chinese, Vietnamese and in French, under the title *Le Cambodge* — were published. After 1967, a few private dailies began to appear (or reappear), and these (*Khmaer Ekaraj, Koh Santibhab, Suvannabhumi,* and *Nagar Dham*) continued after the proclamation of a republic in October 1970. Many new periodicals also appeared in this period, but they soon ran into practical and political difficulties (lack of paper, scarcity of funds, censorship) as war overtook the nation.

The Khmer Rouge published only propaganda bulletins. The Cambodian refugee community, especially in France, has published many Khmer and French journals representing different political viewpoints. These include: *Serika, La Voix du Cambodge Libre, Lettre d'Information de l'A.G.K.E., Nagar Dham/Nokor Thom, Journal des Refugiés Cambodgiens, Samagan kar bar tampun khmaer/Préserver la culture khmère*.

On the development of printing and literature, see **Nepote** and **Khing Hoc Dy** (1981). For information on the press in general, see **Nepote** (1979) and **Soth Polin** and **Sin Kimsuy** (1982). For listings of Cambodian newspapers and periodicals in libraries, see **Moon** (1979) and **Nunn** (1972 and 1977).

Literature

Cambodian literature has been little studied. As with other South-East Asian literatures, it is difficult to apply to Cambodian literature classification by genres used in Europe. Historians and archaeologists generally speak of five periods of development: pre-Angkorian, Angkorian, post-Angkorian, French Protectorate, and contemporary. Linguists and philologists, however, distinguish three periods based more closely on the evolution of the language: the Old Khmer period of the inscriptions (7th to 14th centuries); the Middle Khmer period of inscriptions and manuscripts (15th to 19th centuries); and the modern period.

The inscriptional literature of Cambodia spans several of the eras carved out by the periodization systems above and has received a great deal of scholarly attention by such early scholars as Barth, Bergaigne, Finot, Coedès, and, more recently, Jacques. Inscriptions from the 14th century onwards have been discussed by Coedès and Lewitz [Saveris Pou]. All inscriptions discovered to date in Cambodia and the former Khmer regions of Thailand, Laos and Vietnam are listed in a general inventory of over 1,000 items; rubbings of these inscriptions are preserved in Paris at the Ecole Française d'Extrême-Orient and at the Bibliothèque Nationale.

The writing of the period that begins with the 16th century and runs to the middle of the 19th century is usually regarded as 'classical' Khmer literature. This classification has been the subject of some debate, however, and scholars such as **Au Chhieng** (1953) and **Saveros [Lewitz] Pou** (1977) have adopted various differing categorizations. For convenience of discussion, literature is divided below into religious, didactic, fictional, historical and technical genres.

Khmer religious literature comprises all works of religious instruction, faithfully derived from the Pali texts of the Theravada Buddhist canon, the *Tripitaka*. In Cambodia, the *Vinayapitaka* and the *Suttapitaka* sections of the *Tripitaka* are better known and more commonly preserved in manuscript collections than the *Abhidammapitaka*. In 1969 the Buddhist Institute brought out in 110 volumes the complete Pali text of the *Tripitaka*, together with a Khmer translation. The *Jataka* stories of the Buddha's previous lives, especially the last ten great *Jataka*, are well-known in Cambodia and the fifty extra-canonical *Jataka* stories composed in Pali (probably in the 15th and 16th centuries) are especially popular. Several Cambodian verse adaptations have been made from these texts. *Samray* is the name given to religious texts in Pali accompanied by a translation and explanatory commentary. The famous *Traibhumi* cosmological text (about which, see the Thailand section) has much influenced Cambodian literature.

Didactic literature comprises verse works called *cpap,* which are moral treatises or codes of conduct, generally undated and relatively short in length. These works are divided into two categories: the old *cpap* (*cas* or *puran*) which present an idealized society, and the modern *cpap* (*thmi*), which deal with the everyday concerns of the peasantry. It has been argued that this didactic literature was the product of an ardent proselytization by Buddhist monks in the 14th to 18th centuries, who composed these verse texts as practical and moral guides for the people. Pupils in traditional Buddhist schools always learned *cpap* texts by heart.

Fictional literature is diverse in Cambodia and includes the *lpaen*, which have been defined as texts that entertain through their beauty of expression. *Lpoek* are middle length verse works treating a specific theme, and sometimes included in the *lpaen* genre. *Rioen bren* (folk stories) are short, traditional texts which were first transmitted orally and only much later written down to ensure their preservation. They are mostly in prose and are not dated. These traditional Cambodian stories have been classified variously, and include fables, etiological tales and stories whose chief purpose is edification of the audience. *Rioen*, or verse fiction, includes histories, stories, legends and fables. These works come mostly from the 18th and 19th centuries and are generally long, averaging 8,000 verses. The oldest dated verse work is of *Saka* 1651 (1729 AD) and is called *Rioen khyan sankh* (The conch shell story). Other dated works are: *Lokanayapakar (n)* (1794), *Pannasar sirasa* (1797), *Krun sabhamitr* (1798), *Bhogakulakumar* (1804), *Varanetr varanuj* (1806), *Kaki* (1815), *Brah candagorab* (1833), *Tav rioen* (1837), *Brah samudr* (1847-60), *Brah Jinavans* (1856), *Nan vimancand* (1858), *Maranamata* (1877), *Sugandh thon* (1883), *Cau sradap cek* (1889), and *Sabv siddh* (1899). There are also many undated works which can be ascribed to the same period. These *rioen* were written by monks, scholars and palace mandarins; they drew their inspiration from Buddhist texts, particularly the *Jatakas*.

Cambodian epics are not always easily distinguishable from verse fiction. But while fiction tends to be concerned with amorous intrigue and daring exploits, epic literature glorifies and elevates its heroes to the status of gods. The two great Khmer epics are *Lpoek Angar Vatt* ('The poem of Angkor Vat') and the *Ramakerti*. The first is the story of a certain Prince Ketumala, son in a previous existence to the god Indra, who sends his personal architect to earth to build a palace for Ketumala. The epic eulogizes the prince and celebrates the glory of his palace, Angkor Vat. A philological study of this text by Saveros Lewitz/Pou has established its date of composition as *Saka* 1542 (1620 AD). The *Ramakerti* is the best-known epic deriving from the *Ramayana*. Saveros Lewitz/Pou's examination of the text led her to distinguish between a *Ramakerti* I, composed between the 16th and 17th centuries, and a *Ramakerti* II, composed in the mid-18th century.

Historical literature consists largely of inscriptions from Angkor Vat and the Cambodian royal chronicles. The inscriptions, forty in number, are engraved on the walls of Angkor Vat and are of great historical and literary value. They were first studied by Aymonier, and most recently translated, edited and analyzed by **Lewitz [Pou]** (1970-75 and 1972). Inscription 38 is dated *Saka* 1623 (1702 AD) and is the oldest dated Cambodian verse work.

The royal chronicles (*Rapa Ksatr* or *Brah raj bangsavatar*) are based on old traditions and on texts which have not survived the passage of time. The oldest fragment of a chronicle is dated 1796 and the most recent dates from 1941. The first known author of a royal chronicle is the scholar Nong, whose work is dated 1818. The most complete chronicle is called *Veang Chuon* (*Vamn Juon*), begun in 1903 by order of King Norodom. The royal chronicles have two parts: a legendary section derived from popular oral tradition, starting with the

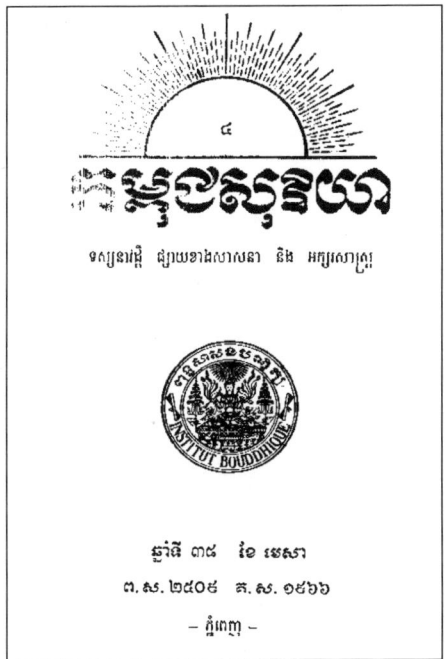

Kambuja Suriya magazine

mythological origins of the kingdom of Cambodia and continuing to the mid-14th century; and a historical section dealing with kings' reigns. In general, older versions of the chronicles are very concise, while later versions record more detailed descriptions.

Cambodian technical literature consists of specialized texts learned by heart from a master and subsequently consulted at certain periods to verify the knowledge acquired. The texts are generally considered sacred and cover such subjects as astrology, magic, divination, ritual and medical prescriptions.

Classical literature continued to appear in the colonial period, and often traditional verse fiction was rewritten in another verse form. Sou Seth's *Bimba bilap* (1901) is a work of this type, for example, as are the Venerable Som's *Dik ram phka ram* (1911) and *Dum Dav* (1915), and Nou Kan's *Dav Ek* (1942). But with the development of printing and modern education in the French period, new literary genres were created. The term *pralom lok,* for example, was coined to signify novel. The new kind of literature dates from 1938, when the first novel in prose form - *Suphat* by Rim Kin (1911-1959) - was published. In the period 1939-53, only about 30 new works appeared, but with the end of the French

Protectorate Cambodian literary production soared and in the period 1953-70, 555 novels were published. In the period between the coup d'etat of March 1970 to 1972, some 123 new works saw print.

French literature has had a great influence on modern Cambodian writing. Molière and Corneille, as well as modern French novelists, have been translated into Khmer. Alexandre Dumas and Hector Malot have been especially popular. Chinese literature has also had some influence, and Chinese epics have been adapted and translated into Khmer. *Sam Kuk* (The three kingdoms), for example, was translated by Nou Kan and serialized in *Kambuja Suriya* beginning in 1948. Literature appears to have ceased with the regime of Pol Pot and the Khmer Rouge. Little is known of the literary situation under the current Vietnamese administration. Cambodians who have take refuge in exile abroad continue to write novels in their own language, however.

On inscriptional literature, see **Jacques** (1968-78); for inscriptions from the 14th century onwards, see **Coedès** (1958) and **Lewitz [Pou]** (1970-75 and 1972). For an index to the inscriptions in Khmer, see volume VIII (1966) of **Coedès'** *Inscriptions du Cambodge* (1937-66) and the supplement by **Jacques** (1971); for a chronological inventory, see **Jenner** (1980) and for a lexicon, **Jenner** (1980-82). On didactic literature (*cpap*), see **Saveros [Lewitz] Pou** (1979 and 1981); a study of different *cpap* texts is **Saveros [Lewitz] Pou** and **Jenner** (1975-79); for a listing of *cpap* works, see **Saveros [Lewitz] Pou** and **Kuoch Haksrea** (1981). On *lpeok* works, see **Khing Hoc Dy** (1983). On traditional stories and folk tales, and their classification, see especially **Martini** and **Bernard** (1946), **Saveros [Lewitz] Pou** (1977a) and **Thierry** (1978 and 1985). The Buddhist Institute in Phnom Penh edited and issued a compilation of these stories in nine volumes, *Prajum rioen bren khmaer* (1963-74); altogether some 250 Khmer stories were published in this compilation. For translations of traditional stories, folk tales and legends, see **Carrison** (1987), **Chandler** (1976), **Leclère** (1895), **Martini** and **Bernard** (1946), and **Milne** (1972). For a translation of a portion of *Lpoek Angar Vatt,* see **Saveros [Lewitz] Pou** (1977a, b). On the *Ramakerti,* and a French translation, see **Saveros [Lewitz] Pou** (1977b) and **Martini** (1978); an English translation is **Jacob** (1986a). For a bibliography on the *Ramayana* in Cambodia, see **Saveros [Lewitz] Pou**, **Lan Sunnary** and **Kuoch Haksrea** (1981). A Khmer text of the *Ramakerti* was first published in sixteen parts and twelve volumes by the Buddhist Institute in 1937. On the chronicles, see **Vickery** (1977 and 1979), **Chandler** (1979), **Khin Sok** (1975 and 1977), and **Mak Phoeun** (1980 and 1981). On modern Cambodian literature, see the articles of **Bernard-Thierry** (1949-55), **Bitard** (1951), **Jacob** (1982), **Nepote** and **Khing Hoc Dy**, and **Piat** (1974 and 1975). For analysis and references to ancient Cambodian law, see **Ishizawa** (1986).

Bibliography

Au Chhieng
1953 *Catalogue du fonds khmer.* Paris: Imprimerie nationale.

BEFEO
1902 "Liste des manuscrits khmers de l'Ecole Française d'Extrême-Orient." *BEFEO* 2: 387-400.

Bernard-Thierry, S.
1949-55 "Le Cambodge à travers sa littérature." *France-Asie* 4, 37/38 (Spring, 1949): 910-921; 12, 114/115 (Nov-Dec., 1955): 351-354 and 440-450.

Bhattacharya, K.
1961 *Les religions brahmaniques dans l'ancien Cambodge d'après l'épigraphie et l'iconographie.* Paris: EFEO. (Publications de l'EFE0, 49).

Bitard, P.
1951 "Etude sur la satire sociale dans la littérature du Cambodge." *BSEI* 26, 2: 189-218.

Bizot, F.
1976 *Le figuier à cinq branches: recherche sur le bouddhisme khmer, I.* Paris: EFEO. (Publications de l'EFEO, 107).
1979 "La grotte de la naissance: recherches sur le bouddhisme khmer, II." *BEFEO* 66: 221-273.
1981 *Le don de soi-même: recherches sur le bouddhisme khmer, III.* Paris, EFEO. (Publications de l'EFE0, 130).

Briggs, L. P.
1951 *The ancient Khmer empire.* Philadelphia: American Philosophical Society.(Reprinted 1974).

Cabaton, A.
1927 "L'Islam dans l'Indochine française." In *Encyclopédie de l'Islam.* vol. 2. Leiden: Brill.

Cambefort, G.
1950 *Introduction au cambodgien.* Paris: Maisonneuve.

Carrison, M. P.
1987 *Cambodian folk stories from the Gatiloke.* Rutland, Vermont; Tokyo: Charles E Tuttle.

Chandler, D. P.
1975 *Cambodia before the French: politics in a tributary kingdom, 1794-1848.* Ann Arbor, Michigan: University Microfilms International.
1976 *Two friends who tried to empty the sea: eleven Cambodian folktales.* Victoria: Monash University Centre for Southeast Asian Studies (Working Papers, No.8).

1979 "Cambodian palace chronicles (*Rajabang savatar*), 1927-1949: kingship and historiography at the end of the colonial era." In A. J. S. Reid and D. G. Marr, eds. *Perceptions of the past in Southeast Asia*. Singapore: Heinemann, pp. 207-217.
1983 *A history of Cambodia*. Boulder, Colorado: Westview.

Chandler, D. P. and B. Kiernan (eds.)
1983 *Revolution and its aftermath in Kampuchea: eight essays*. New Haven: Yale University Southeast Asia Studies.

Coedès, G.
1937-66 *Inscriptions du Cambodge*. 8 vols. Hanoi: Imprimerie d'Extrême-Orient, and Paris: EFEO.
1958 *Inscriptions modernes d'Angkor Vat*. 2nd. edn. Phnom Penh: Institut Bouddhique.
1962 *Les peuples de la péninsule Indochinoise*. Paris: Dunod. (Translated into English as *The making of Southeast Asia*. London: Routledge & Kegan Paul, 1966; and Berkeley: University of California Press, 1969).
1964 *Les états hindouisés d'Indochine et d'Indonésie*. Paris: E. de Boccard, 1964. (Translated into English as *The Indianized states of Southeast Asia*. Honolulu: East-West Center Press, 1968; and Canberra: Australia National University Press, 1975).

Delvert, J.
1961 *Le paysan cambodgien*. Paris, The Hague: Mouton.

Dumarçay, J.
1967 *Le Bayon: histoire architecturale du temple*. Paris: EFEO. (Publications de l'EFEO, Mémoire Archéologique, 3).

Faraut, F. G.
1910 *Astronomie cambodgienne*. Phnom Penh: the author.

Forest, A.
1980 *Le Cambodge et la colonisation française: histoire d'une colonisation sans heurts (1897-1920)*. Paris: L'Harmattan.

Giteau, M.
1974 *Histoire d'Angkor*. Paris: Presses Universitaires de France.
1976 *Angkor: un peuple, un art*. Paris: Bibliothèque des Arts. (Translated into English as *The civilization of Angkor*. New York: Rizzoli, 1978).

Groslier, B. P.
1958 *Angkor et le Cambodge au XVIe siècle d'après les sources portugaises et espagnoles*. Paris: Presses Universitaires de France.
1973 *Inscriptions du Bayon*. Paris: EFEO.

Groslier, G.
1921 *Recherches sur les cambodgiens*. Paris: Challarmel.

Guesdon, J.
1930 *Dictionnaire cambodgien-français.* 2 vols. Paris: Librairie Plon.

Headley, R. K., et al.
1977 *Cambodian-English dictionary.* 2 vols. Washington D.C.: Catholic University Press of America.

Henderson, E. J. A.
1952 "The main features of Cambodian pronunciation." *BSOAS* 14: 149-174.

Huffman, F. E.
1967 *Outline of Cambodian grammar.* Ph.D. dissertation, Cornell University.
1970a *Cambodian system of writing and beginning reader.* New Haven; London: Yale University Press.
1970b *Modern spoken Cambodian.* New Haven; London: Yale University Press.
1972 *Intermediate Cambodian reader.* New Haven; London: Yale University
1986 *Bibliography and index of mainland Southeast Asian languages and linguistics.* New Haven; London: Yale University Press.

Huffman, F. E., and Im Proum
1974 "Transliteration system for Khmer." *CORMOSEA Newsletter* 8, 1: 8-11
1977a *Cambodian-English glossary.* New Haven; London: Yale University Press.
1977b *Cambodian literary reader and glossary.* New Haven; London: Yale University Press.
1978 *English-Khmer dictionary.* New Haven; London: Yale University Press.

Ishizawa, Y.
1986 "Remarks on the epigraphy of Angkorian Cambodian." In M. B. Hooker, ed. *Laws of South-East Asia, Vol 1: the pre-modern texts.* Singapore: Butterworth, pp. 205-240; bibliography, pp. 518-532.

Jacob, J. M.
1968 *Introduction to Cambodian.* London: Oxford University Press.
1974 *A concise Cambodian-English dictionary.* London: Oxford University Press.
1982 "The short stories of Cambodian popular tradition." In J. H. C. S. Davidson and H. Cordell, eds. *The short story in South East Asia.* London: School of Oriental and African Studies, pp. 37-62

Jacob, J. M. (trans.)
1986a *Reamker (Ramakerti): the Cambodian version of the Ramayana.* London: Royal Asiatic Society.
1986b "The deliberate use of foreign vocabulary by the Khmer: changing fashions, methods and sources." In M. Hobart and R. H. Taylor, eds. *Context, meaning and power in Southeast Asia.* Ithaca: Cornell University Southeast Asia Program, pp. 115-130.

Jacques, C.
1968-78 "Etudes d'épigraphie cambodgienne." Series of articles in *BEFEO*, vols 54-65.
1971 "Supplément au tome VIII des Inscriptions du Cambodge." *BEFEO* 58: 177-195.

Jenner, P. N.
1980 *A chronological inventory of the inscriptions of Cambodia.* Honolulu: University of Hawaii. (Southeast Asia Studies Working Paper No. 19).
1980-82 *A chrestomathy of pre-Angkorian Khmer.* Honolulu: University of Hawaii. (Southeast Asian Studies Working Paper No. 20, parts 1-4.).

Jenner, P. N. and Saveros Pou
1980-81 "A lexicon of Khmer morphology." *Mon-Khmer Studies* IX-X.

Keyes, C. F.
1979 *Southeast Asian research tools: Cambodia.* Honolulu: University of Hawaii. (Southeast Asia Paper, No 16, part VIII).

Khing Hoc Dy
1983 "Note sur le genre *lpoek* dans la littérature khmère." *Seksa Khmer* 6: 11-18.

Khin Sok
1975 *Les chroniques royales du Cambodge (de Bana Yat jusqu'à la chute de Lanvaek).* Thèse de 3e cycle, Université de Paris.
1977 "Les chroniques royales khmères." *Mon-Khmer Studies* 6: 191-215.

Khy Phanra.
1974 *La communauté vietnamienne au Cambodge a l'époque du protectorat français (1863-1953).* 2 vols. Thèse de 3e cycle, Université de la Sorbonne Nouvelle.
1978 "L'immigration vietnamienne au Cambodge à l'époque du protectorat français (1863-1940)." *Cahiers de l'Asie du sud-est* 2: 45-58.

Kiernan, B.
1985 *How Pol Pot came to power: a history of communism in Kampuchea 1930-1975.* London: Verso.

Kiernan, B. and Chantou Boua
1982 *Peasants and politics in Kampuchea, 1942-81.* London: Zed Press; New York: M. E. Sharpe.

LeBar, F. M., G. C. Hickey. and J. K. Musgrave.
1964 *Ethnic groups of mainland Southeast Asia.* New Haven: HRAF.

Leclère, A.
1895 *Cambodge, contes et legendes.* Paris: E. Bouillion.
1975 *Le Bouddhisme au Cambodge.* New York: AMS Press. (Reprint of original 1899 Paris edition).

Lent, John A. (ed.)
1982 *Newspapers in Asia: contemporary trends and problems.* Hong Kong: Heinemann.

Lewitz [Pou], S.
1967- "Recherches sur la vocabulaire cambodgien." *Journal Asiatique.* Series of articles beginning in Volume 225. (Later articles in name of Saveros Pou).
1968 *Lectures cambodgiennes (reader), notions succintes.* Paris: Librairie d'Amérique et d'Orient.
1969 "Note sur la translittération du cambodgien." *BEFEO* 55: 163-169.
1970-75 "Inscriptions modernes d'Angkor." *BEFEO* series of articles in volumes 57-62. (From 1974 articles in name of Saveros Pou).
1972 "Les inscriptions modernes d'Angkor Vat." *Journal Asiatique* 260: 107-129.

Mak Phoeun
1980 "L'introduction de la chronique royale du Cambodge du Lettré Nong." *BEFEO* 67: 135-145.
1981 *Chroniques royales du Cambodge (de 1594 a 1677)* Paris: EFEO. (Collection des textes et documents sur l'Indochine 13).

Malleret, L.
1959-63 *L'archéologie du delta du Mekong.* 4 vols. Paris: EFEO (Publications de l'EFEO, 43).

Martini, F.
1978 *La gloire de Rama, Ramakerti.* Paris: Société d'édition Les Belles Lettres.

Martini, F., and S. Bernard
1946 *Contes populaires inédits du Cambodge.* Paris: Maisonneuve. (Collection documentaire de tous les pays, tome II).

Maspero, G.
1915 *Grammaire de la langue khmère.* Paris: Imprimerie nationale.

Midoux, M.
1973-74 *La dérivation en langue cambodgienne moderne.* Thèse de 3e cycle, Ecole Pratique des Hautes Etudes.

Milne, A.
1972 *Mr. Basket-knife and other Khmer folktales.* London: Allen and Unwin.

Mon-Khmer Studies
1964-1979 *Mon-Khmer Studies,* vols. 1-8. Saigon: Linguistic Circle of Saigon and Summer Institute of Linguistics. (Ongoing under the editorship of P. N. Jenner; later volumes published by the University Press of Hawaii).

Moon, B. E.
1979 *Periodicals for South-East Asian studies: a union catalogue of holdings in British and selected European libraries.* London: Mansell.

Nafilyan, G
1969 *Angkor Vat: description graphique du temple.* Paris: EFEO.

Nepote, J.
1979 "Introduction à une histoire de la presse au Cambodge." *Présence indochinoise* 2: 96-129.

Nepote, J. and Khing Hoc Dy
1981 "Literature and society in modern Cambodia." In Tham Seong Chee, ed. *Essays on literature and society in Southeast Asia.* Singapore: Singapore University Press, pp. 56-81.

Nunn, G. R. and Do Van Anh
1972 *Vietnamese, Cambodian and Laotian newspapers: an international union list.* Taipei: Chinese Materials and Research Aids Service Center.
1977 *Southeast Asian periodicals: an international union list.* London: Mansell.

Osborne, M. E.
1969 *The French presence in Cochinchina and Cambodia: role and response, 1859-1905.* Ithaca: Cornell University Press.
1973 *Politics and power in Cambodia: the Sihanouk years.* Camberwell, Victoria: Longman.

Piat, M.
1974 "La littérature populaire cambodgienne contemporaine." In P. B. Lafont and D. Lombard, eds. *Littératures contemporaines de l'Asie du Sud-Est.* Paris: Asiathèque, pp. 19-28 (Colloque du XXIXe Congrès International des Orientalistes).
1975 "Contemporary Cambodian literature." *Journal of the Siam Society* 63, 2: 251-259.

Po Dharma
1981 "Notes sur les Cam du Cambodge." *Seksa Khmer* 3-4: 161-183.
1982 "Notes sur les Cam du Cambodge: religion et organisation." *Seksa Khmer* 5: 103-116.

Ponchaud, F.
1977 *Cambodge, année zéro.* Paris: Julliard. (Translated into English as *Cambodia, year zero.* London: A. Lane, 1978).

Porée-Maspero, E.
1954 "Notes sur les particularités du culte chez les cambodgiens." *BEFEO* 44, 2: 619-641.
1958 *Cérémonies privées des cambodgiennes.* Phnom Penh: Editions de l'Institut Bouddhique.

1962-69 *Etudes sur les rites agraires des cambodgiens.* Paris; The Hague: Mouton. 3 vols. (Le monde d'outre mer passé et présent, première série, étude 14).

Pouvatchy, J.
1975 *Les Vietnamiens au Cambodge: étude d'une minorité étrangère.* Thèse de 3e cycle, Université de Paris.
1986 "Le peuplement vietnamien au Cambodge historique." *Cahiers de l'Asie du sud-est.* 19: 121-143.

Preschez, P.
1961 *Essai sur la démocratie au Cambodge.* Paris: Foundation nationale des sciences politiques.

Régamey, C.
1948 *Manuscrits sur feuilles de palmier: les manuscrits indiens et indochinois de la Section Ethnographique du Musée Historique de Berne. Catalogue déscriptif.* Bern: Buchdrückerei K. J. Wyss Erben Aktiengesellschaft.

Saveros [Lewitz] Pou
1977a *Ramakerti (XVIe-XVIIe siècles): traduit et commenté.* Paris: EFEO. (Publications de l'EFEO, 110).
1977b *Etudes sur le Ramakerti.* Paris: EFEO. (Publications de l'EFEO, 111).
1979 "*Subhasit* and *cpap* in Khmer literature." In J. P. Sinha, ed.*Ludwik Sternbach felicitation volume, part 1.* Lucknow: Akhila Bharatuya Sanskrit Parishad, pp. 331-348.
1981a La littérature didactique khmère: les *cpap. Journal Asiatique* 269, 3-4: 453-466.
1982 *Ramakerti 11 (Deuxième version du Ramayana khmer, traduction et annotations.* Paris: EFEO. (Publications de l'EFEO, 132).

Saveros [Lewitz] Pou and Kuoch Haksrea
1981 "Liste d'ouvrages de *cpap.*" *Journal Asiatique* 269, 3-4: 467-483.

Saveros [Lewitz] Pou and P. Jenner
1975-79 "Les *'cpap'* ou 'codes de conduite' khmers." Series of articles in *BEFEO,* volumes 62-66.

Saveros [Lewitz] Pou, Lan Sunnary and Kuoch Haksrea
1981 "Inventaire des oeuvres sur le Ramayana khmer (Ramakerti)." *Seksa Khmer 3-4: 111*-126.

Soth Polin and Sin Kimsuy
1982 "Kampuchea." In J. A. Lent, ed. *Newspapers in Asia: contemporary trends and problems.* Hong Kong: Heinemann, pp. 219-239.

Le Temple d'Angkor Wat
1929-32 7 vols. Paris: EFEO.

Tep-Yok and Thao-Kun
1962-64 *Dictionnaire français-khmer.* 2 vols. Phnom Penh: Kim Libraire Bouth-Neang.

Thierry, S.
1978 *Etude d'un corpus de contes cambodges traditionnels.* Thèse de doctorat d'Etat, Université de Paris. Lille: Atelier réproduction des thèses.
1985 *Le Cambodge des contes.* Paris: Editions l'Harmattan.

Vacananukram Khmaer (Cambodian dictionary)
1967-68 5th edn. Phnom Penh: Institut Bouddhique. (First edition published 1939-43).

Vickery, M.
1977 *Cambodia after Angkor, the chronicular evidence for the fourteenth to sixteenth centuries.* 2 vols. Ann Arbor, Michigan: University Microfilms International.
1979 "The composition and transmission of the Ayudhya and Cambodian chronicles." In A. J. S. Reid and D. G. Marr, eds. *Perceptions of the past in Southeast Asia.* Singapore: Heinemann, pp. 130-154.
1984 *Cambodia, 1975-1982.* Hemel Hempstead: Allen & Unwin; Boston: South End Press.
1986 *Kampuchea: politics, economics and society.* London: Frances Pinter; Boulder, Colorado: Lynne Rienner Publishers. (Marxist Regimes Series).

Whitaker, D. P., et al.
1973 *Area handbook for Cambodia.* Washington, D.C.: American University.

Wilmott, W. E.
1967 *The Chinese in Cambodia.* Vancouver: University of British Columbia Press.
1970 *The political structure of the Chinese community in Cambodia.* London: Athlone Press.

Laos

Laos is a landlocked country, bordered by China and Burma in the north and northwest, by Cambodia in the south and by Vietnam in the east. The Mekong river is the major communication line between north and south; it also marks a large section of the western frontier with Thailand.

The different ethnic groups of Laos (total population, 1985 census: 3,584,804) are divided by altitude rather than by region. The Lao (numbering just over 1,500,000) are the largest group and predominate in the rich, low valleys of the Mekong and its tributaries. The Tai minority groups (Black Tai, Red Tai, Tai Loe, Tai Noea, etc.), who together number about 1,000,000, live in high valleys to the north. The 'proto-Indochinese', who speak a Mon-Khmer language and number about 600,000, are now located at altitudes of about 500 to 1,000 metres in both north and south Laos. They were pushed from the good lands they formerly occupied by the Lao and Tai in the 12th and 13th centuries. The most recent immigrants are the Hmong (also called Meo), Yao, Lanten, and others who speak a Miao-Yao language and number about 300,000. They entered Laos in the 19th century and live at altitudes of between 1,000 and 1,500 metres, where they grow opium and maize.

The earliest traces of settlement in Laos, which date from the prehistoric period, are circles of standing stones and giant jars. As in other parts of South-East Asia, Indian influence was established in Laos from the beginning of the Christian era. The areas now comprising Laos then came under Khmer influence until the 13th century, when the Tai became dominant in the region. The founding of the first Lao state, Lan Xang, by the Tai led to the establishment of Theravada Buddhism, which quickly became the religion of the Lao. Animistic and spirit cults continued to attract popular enthusiasm then, as today, when they tend to complement rather than compete with Buddhism among the populace. In the following centuries, the Tai-Lao waged war against Siam, Burma and Vietnam. In the 16th century, Lan Xang's territory covered not only present-day Laos but much of the northern and eastern territories of modern Thailand. From the 18th century, however, Lan Xang declined and was divided into three rival states. Had it not been for French intervention in 1893, these states would probably have come under Thai control. The French Protectorate lasted until 1949. After regaining independence, Laos suffered both invasion and civil war for decades. The revolutionary forces of Neo Lao Haksat (Lao Patriotic Front) were victorious; the monarchy was abolished and the Popular Democratic Republic was established on December 2, 1975.

For a general introduction to Laos, see **Reinach** (1901), **Deydier** (1952), **Lafont** (1959), and **LeBar** (1960). On religious practices, see **Archaimbault** (1973), and **Zago** (1972). For a comprehensive annotated bibliography of pre-1975 publications, see **Lafont** (1978a and 1978b), and for post-1975 publications, see **Sage** and **Henchy** (1986). On research tools, see **Keyes** (1979). For minority groups, see **Kunstadter** (1967), **LeBar** (1964), and **Moerman** (1965). For Laos since 1975, see **Stuart-Fox** (1982 and 1986). On communism in Laos, see also **Brown** and **Zasloff** (1986).

South-East Asia

Detail from the Lao calendar published in the Bulletin des Amis du Laos

Dating Systems

As well as the Christian era, which was introduced by the French at the end of the 19th century, the Lao have the following dating systems: the *Cullasakaraj* era (beginning March 21st, 639 AD); the *Buddhasakaraj* era (beginning in 543 BC and used primarily in Buddhist texts); and the *Mahasakaraj* era beginning March 15th, 79 AD). Like the Cambodians, Thai and Burmese, the Lao use a lunar calendar, and adjustments were made for closing the gap between a lunar and solar year. In Laos, as also in Thailand and Cambodia, there is an additional method for designating years by a combination of two names: the first is borrowed from a series of ten terms, and the second from a series of twelve animals. When the twelve-name cycle has been repeated five times, the complete combination (of the ten-name and twelve-name cycles) totals a larger cycle of sixty years, each having a different name. Approximately forty years ago, the Laotian New Year's Day was arbitrarily fixed as April 15th of the Gregorian calendar.

On the Laotian calendar, see **Dupertius** (1981), and **Phetsarath** (1940).

Language

Each of the peoples inhabiting Laos has its own language. The following discussion deals only with the Lao language in the central region of Laos.

Lao is a Tai language; it is tonal (with six tones) and monosyllabic (words of more than one syllable being borrowings from Sanskrit, Pali, and Khmer). The vowel system of Lao is made up of twelve phonemes: nine monophthongs and three dipthongs. The long-short opposition, which is characteristic of primitive Tai and maintained in modern Thai, tends in the Lao language toward an opposition between tonal qualities. Finally, a word cannot end in a vowel unless this vowel is long.

Lao's consonantal system has 28 phonemes; only 9 consonants can be final. Every Lao word is unalterable, and its grammatical function is determined by its class and by its position in a sentence. The typical order of syntax is: subject-verb-complement, with the determiner placed after the determinated. Auxiliary words and classifiers give the necessary indication for understanding the sentence and mark the gender and number. Verb tense and case is understood by the context and by the use of adverbs; special particles indicate different verbal aspects.

The Lao vocabulary is rich in concrete terms and, as spoken up to the revolution of 1975, used a hierarchy of personal pronouns varying with the status and age of the speaker and person addressed. Lao possessed until recently special vocabularies to be used in conversation with members of royalty and the monkhood. To these may be added special political and technical vocabularies.

Dictionaries: Lao-Lao, **Laos** (1962); Lao-French, **Reinhorn** (1970); French-Lao, **Nginn** (1969); Lao-English, **Kerr** (1972); English-Lao, **Boon Thom Boonyavong** (1962); English-Lao, Lao-English, **Bounmy Soukbandith** (1983). Grammars: **Hospitalier** (1937), **Morev** (1979). Teaching aids: **Hoshino** and **Marcus** (1981), **Yates** and **Souksomboun** (1974). For a comprehensive language bibliography, see **Huffman** (1986).

Script

The Lao language has two scripts: the Lao and the Lao Tham scripts, both written from left to right with no spacing between words. The Lao Tham (*dham*) script was used for writing religious texts in the Pali language; the ordinary Lao script is used for lay texts and also, from about 1930 onwards, for religious texts. To adapt the ordinary script to Pali writing, twelve letters used in Pali but lacking in Lao had to be added.

The Lao script has 27 consonant signs which, when written in isolation, have an inherent short vowel, 'a'. Two consonants are traditionally divided into three groups: high, middle, and low. Twelve vowel signs denote simple long and short vowels, and two additional signs denote the short vowel 'a' and the short vowel 'o'. Two special signs are used to denote 'ai' and 'aï'. Finally, ten simple signs indicate the numbers 0 to 9.

Until recently, spelling was not standardized and scribes often changed spellings when copying works. Until 1975, four types of spelling systems were used: that of the Comité Littéraire (Académie Royale), which used a predominantly phonetic script; that of the Buddhist clergy, which used spellings according to the original etymology of the words; that of Lao who had studied in Thailand and adopted Thai orthography; and that of the Lao Patriotic Front, which adopted a completely phonetic script with the aim of achieving literacy rapidly. Since the victory of the revolutionary forces in 1975, the system of the Lao Patriotic Front has been officially adopted.

Of the approximately 2,000,000 minority peoples in Laos, only the Tai possess a written culture. The Tai minorities are situated in the high valleys of the northwest (Tai Loe, Yun, Black Tai) and of the northeast (Red Tai, Tai Noea, Black Tai). Each group has its own dialect and script. Like Lao itself, these dialects belong to the Tai language family and can be differentiated from one another by their vocalic systems (by such features, for instance, as their retention or abandonment of the long-short vowel opposition).

Although the Yun and Tai scripts are quite similar, they do not resemble any of the other scripts; and whereas the Black Tai script differs from the two Red Tai scripts used in the region of the Hua Phan, all three scripts belong to the same type. The Tai Noea script differs through its affiliation to a western region type of the script and through having only one series of initial consonants. The Tai Loe and Tai Noea scripts are also used in China, where the Linguistic Commission on Minorities standardized these scripts in 1957. Although a Tai

Noea Bible was published in 1932, and although China has printed some newspapers and other materials for its Tai Loe and Tai Noea peoples, no text using any of these scripts has ever been published in Laos.

For more information on scripts, see **Lafont** (1961a and 1961b).

Manuscripts

Laos has two basic types of manuscripts: folding books made of thick local paper and with a text written in ink; and palm leaf manuscripts with the text incised with a stylus. Palm leaf manuscripts generally measure 50 x 4 cm, with four lines of text per side; they are grouped into sections of 20 leaves (*phuk*), which in turn are grouped into bundles (*mat*). Extra leaves are often stitched together to mark the beginnings and ends of sections. The copying of manuscripts by scholars and monks has continued into recent times. The late introduction of printing into Laos has encouraged the continuance of the art of copying texts. Nowadays works are copied into exercise books instead of folding books or palm leaves.

Lao manuscripts are found in the former Royal Palace (now a Museum) in Luang Prabang, in the Ministry of Culture in Vientiane and in temple libraries. For an inventory, see **Lafont** (1965). There are also Lao manuscripts in the National Library, Bangkok, the Bibliothèque Nationale, Paris, in Germany (for which, see **Wenk** [1975]), and other scattered locations. For further details regarding collections of manuscripts, most of which possess no published catalogues, see **Lafont** (1978a).

Printing and Development of the Press

The late introduction of printing to Laos — the government press was only installed just before World War II — is sometimes considered to have handicapped the publication of Lao works because they had to be printed in Vietnam or France. Yet even after the installation of several presses in Vientiane, the cost of printing and the small market led to very few books being published. Organizations such as the Comité Littéraire Lao (later named the Académie Royale), the Phone Phra Nao Pagoda, the Institut d'Etudes Bouddhiques, the Ministère des Cultes and the Bibliothèque Nationale preferred to make multicopies or xerox copies of their publications in order to reduce costs. This limited the edition of a given work, often to about 100 copies but sometimes to as much as 1,000 copies.

In the area controlled by the revolutionary Neo Lao Haksat (NLH), the aim of literature was to mobilize the country against American aggression and to build a socialist state. Tracts and books were printed in editions of several thousands and distributed freely to the cadres of the NLH. Since 1975, this kind of literature has become a mass literature, designed to popularize government policy and ideology. Works are printed in editions of 10,000 to 50,000 copies and, though usually bearing a printed price on the inside cover, are distributed free of charge.

Regular newspaper publication began in 1941, when *Lao Nhay* and *Pathet Lao* were promoted by the French Protectorate. The development of newspaper publishing has been slow. Up until 1975, in the area controlled by the Vientiane

19th century manuscript of Lao dictionary

government, two daily information bulletins in French and in Lao were published by the official news agency, Agence Lao Presse. A few other reviews and papers were also published. These tended to have brief lives, were distributed in printed or mimeographed form free of charge and served as the official voice of such influential groups as the police, the army and political parties.

From 1969-75, in the area under NLH control, an information bulletin was published in Lao and French (and at one period in English), together with a daily paper, *Neo Lao Haksat,* which presented the views of the Lao Patriotic Front. Since 1975 the Ministry of Information has continued the publication of the information bulletin in a Lao and a French edition; the daily newspaper, renamed *Siang Pasasonh,* remains the only daily in circulation and it is the central organ of the government.

For further bibliographical references, see **Lafont** (1978b); on modern publishing activities, see **Lafont** (1974) and **Saveng Phinith** (1974); for a profile of Lao newspapers, see **Lent** (1977 and 1982). A brief list of newspapers is available in **Lafont** (1978a and 1978b) and **Nunn** and **Do Van Anh** (1972).

Literature

Lao religious literature comprises the Theravada Buddhist canonical texts, of which the best known in Laos are the five *Vinaya,* the *Dighanikaya* and the *Abhidhamma.* The most popular texts are undoubtedly the *Jataka* stories. Various standard collections of these exist: there are some complete collections of 500 *Jataka,* some of the last ten great *Jataka* (*sip jat*), and some collections of the fifty extra-canonical, or apocryphal, *Jataka.* Also important in Laos are the Pali verse texts called *parittam,* which monks chant for lay people in order to invoke protection against various dangers. Religious literature also includes edifying lessons regarding the gods (particularly Indra), the saints (especially Upagutta and Ananda), and the sites containing relics of the Buddha. An extremely popular set of extra-canonical texts is the *anisamsa,* which are short texts aimed at explaining the practical advantages of pious deeds.

The secular literature of Laos comprises popular literature, classical or ancient literature and modern literature. The body of secular writing is much richer than that of the religious sort. Popular and classical literature are well known at all levels of society, and have two characteristics in common: the authors' names are not known and texts are both undated and undatable (because of the way copyists modernize texts). Popular literature includes all the stories, legends and poems of oral tradition. In the course of time much of this literature has been written down by scribes. Some stories have a satirical tone that is on occasion quite sharp, but which is normally simply light, sometimes burlesque-like in tone. Others, such as the collection of stories called *sysvat* have a strong moral and educational content. Some tales comment on the naivety of the peasantry, the avarice of the wealthy, or the demands of princes. There exist also judicial stories which include commentaries on ancient Lao codes, and the stories known collectively as the 'Tales of Nantantai', a Lao version of the Indian *Pancatantra* taking the form of a discussion among several people. There are as well numerous legends, some of which claim historical basis. For example, those under the title 'History of Khun Purom' recount the legendary migration of the Tai peoples from China to Luang Prabang. Lao popular poetry ranges from the predominantly Buddhist-inspired to the licentious.

Between 1965 and 1975 the Comité Littéraire and the Bibliothèque Nationale rehabilitated these popular literary forms, which had been relegated to a secondary position in oral literature, and published the most representative stories, legends, and poems. Unfortunately, the editors censored all passages they considered to be too risqué or critical of the princes or others holding power; they also removed passages which they found trivial or vulgar, and rewrote certain paragraphs which they judged to be archaic in literary style or vocabulary.

Classical Lao literature, written in both prose and verse form, is generally lengthy and not remarkably original. The hero is always a handsome prince who is irresistible to women and who has been instructed in the occult by a *rsi* or wizard; the heroine is beautiful, the daughter of a king (frequently made out to be a rather ridiculous figure), and faithful to her hero; the hero's enemy is a *yaksa* or demon who, despite his magical powers and enchanted weapons, is destined to be conquered through the intervention of the god Indra. Recitals of such stories, with their complex and numerous battles and intrigues, are listened to with devotion. The best-known epic poem in Laos is the Lao version of the *Ramayana, Prah lak Prah lam*. It bears few similarities with the classical *Ramayana* of Valmiki, for it is set in the Mekong Valley, gives only secondary importance to Rama and makes Ravana the real hero of the epic. In the Lao version, Ravana is no longer the four-headed demon of the Indian version, but a boy of great beauty who conducts himself like a Lao prince and is a protégé of Indra. The originality of the Lao *Ramayana* no doubt explains the immense popularity of the text: it is the subject of theatrical representations in the Luang Prabang region, and excerpts are regularly recited during evening social gatherings.

Technical treatises constitute another type of classical literature and include juridical texts (which present rules of law in the form of stories), anatomy texts (which assign great importance to the 'winds' circulating in the body), governmental texts (on the rights and duties of princes) and prediction manuals or *horasastra,* which until recent times guided Lao daily life and conduct.

In the 1960s a modern literature arose. It displayed two opposing tendencies that have their origin in the division of the country between partisans of a pro-Western regime and those of a socialist regime. Under the Lao Patriotic Front, a revolutionary literature developed under party control. It praised the exploits of the people in their struggle against the Americans and their Lao supporters. This literature used a new and often aggressive style of writing, and the terminology of international revolution. In the area under the control of the Vientiane government, young authors published (by themselves, as there were no publishing agencies) soap opera novels, humorous histories and poorly-written works of social criticism that featured dishonest officials and scheming politicians. Since 1975, the only modern Lao literature appears to consist of works urging the consolidation of socialism and emphasizing ideology and internationalism.

The Tai minorities of Laos possess a very rich literature, preserved in manuscript form and including, above all, magical and astrological texts. Juridical texts, which are the next largest category of minority literature, are divided into small chapters describing specific cases and presenting appropriate decisions. There are also Tai pharmaceutical texts dealing with the treatment of certain illnesses by medicinal plants and other preparations. Additional texts of this sort list the supernatural origins of illnesses and give remedies. The Tai minority groups also possess a rich religious literature, including rituals, prayers, and texts written in praise of spirits, especially of Phi Moeang, who is widely venerated. Finally, each minority group has its own popular and classical texts. This literature includes epics, stories, legends, and cosmographical works. The cosmogonies present visions of the creation of the worlds proper to each particular group. Some epics have a Buddhist flavour. For example, in *P'ommacak,* the Tai-Loe version of the *Ramayana,* Rama has been assimilated with the Buddha and his struggle against Ravana is depicted as a struggle between the Buddha and the evil Mara. This differs radically from the Lao version, and indeed the story has been virtually transformed by the monks into a *Jataka.*

For an introduction to Lao literature, see **Thao Pouvong** (1949). On Lao legends, see **Archaimbault** (1980); on a form of oral literature called *lam,* see **Compton** (1979). For classical literature, see **Finot** (1917), **Manich Jumsai** (1973), and **Peltier** (1971). On the *Ramayana,* see **Sahai** (1973 and 1976). For an introduction to modern Lao literature, see **Saveng Phinith** (1974) and **Lafont** (1974). On *P'ommacak,* see **Lafont** (1957).

Bibliography

Archaimbault, C.
1973 *Structures religieuses lao: rites et mythes.* Vientiane: Editions Vithagna.
1980 *Contribution à l'étude d'un cycle de legendes lau.* Paris: EFEO (Publications de l'EFEO, 119).

Boon Thom Boonyavong
1962 *English-Lao dictionary.* Vientiane: Lao-American Association.

Bounmy Soukbandith
1983 *Modern English-Lao, Lao-English dictionary.* San Diego: Kongseng Soukbandith.

Brown, M. and J. J. Zasloff (eds.)
1986 *Apprentice revolutionaries: the communist movement in Laos, 1930-85.* Stanford: Hoover Institution Press, Stanford University. (Histories of Ruling Communist Parties, vol. 11).

Compton, C. J.
1979 *Courting poetry in Laos: a textual and linguistic analysis.* DeKalb, Illinois: Northern Illinois University Center for Southeast Asian Studies (Special Report no.18.)

Deydier, H.
1952 *Introduction à la connaissance du Laos.* Saigon: Impr. Française d'outre mer.

Dupertius, S.
1981 "Le calcul du calendrier laotien." *Peninsule* (Paris) 2: 25-118.

Finot, L.
1917 "Recherches sur la littérature laotienne." *BEFEO* 17: 1-28.

Hoshino, T., and R. Marcus
1981 *Lao for beginners: an introduction to the spoken and written language of Laos.* Rutland, Vermont; Tokyo: Charles E. Tuttle.

Hospitalier, J. J.
1937 *Grammaire laotienne.* Paris: Geuthner.

Huffman, F. E.
1986 *Bibliography and index of mainland Southeast Asian languages and linguistics.* New Haven; London: Yale University Press.

Kerr, A. D.
1972 *Lao-English dictionary.* 2 vols. Washington, D.C.: Consortium Press/Catholic Church of America Press.

Keyes, C. F.
1979 *Southeast Asian research tools: Laos.* Honolulu, University Press of Hawaii. (Southeast Asia Paper no.16, part VII).

Kunstadter, P.
1967 *Southeast Asian tribes, minorities, and nations.* 2 vols. Princeton: Princeton University Press.

Lafont, P. B.
1957 *P'ra Lak-P'ra Lam. P'ommacak.* Vientiane: EFEO.

1959   *Aperçus sur le Laos*. Vientiane: Alliance Française.
1961a "Les écritures 'tay du Laos." *BEFEO* 50, 2: 367-393.
1961b "Les écritures du Pali au Laos." *BEFEO* 50, 2: 395-405.
1965   "Inventaire des manuscrits des pagodes du Laos." *BEFEO* 52: 429-545.
1974   "La littérature politique lao." In P. B. Lafont and D. Lombard, eds., *Littératures contemporaines de l'Asie du sud-est*. Paris: Asiathèque, pp.41-55. (Colloque du XXIXe Congrès Internationale des Orientalistes).
1978a B*ibliographie du Laos. Vol.1 (1666-1961)*. Paris: EFEO. (Publications de l'EFEO, 50).
1978b *Bibliographie du Laos. Vol.2 (1962-1975)*. Paris: EFEO. (Publications de l'EFEO, 50).

Laos, Ministère de l'Education
1962   *Wachananukom phasa lao. Dictionnaire lao*. Vientiane: Ministère de l'Education Nationale.

LeBar, F. M., et al.
1960   *Laos: its people, its society, its future*. New Haven: HRAF Press.

LeBar, F. M., G. C. Hickey and J. K. Musgrave
1964   *Ethnic groups of mainland Southeast Asia*. New Haven: HRAF Press.

Lent, J. A.
1977   "Newspapers of contemporary Laos." In Asia Library Services, *A guide to research materials on Thailand and Laos*. Auburn, N.Y.: Asia Library Services, pp.29-35.
1982   "Laos." In J. A.Lent, ed., *Newspapers in Asia: contemporary trends and problems*. Hong Kong: Heinemann, pp.240-251.

Manich Jumsai
1973   *History of Thai Literature (including Laos, Shan, Khamti, Ahom and Yunnan-Nanchao)*. Bangkok: Chalermnit Press.

Moerman, M.
1965   "Ethnic identification in complex civilization: who are the Lue?" *American Anthropologist*. 67, 5: 1215-1230.

Morev, L. N., et al.
1979   *The Lao language*. Moscow: Nauka.

Nginn, P. S.
1969   *Dictionnaire français-lao*. Vientiane: Nal Sal.

Nunn, G. R. and Do Van Anh
1972   *Vietnamese, Cambodian and Laotian newspapers: an international union list*. Taipei: Chinese Materials and Research Aid Center.

Peltier, A.R.
1971   *Une texte classique lao, le Sysvat: traduction et notes*. Paris: EFEO. (Collection textes et documents sur l'Indochine, X).

Phetsarath, Prince.
1940 "Calendrier laotien." In *Bulletin des Amis du Laos,* 4 (August): 107-140.

Reinach, L. de.
1901 *Le Laos.* 2 vols. Paris: A. Charles.

Reinhorn, M.
1970 *Dictionnaire laotien-français.* 2 vols. Paris: C.N.R.S.

Sage, W. S. and J. A. N. Henchy
1986 *Laos: a bibliography.* Singapore: Institute of Southeast Asian Studies. (Library Bulletin no. 16).

Sahai, S.
1973 *The Phra Lak Lam or the Pra Lam Sadok.* 2 vols. New Delhi: Indian Council for Cultural Relations.
1976 *The Ramayana in Laos: a study in the Gvay Dvorahbi.* Delhi: B.R. Publishing.

Saveng Phinith
1974 "La littérature lao contemporaine." In P. B. Lafont and D. Lombard, eds. *Littératures contemporaines de l'Asie du sud-est,* Paris: Asiathèque, pp. 29-40.

Stuart-Fox, M.
1986 *Laos: politics, economics and society.* London: Frances Pinter; Boulder: Lynne Rienner Publishers.

Stuart-Fox, M., (ed.)
1982 *Contemporary Laos: studies in the politics and society of the Lao People's Democratic Republic.* St.Lucia; London: University of Queensland Press.

Thao Phouvong
1949 *Initiation à la littérature laotienne.* Hanoi: EFEO.

Wenk, K.
1975 *Laotische Handschriften.* Wiesbaden: F. Steiner Verlag. (Verzeichnis der Orientalischen Handschriften in Deutschland, Band 32.)

Yates, W. G., and Souksomboun Sayasithsena
1974 *Reading Lao: a programmed introduction.* Washington, D.C.: Foreign Service Institute.

Zago, M.
1972 *Rites et ceremonies en milieu bouddhiste lao.* Rome: Universita Gregoriana Editrice. (Documenta Missionalia 6).

Vietnam

Vietnam is shaped like an elongated 'S' and stretches along a coastline of nearly 2,000 kilometres, from the China frontier to the Ca-Mau peninsula. Seven natural geographic regions can be distinguished: three lowland zones (the deltas of the Red River and the Mekong and the smaller central delta region); two mountainous zones (the Annamite Chain separating Vietnam and Laos and the ring of high mountains of the Upper Red River basin); and two zones intermediate in height and structure (the midlands of northern Vietnam and the vast plateaus to the south of the 17th parallel). Historical accident brought about a somewhat artificial division of this disparate whole into three regions: the North (Tonkin, Bac-ky or Bac-bo), the Centre (Annam, Trung-ky or Trung-bo) and the South (Cochinchina, Nam-ky or Nam-bo). The cradle of Vietnamese civilisation was the Red River basin, from which, in a slow process of territorial expansion over several centuries, the Vietnamese people gradually spread southward along the coastal plains.

The overwhelming numerical superiority of the ethnic Vietnamese, who make up 87% of a population of approximately 62,000,000, should not be allowed to disguise the immense ethnic diversity of Vietnam. Besides the Chams and the Khmers and the many descendants of early Chinese immigrants in the south, some 60 additional minority groups can be distinguished. These groups, which belong to the Sino-Tibetan and Austro-Asiatic language families and possess distinctive cultures, live in the hinterlands and occupy a total area equal to two-thirds of Vietnam. The ethnic Vietnamese have kept to their traditional rice cultivation and are generally settled in the delta areas and coastal plains.

Vietnam's long and stormy history has been marked by outside challenges and intervention. In the course of China's long domination of Vietnam from the 2nd century BC to the 10th century AD, Vietnam was to a large extent initiated into Chinese political theories, social organization, bureaucratic practices, religious beliefs and other cultural attributes. The depth of the Chinese imprint may be illustrated by the fact that Vietnamese rulers, even when they maintained their political independence, continued to derive their cultural inspiration from China. The wisdom and techniques of the Chinese were seen by the Vietnamese as part of a universal heritage, in much the same way as Europeans viewed the legacies of Greece and Rome.

The years of French administration from the 19th century to 1954 — a brief period indeed when set against 1,000 years of Chinese occupation — have also had a great influence. French rule brought Western material civilisation, modern techniques and social concepts; it also inspired modern nationalist desires. The ending of colonial rule gave rise to profound upheavals complicated by the advent of international power struggles; Vietnam was divided in 1954 and reunified only in 1975.

Despite cultural borrowings from China and France, certain specifically Vietnamese traditions survive, particularly in the field of religion. For instance, archaic beliefs in spirits and cults of ancestors were not ousted by the arrival of the major foreign doctrines of Confucianism, Taoism, Buddhism and Christianity. Nor have the Vietnamese been hesitant to attempt syncretic

South-East Asia

approaches to outside influences and their own traditions. The best known of these today is probably the Cao Dai religious movement, which arose in southern Vietnam in the 1920s and attempts to synthesize the principal world religions at the same time as restating traditional Vietnamese values.

For a profile of Vietnam, see **Duiker** (1983); and for a general introduction to the Vietnamese, see **Huard** and **Durand** (1975) and **Phan Ke Binh** (1975-80); for ethnic groups of Vietnam, see **LeBar** (1964) and **Schrock** (1972) and on the montagnards (hill peoples), see **Legay** and **Tran Van Tot** (1967) and **Mole** (1970). On general bibliography, see **Chen** (1973) and **Cotter** (1977); bibliographies covering archaeology in Vietnam are **Bayard** (1980) and **Ha Van Tan** (1980); for a bibliography on relations between Vietnam and the West, see **Nguyen The Anh** (1967); a bibliography on Vietnamese communism is **Phan Thien Chau** (1977); for a bibliography of the Vietnam War, see **Burns** and **Leitenburg** (1984) and **Sugnet** and **Hickey** (1983); research guides are **Cotter** (1979) and **Descours-Gatin** (1983); a useful reference dictionary is **Whitfield** (1976).

For recent work on the prehistory of Vietnam, see **Davidson** (1976 and 1979); on history see **Buttinger** (1968), **Hodgkin** (1981), **Isoart** (1969), **Le Thanh Khoi** (1955 and 1982), **Marr** (1971 and 1981), **Smith** (1971), **Taylor** (1983), and **Woodside** (1976). On the Vietnam War, see especially **Smith** (1983-) and **Turley** (1986). For more recent events, see **Beresford** (1988) and **Duiker** (1986); for communism and modern Vietnam, see also **Duiker** (1981), **Huynh Kim Khanh** (1982), **Nguyen Van Canh** (1983) and **Pike** (1978). On religion in general, see **Cadière** (1944-57); on the Cao Dai sect, see **Oliver** (1976) and **Werner** (1981).

From The Ivory Comb, short stories published by Giai Phong, 1967

Dating Systems

The old Vietnamese calendar followed that of China. Years were recorded using a method of cyclical characters (*giap ty* or *can chi*) and year periods (*nien hieu*) which designated the divisions into different periods or eras of a ruler's reign. Dates were thus reckoned from the number of years elapsed since the adoption of a particular year-period and not from the ruler's accession. The years were divided into twelve lunar months of 29 or 30 days. In order to bring the lunar cycle into accord with the solar cycle, seven intercalary months (*nhuan nguyet*) were added over a period of nineteen years. These intercalary months were sometimes inserted differently from Chinese months, so it is not always possible to obtain the correct conversion of Vietnamese dates by using the conversion tables drawn up for the Chinese and Gregorian calendars. The lunar calendar was replaced for official purposes in the 20th century by the solar calendar, but the lunar calendar is still used in certain areas of everday life, particularly for the agricultural cycle and the performing of religious ceremonies and revering of ancestors.

On these and related subjects, see **Bui Quang Tung** (1963), **Nguyen Trong Binh** (1976) and **Zhang Huang** (1968).

Language

Vietnamese, a tonal language, is the product of a mixture of elements from Mon-Khmer and Thai language groups, together with elements of the Chinese language absorbed during the long period of Chinese rule. Vietnamese words are therefore something of a challenge to etymologists. The original linguistic substratum has not been effaced, however. Chinese words have formed a learned vocabulary, often inaccessible to the common people, while non-Chinese words have formed a popular vocabulary; frequently two words are found side by side, designating the same concept. Pronounciation of Chinese words tend to be in accordance with Vietnamese phonetics and there are syntactical differences between the two languages. Although there are phonetic, dialectical and lexical variations in the Vietnamese language, these must be considered relatively minor, especially taking into account the geographical extent of the country.

On the Vietnamese language in general, see **Nguyen Dinh Hoa** (1987), **Thompson** (1965) and **Truong Van Chinh** (1970). On the spoken language, see **Jones** (1979), **Le Van Ly** (1960) and **Nguyen Dinh Hoa** (1974); for grammar, see **Cadière** (1958), **Emeneau** (1951), **Nguyen Phu Phong** (1975 and 1976); and for teaching aids, see **Nguyen Dinh Hoa** (1963), **Thompson** and **Nguyen Duc Hiep** (1952) and **Dauphin** (1984). A survey and bibliography of linguistic studies of Vietnamese is available in **Thompson** and **Thomas** (1967) and **Huffman** (1986) is a more up-to-date bibliography.

Dictionaries are as follows: Vietnamese-Vietnamese, **Le Van Duc** and **Le Ngoc Tru** (1970), **Van Tan** and **Nguyen Van Dam** (1977), and (in *nom* or Vietnamese demotic characters) **Nguyen Quang Xy** and **Vu Van Kinh** (1971); Vietnamese-English, **Nguyen Dinh Hoa** (1971), **Nguyen Van Khon** (1966), **Bui Phung** (1978); English-Vietnamese, **Nguyen Dinh Hoa** (1980), **Nguyen**

Van Khon (1962); Vietnamese-Chinese-French, **Gouin** (1957), **Hue** (1971); Vietnamese-French, **Dao Van Tap** (1982); French-Vietnamese, **Truong Vinh Ky** (1884), **Dao Duy Anh** (1950), **Thanh Nghi** (1979); Vietnamese-German, **Boscher** (1978), **Karow** (1972); German-Vietnamese, **Boscher** (1964).

Script

Under Chinese domination, the Vietnamese adopted Chinese ideograms. These continued in use down to the beginning of the 20th century. During this period, classical Chinese was established as the official language of Vietnam and was the vehicle for Vietnamese intellectual expression. A need was early felt, however, to find a written form for that part of the Vietnamese vocabulary which had nothing to do with Chinese. A hybrid script called *nom* (or *chu nom*, meaning 'southern characters') was created with definite, but not always consistent, rules of construction. *Nom* script is also ideographic and is formed with the help of Chinese characters used either alone (but pronounced differently and having a different meaning) or used together (generally by bracketing two characters, with one character conveying the meaning and another its sound).

The codification of the *nom* script is traditionally dated from 1282. In the 14th and 15th centuries, *nom* was used in literary works concurrently with classical Chinese. The use of *nom* was especially significant in that it gave poets an opportunity to detach themselves from the rules of Chinese prosody and to develop purely Vietnamese metres such as the *luc bat* (six-eight). The *nom* script was also used for official edicts of the Ho (beginning of the 15th century), the Tay-son (end of the 18th century) and the first years of the Nguyen dynasty (early 19th century). In general, however, *nom* tended to be used most in works of a non-official nature and of popular literature.

Contact with Europeans introduced a script of foreign origin, using letters of the Latin alphabet and a number of diacritical signs to transcribe Vietnamese phonetically. Catholic missionaries helped create this Latin script, using it in preparing texts of their sermons and in translations of Christian texts. By 1651, when the Jesuit missionary Alexandre de Rhodes published his *Dictionarium Annamiticum Lusitanum et Latinum*, the use of a Latin script for Vietnamese was well established.

Until the end of the 19th century, this script, which later came to be called *quoc ngu* ('national language'), remained confined to Catholic circles and was not used in official teaching or by the general populace; French colonial rule led directly and indirectly to its diffusion throughout the country, however. The colonial authorities used *quoc ngu* initially in Cochinchina as a political instrument to break the national and traditional culture of the Vietnamese. In 1865 it was the French who, for instance, established the first Vietnamese-language newspaper to appear in *quoc ngu*, *Gia Dinh Bao* (Gia Dinh Gazette). The use of the new script spread rapidly, aided by the efforts of such Catholic scholars as Truong Vinh Ky and Huynh Tinh Cua (editors of *Gia Dinh Bao*) and by its use in schools.

But *quoc ngu* also became a tool and symbol of modernity for Vietnamese reformists and revolutionaries who, although still mostly Confucian scholars, soon came to recognize the Latin script's potential for reaching the masses. The

Dong Kinh Nghia Thuc (Tonkin Free School) movement, for example, proposed in the early 1900s to modernize the country and popularize western scientific knowledge and political concepts by means of *quoc ngu*, which was much more easily learned than the old scripts. The abolition in 1918 of classical examinations for the civil service helped spread the use and understanding of *quoc ngu*. The editors of such reviews in the north as *Dong Duong Tap Chi, Trung Bac Tan Van* and *Nam Phong Tap Chi,* as well as the different literary movements of the post-1930 period, particularly that of the *Tu Luc Van Doan* group, played an important role in shaping and enriching *quoc ngu*. Under their influence *quoc ngu* was liberated from Chinese: use of Chinese words where there were non-Chinese expressions available came increasingly to be considered pedantic. By 1945, *quoc ngu* had assumed its present form; it has, however, continued to add new words and in particular to build up a precise scientific terminology.

On *nom*, see **Nguyen Dinh Hoa** (1959); for a discussion of colonialism and language policy, see **De Francis** (1977); on *quoc ngu* and the development of modern literature, see **Hoang Ngoc Thanh** (1973), **Marr** (1981) and **Nguyen Khac Kham** (1976).

Manuscripts

The transmission of texts in pre-colonial Vietnam was carried out above all by scribes. The number of manuscripts in existence today considerably exceeds the number of old printed texts. Even during the last Nguyen dynasty, when a fair number of texts were block printed, many works remained in manuscript form only. A concern with expurgating and restoring texts has often led copyists of manuscripts from one generation to another to make profound changes in the texts as they copied them. As a result, the collation of different copies of a single work can present a great many problems for the contemporary scholar.

Manuscripts were written on different grades of paper made from the bark of the mulberry tree (*giay ban, giay lenh*) and varied considerably in size from an oblong format of about 14 x 25 cm to a large format of about 22 x 32 cm, with both standard and cursive calligraphy. Early wood-block printed texts are often included by scholars in the category of manuscripts.

The manuscript collection of the Ecole Française d'Extrême-Orient was left behind in Hanoi in 1955, but microfilms of the collection are preserved in Paris and some are also preserved at the School of Oriental and African Studies, London. Much of the old imperial library of Hue is now stored in Ho Chi Minh City; on historical sources in this library see **Smith** (1967). **Tran Van Giap** (1984) began listing Sino-Vietnamese and *nom* works, but his work remains unfinished. The manuscripts in the collections of the Bibliothèque Nationale, Paris, have not been fully catalogued. For further details on manuscript sources, see **Chen** (1962) and **Whitmore** (1970).

Printing and Development of the Press

The beginnings of printing in Vietnam are not precisely known, though woodblock (xylograph) editions of books were mentioned in 1295 and 1299 and tradition attributes the spread of such printing to the efforts of a 15th century scholar named Luong Nhu Hoc. The beginnings of paper-making in Vietnam are also unknown. Vietnam's troubled history and tropical climate have contributed to the rapid deterioration and destruction of books so that there are few early works surviving in their original editions. Acknowledging this unfortunate circumstance, it would seem that the majority of early editions alluded to in works composed at a much later date cannot be placed earlier than the second half of the 17th century. Indeed, the first definite dated work is the 1697 edition of the great official history, *Dai Viet su ky toan thu.*

Until the 19th century, the printing technique used in Vietnam was woodblock engraving; movable characters, although known, were not used. Woodblock printing was a limited art, confined for the most part to certain temples and villages of northern Vietnam specializing in the making of paper and ink and in the art of engraving. Printed books were rare therefore and the copying of texts by scribes remained the principal means of transmitting texts. Old wood-block editions bore only such inscriptions as 'engraved by the woodblock cutters of (such and such) village', with no names of publishers given.

Modern printing was instituted in Vietnam by the French. Western typographic processes were introduced into Cochinchina in 1862 and in Tonkin in 1883, with the establishment of official presses (publishing *Bulletin official de l'expédition de la Cochinchine, Bulletin du Comité d'Etude Agricole, Industrielle et Commerciale de l'Annam et du Tonkin,* etc.). But the development of book publishing was brought about all by the rise of *quoc ngu*. One of the earliest Vietnamese publishers was Dinh Thai Son, who, in the late 19th century, established the Imprimerie de l'Union to compete with the French publishing houses in Saigon. After World War I, publishing houses established largely with Vietnamese capital multiplied in Hanoi, Hue and Saigon. In the field of periodical publications, 420 titles appeared between 1932 and 1945, compared with a total of only 97 for the period 1865 to 1930. A sytem of copyright deposit was begun in 1881, but only applied after 1922. The *Liste des imprimés déposés au Service du Dépôt Légal,* published annually by the Direction des Archives et Bibliothèque de l'Indochine from 1922 to 1940 testifies to the development of publishing during this period.

The division of Vietnam from 1954 to 1975 also entailed a separate evolution in the publishing field. In the socialist North, where culture and literature were placed under the direction of the state, publications were often in large editions and played an important role in society. In the South, where free enterprise reigned, publishing benefited from the latest technical innovations but was often disorderly, with a proliferation of limited and poorly distributed editions.

The idea of a daily press was a Western introduction to Vietnam and journalism as a literary genre can thus be said to have developed with the establishment of French colonial rule. Vietnamese newspapers were modelled on the French papers published in Indochina, but they also had from the start special literary features such as 'literary corners' (*van uyen*) and translations into Vietnamese of French and Chinese literary works. The press played an important part in disseminating and developing *quoc ngu* and contributed greatly to the formation of the modern Vietnamese language and literature. Not only were many new literary, philosophical and scientific terms introduced into the language, but the language itself became more standardized. Reviews such as *Nam Phong Tap Chi* and *Phu Nu Tan Van* were read throughout the country and through them journalists gave terms of speech once restricted to a particular region a much wider currency.

The first Vietnamese gazette or paper was *Gia Dinh Bao*. It was started in Saigon in 1865 as a means of publishing official texts pertaining to the administration of Cochinchina and was soon followed by other papers such as *Nong Co Min Dam* and *Luc Tinh Tan Van*. With the appearance in Hanoi of *Dang Co Tung Bao* in 1907, of *Dong Duong Tap Chi* in 1913 and of *Trung Bac Tan Van* in 1915, journalism became concerned with politics as well as with literature and poetry. From 1919 onwards, preoccupation with political matters led to the establishment of many periodicals, although most were short-lived. The development of journalism was much influenced by the activities of such literary groups as the *Tu Luc Van Doan* (whose irreverent publication *Phong Hoa*, begun in 1922, was very successful) and of individuals such as Nguyen Van Vinh and Pham Quynh. Pham Quynh was chief editor of the review *Nam Phong*, published 1917-1934, which did much to free Vietnamese literature and language from Chinese cultural influence and models. After the colonial authorities proclaimed freedom of the press and abolished censorship in 1935 many different journals flourished. In 1937 there were 110 dailies and 159 periodicals; in 1938, 128 dailies and 160 periodicals; and in 1939, 128 dailies and 176 periodicals. After 1939, due to the reimposition of censorship and then to the war, a drastic drop in the number of publications occurred.

Despite its growth, the press did not become a powerful social force. Generally speaking, newspapers lacked financial resources and were short-lived. The privately owned press in Vietnam has never achieved a truly mass circulation, but has consisted of a large number of dailies and weeklies with only a limited, predominately urban, readership. For example, in 1929 the total annual circulation of the most important paper in central Vietnam *Tieng Dan (Voice of the People)*, published twice weekly, amounted to only 336,331 copies. This limited circulation of newpapers continued until 1975 in the south, where there was no true freedom of the press. In contemporary socialist Vietnam there is a tendency to utilise news items as a means of political and moral indoctrination. There are currently about 200 government-sponsored periodicals and newspapers published in Vietnam. They cover a range of subjects in the sciences, technology, social sciences and humanities. They are all distributed overseas through the state enterprise for the export of books, Xunhasaba.

On early printed works, see **Gaspardone** (1934) and **Tran Van Giap** (1938); for publication of texts in Chinese or *nom* with parallel *quoc ngu* transcription/translation, see **Nguyen The Anh** (1968, 1972-1973) and **Vo Long The** (1971). On early printing techniques in Vietnam, see **Oger** (1909). The journal *Nam Phong* and literary developments of the early 20th century are covered in **Pham Thi Ngoan** (1973); works on newspapers are **Guimary** (1982), **Huynh Van Tong** (1973), **Nguyen Viet Chuoc** (1974) and **Tran Van Dinh** (1982). The Bibliothèque Nationale's important holdings of Sino-

Vietnamese and *Nom* printed works are partially listed in **Yamamoto** (1953); the Ecole Française d'Extrême-Orient in Paris and the Han Nom institute in Hanoi are compiling an inventory and bibliography of Sino-Vietnamese and *nom* works, of which the first volume, covering collections in Paris, is in press. For a microfiche catalogue of *quoc ngu* holdings in the Bibliothèque Nationale, see **Rageau** (1979). Other library catalogues are **Cornell University** (1979 and 1983) and for the Library of Congress, **Rony** (1982 and 1987). An international union list of Vietnamese newspapers is in **Nunn** and **Do Van Anh** (1972); periodicals are covered in **Moon** (1979) and **Nunn** (1977).

Literature

Popular Vietnamese literature is varied and rich, expressing over the centuries the humour, realism and irony of the people. Only part of this mostly anonymous literature has been written down. Consequently, it is difficult to date this orally transmitted stock of stories, legends, proverbs and popular songs that depicts a great many aspects of traditional Vietnamese society. Vietnamese folk literature was enriched in the 17th and 18th centuries by new genres such as fables, satirical and narrative poems, and above all verse novels (*truyen*). The latter are stories in 6-8 verse form, in which the first verse has six 'feet' and the second eight, and the sixth character of the second verse rhymes with the last character of the first verse and so on. These verse novels were recited and sung from village to village. Folk literature was a source of inspiration for the intellectual elite, who borrowed simple everyday speech and colourful, often satirical, expressions from proverbs and songs in order to create their own literary works. Folk songs (*ca dao*) however, have not always been entirely the creations of the people. Scholars sometimes composed for their own enjoyment and for such occasions as spring and agricultural festivals. In the 19th century, anonymous scholars produced ballads that were full of desperation and disrespect for authority, occasioned by the misfortunes of the reign of Tu duc (1848-1883).

Vietnamese literature from its beginnings until the 18th century, was dominated by Chinese influence. At first Chinese characters and Chinese conceptions of literary style were used exclusively, but gradually the literature distanced itself from these models as authors attempted to preserve the popular oral literature and to create a national literature in *nom*. Different stages mark the development of this literature. During the Ly and Tran dynasties (11th to 14th centuries), the Chinese influence lost its association with Buddhism ; Confucianism was instituted as the state doctrine and an official educational structure was established. This structure supported Chinese official literature, tied as it was to a moral conception of society, one not popular or national but Confucian and inspired by a class of literati. A literature reflecting these changes arose in the first period of the Le dynasty (15th century). Many different Sino-Vietnamese works (historical chronicles and especially poetry), some attaining perfection of classical form and a high level of sophistication, were composed. Some examples are *Thien Nam du ha tap,* an encyclopaedic collection of documents relating to the reign of Le Thanh-tong (1460-1497); *Linh Nam trich quai,* a collection of legends edited by Vu Quynh and Kieu Phu; and the historian Phan Phy Tien's *Ban thao thuc vat toat yeu.*

Vietnam

But thinkers were already concerning themselves with the weakening of the national conscience, which was aggravated, in the opinion of many, by the insufficient preservation and study of purely Vietnamese culture. This concern is apparent in the *Dai Viet su ky* (*Records of Dai Viet*, compiled and revised in the 13th century by Le Van Huu, supplemented and edited by Ngo Si Lien in 1479), which justified, through legend and myth, the independent personality of the Vietnamese people and the Vietnamese state.

It is against this background that the interpenetration of two literary traditions — those of the literati on the one hand and the people on the other, which until then had developed separately — is best understood. The interpenetration was made possible by the development of *nom* and its acceptance as a vehicle adapted to literary and poetic expression. The first great works in *nom* date from the 15th century. In their simplicity of language and the immediacy of their concerns, they constitute the point of departure for a purely Vietnamese literature. From the 16th to the 18th centuries, Vietnam went

Title page of de Rhodes' dictionary, 1651

through a long, troubled period in the course of which Confucian idealogy experienced an unprecedented crisis. Poets and writers, liberated from an increasingly sterile formalism, took a critical look at the old society and sought to express new aspirations. New themes appeared, requiring new forms; the language became both more concise and more flexible. Compilations in classical Chinese continued to be made, but in literature *nom* predominated. Though in the 18th century Chinese genres of composition had a certain revival and were even adapted into *nom*, *nom* poems in 6-8 verse multiplied until, by the end of the century, they constituted the most important and original form of literary expresssion in Vietnam. Among the best-known *nom* poems from this period are *Chinh phu ngam* (*Lament of a soldier's wife*), a moving anti-war poem usually attributed to the famed Doan Thi Diem (1705-1948) but more recently accepted as the work of Phan Huy Ich (1750-1822); and *Cung oan ngam khuc* (*Concubine's complaint*), by Nguyen Gia Thieu (1741-1798).

The Nguyen dynasty gave a legitimist, traditional and authoritarian stamp to the 19th century. It sought to buttress its own legitimacy by reaffirming and sustaining neo-Confucian precepts. At the same time, however, there occurred a flowering of *nom* poetry which, together with the success of the verse novels, put an end to all rules of traditional literature. The political upheavals of the time led people to reflect deeply on political relationships. As loyalty toward one's ruler no longer seemed sufficient and as rulers changed so frequently in the constant struggle for power, to whom or to what was allegiance due? In the 19th century, authors gave different replies to this basic question. Some interpreted new events in the light of traditional values, while others turned to social criticism or reflected in their writings the irreverent and anarchistic strains of humour characteristic of the day. The social upheavals and the ferment of ideas in this period were best reflected in the greatest of all works of Vietnamese literature, *Kim Van Kieu* or *Truyen Kieu* (*The Tale of Kieu*). The genius of the author, Nguyen Du (1765-1820), lay partly in the fact that he was a man very much of his time, expressing its contradictions and using them to present universal truths. He was, however, only the most durable of a profusion of talented writers who in the second half of the 18th century perfected the use of *nom* and built a literature upon it. In this period, language freed itself from Chinese influence, a stage of development which was perhaps necessary before Vietnamese could successfully be cast in the mould of *quoc ngu*.

Modern Vietnamese literature began with the French colonization of Vietnam. The influence of European education, with its intellectual and moral repercussions and the general diffusion of *quoc ngu*, transformed literature. Modern Vietnamese literature has been described as the expression of a creative synthesis in which the Western critical apparatus was applied to the Vietnamese past, leading to the preservation of only the best of traditional Vietnamese values. Western literary concepts and techniques were absorbed into the existing literary tradition in order to create an entirely new literature. This process of literary modernization, which began in the first years of the 20th century, occurred in several stages. The important break, however, took place around 1930; until that time, despite the initiation of new disciplines (journalistic reporting, literary criticism, short stories and novels), literary forms were still limited by classical rules entailing a narrative style and appropriate alliterations, assonance and symmetry. A cultural revolution took place in 1930, however, accompanying almost exactly the political crisis of the day. This revolution was the work of the first real generation of intellectuals produced by French cultural influence, a generation more Westernized than the preceding one and so attached to liberal ideas as to be intolerant of traditional forms altogether. Because it was difficult to attack the colonial regime, this generation waged literary war against what it considered the decrepit institutions of traditional Vietnamese society. Through literature, this new generation hoped to bring the spirit of reform into all spheres of Vietnamese life, in the process freeing literature itself from the constraints of tradition. All genres of modern writing flourished, especially poetry, exemplified by the *Tho Moi* ('new poetry') movement. A clear concise prose style — copied from the French and stripped as far as possible of classical Chinese terms and allusions — came into existence.

The repercussions of the thirty years of war between 1945 and 1975, which changed the social and political structure of Vietnam so profoundly, are of great significance to modern Vietnamese literature as well. Particularly noteworthy is the literary dichotomy created by the partition of Vietnam in 1954. In the north, where publication was linked to ideological criteria, literature was required to follow the political path defined by the government. A dissident writers' movement called *Nhan van Giai pham* arose in opposition to socialism, but was quickly stamped out. Henceforth, literature was committed to safeguarding and constructing socialism, to reunifying Vietnam and to fighting foreign aggression. Within this framework of socialist realism, themes and styles were obviously limited. In the south, although writers were not obliged to follow so clearly defined a policy, literature was influenced by the general concern of the government with nationalist, anti-communist ideology. There appeared a variety of works with different themes and biases, subject only to rather erratic and inefficient censorship. Many authors catered to the worst tastes of the public while some, distressed by the cultural and economic upheavals accompanying the American presence in their country, criticised the policies of the government. The leading novelist today is Le Luu whose recent novel, *Thoi xa vang* (Time gone by) about a Vietnamese soldier's difficulties on returning to his North Vietnamese village, sets a new personal and critical style.

The **legal literature** of Vietnam prior to French rule divides neatly into works from the Le dynasty (1428-1789) and those from the Nguyen dynasty (1802-1945). The Le code (*Quoc trieu hinh luat* or *Law of the State*) is known in 18th century recensions that retain provisions from the earlier period of the dynasty. A large portion of the text is known from earlier collections, of which the most important are the *Thien Nam du ha tap* (containing laws issued during the reign of Le Thanh-tong, 1460-1497) and the *Hong Duc thien chinh thu* (compiled in the 16th century and containing, as well, laws from the 15th century). Additional material for the laws of this period can be found in the official histories of the period, especially the *Dai Viet su ky toan thu* and its successor, the *Dai Viet su ky toan thu tuc bien*, written in the 18th century. The final essential source is the collection of imperial edicts, the *Quoc trieu chieu lenh thien chinh*, compiled 1705-1709, and containing edicts promulgated in the 17th century, classified according to the governmental ministry responsible.

The major characteristic of the legal system throughout its long history is the parallel incorporation of indigenous elements with Chinese borrowings. This is apparent from the Le code, in which extensive borrowing from the T'ang and Ming codes is demonstrable. More important, the form and arrangement of the Le code is directly derived from the T'ang model. Yet clearly Vietnamese preference and custom is followed in many areas, especially in property and family matters. It is this tension which gives the law of the period its peculiar characteristics.

The early 19th century saw a radical change in the legal literature of Vietnam which is best exemplified in the Gia-long Code, promulgated in 1812 by Emperor Gia-long, the first sovereign of the Nguyen dynasty. This code has nine basic divisions and 22 books; its formal arrangement is taken directly from the laws of the later Ch'ing and the content is considerably more Sinicized than the earlier Le laws, although some distinctly Vietnamese elements are retained.

On the subject of folk literature, see **Duong Dinh Khue** (1976), **Zucchelli** (1968) and the detailed bibliography in **Cao Huy Dinh** (1976); on folk songs see **Vo Phan Thanh Giao Trinh** (1975) and **Balaban** (1980). For an English translation of *Chinh Phu Ngam*, see **Huynh Sanh Thong** (1986). For an English translation of the *Kim Van Kieu*, see **Nguyen Du** (trans. **Huynh Sanh Thong**) (1983). On poetry, see **Nguyen Ngoc Bich** (1975) and **Huynh Sanh Thong** (1979). The traditional theatre is covered in **Huynh Khac Dung** (1970). Historical writing and chronicles are discussed in **Langlet** (1970 and 1985), **Pozner** (1980), **Marr** (1979), **Taylor** (1983) and **Wolters** (1979). On intellectual history and literary developments see **Marr** (1981) and **Woodside** (1982). The development of the modern novel is introduced in **Bui Xuan Bao** (1972), **Dinh Xuan Nguyen** (1961) and **Duong Dinh Khue** (1966); **Duong Dinh Khue** and **Louis-Hénard** (1978) treat the development of modern poetry, on which, see also **Nguyen Tien Lang** (1974). For contemporary literature more generally, see the articles by **Boudarel** (1974), **Dauphin** (1974), **Davidson** (1982) and **Nguyen Tran Huan** (1974 and 1981). On literature in South Vietnam, see **Vo Phien** (1987). A general survey of Vietnamese literature with a critical bibliography is available in **Durand** and **Nguyen Tran Huan** (1985). See also **Duong Dinh Khue** (1966), **Nguyen Khac Vien** and **Huu Ngoc** (1982) and **Pham The Ngu** (1972). **Tran Van Giap** (1972) provides brief biographies of authors. A four-volume collection of Vietnamese literature is *Anthologie de la littérature vietnamienne* (1972-77), of which **Nguyen Khac Vien** and **Huu Ngoc** (1982) is a recast one-volume edition. Useful poetry collections, in addition to **Huynh Sanh Thong** (1979), are *Anthologie de la poésie vietnamienne* (1969 and 1981). For an anthology of short stories, see **Banerian** (1986). For a bibliography of Vietnamese literature in translation see **Jenner** (1973), though this cannot include the recent spate of publications in Vietnam and elswhere. For an extensive treatment of Vietnamese colonial period literature in French, see **Yeager** (1987). The Le legal system is described in **Deloustal** (1908-22) and **Nguyen Ngoc Huy** (1980); a translation and analysis of the Le code is available in **Nguyen Ngoc Huy** and **Ta Van Tai** (1987), while a translation of the Gia-long code is available in **Aubaret** (1865) and **Philastre** (1976), with a summary provided by **Hooker** (1978). There is a bibliography of legal materials by **Nguyen Phuong Khan** (1977); see also the extensive survey and bibliography in **Nguyen Ngoc Huy** and **Ta Van Tai** (1986).

Bibliography

Anthology de la littérature vietnamienne
1972- 4 vols. Hanoi: Editions en langues étrangeres.

Anthologie de la poésie vietnamienne
1969 Paris: Français Réunis.

Anthologie de la poésie vietnamienne: le chant vietnamienne, dix siècles de poésie.
1981 Paris: Gallimard.

Aubaret, G.
1865 *Code Annamite, lois et règlements du Royaume d'Annam.* 2 vols. Paris: Imprimerie Impériale.

Balaban, J.
1980 *Ca dao Vietnam: a bilingual anthology of Vietnamese folk poetry.* Greensboro: Unicorn.

Banerian, J.
1986 *Vietnamese short stories: an introduction.* Phoenix: Sphinx Publishing.

Bayard, D.
1980 "The roots of Indochinese civilisation: recent developments in the prehistory of Southeast Asia." *Pacific Affairs* 53, 1 89-114.

Beresford, M.
1988 *Vietnam: politics, economics and society.* London; New York: Printer. (Marxist Regimes Series).

Boudarel, G.
1974 "Les débuts de la littérature en République Démocratique du Vietnam de 1945 à 1962." In P. B. Lafont and D. Lombard, eds. *Littératures contemporaines de l'Asie du sud-est.* Paris: Asiathèque, pp. 125-142. (Colloque du XXIXe Congrès Internationale des Orientalistes).

Boscher, W.
1964 *Wörterbuch Deutsch-Vietnamesisch.* Leipzig: VEB Verlag Enzyklopädie.
1978 *Wörterbuch Vietnamesisch-Deutsch.* Leipzig: VEB Verlag Enzyklopädie.

Bui Phung
1978 *Tu dien Viet-Anh* (*Vietnamese-English dictionary*). Hanoi: Truong Dai hoc Tong hop.

Bui Quang Tung.
1963 "Tables synoptiques de chronologie vietnamienne." *BEFEO* 51: 1-78.

Bui Xuan Bao
1972 *Le roman vietnamien contemporaine: tendencies et évolution du roman vietnamien contemporaine, 1925-1945.* Saigon: Tu Sach Nhan-van Xa hoi.

Burns, R. D. and M. Leitenburg
1984 *The wars in Vietnam, Cambodia and Laos, 1945-1982: a bibliographic guide.* Santa Barbara, Ca.; Oxford: ABC-Clio Information Services. (War/Peace Bibliography Series, 18).

Buttinger, J.
1968 *Vietnam: a political history.* New York: Praeger.

Cadière, L.
1944-57 *Croyances et pratiques religieuses des Annamites.* 3 vols. Hanoi; Saigon; Paris: EFEO.
1958 *Syntaxe de la langue vietnamienne.* Paris: EFEO.

Cao Huy Dinh
1976   *Tim hieu tien trinh van hoc dan gian Viet-Nam.* (*Understanding the evolution of Vietnamese popular literature*). Hanoi: Nha Xuat Ban Khoa Hoc Xa Hoi.

Chen Ching-ho
1962   "The Imperial archives of the Nguyen dynasty." *JSEAH* 3, 2: 111-128.

Chen, John H. M.
1973   *Vietnam: a comprehensive bibliography.* Metuchen, N.J.: Scarecrow Press.

Cornell University Libraries
1976   *Southeast Asia catalog.* 7 volumes. Boston: G. K. Hall.
1983   *Southeast Asia catalog.* First supplement. 3 volumes. Boston: G. K. Hall.

Cotter, M. G.
1977   *Vietnam: a guide to reference sources.* Boston: G. K. Hall.
1979   *Southeast Asian research tools: Vietnam.* Honolulu: Hawaii University Press. (Southeast Asia Paper No.16, part IX).

Dao Duy Anh
1950   *Phap-Viet tu dien: dictionnaire français-vietnamien, avec transcription en caractères chinois des termes sino-vietnamiennes.* Saïgon: Truong-thi.

Dao Van Tap
1982   *Tu dien Viet-Phap pho-thong: dictionnaire général vietnamien-français.* Paris: Institut de l'Asie du sud-est.

Dauphin, A.
1974   "Le roman en République Démocratique du Vietnam de 1945 a 1970." In P. B. Lafont and D. Lombard, eds. *Littératures contemporaines de l'Asie du sud-est.* Paris: Asiathèque, pp. 143-152. (Colloque du XXIXe Congrès International des Orientalistes).
1984   *Cours de vietnamien.* 2nd edn. Paris: Asiathèque.

Davidson, J. H. C. S.
1976   "Recent archaeological activity in Vietnam." *Journal of the Hong Kong Archaeological Society* 6: 80-99.
1979   "Archaeology in northern Vietnam since 1954," and "Archaeology in southern Vietnam since 1954." In R. B. Smith and W. Watson, eds. *Early South East Asia: essays in archaeology, history and historical geography.* New York: Oxford University Press, pp. 98-124 and 215-222 respectively.
1982   "To aid the revolution: the short story as pro-liberation literature in South Viet-Nam." In J. H. C. S. Davidson and Helen Cordell, eds. *The short story in Southeast Asia.* London: School of Oriental and African Studies, pp. 203-228.

De Francis, J.
1977   *Colonialism and language policy in Viet-Nam.* The Hague: Mouton.

Deloustal, R.
1908-1922 "La justice dans l'ancien Annam, traduction et commentaire du Code des Le." Serialised in *BEFEO* volumes 8-22.

Descours-Gatin, C. and H. Villiers
1983 *Guide de recherches sur le Vietnam: bibliographies, archives et bibliothèques de France.* Paris: Editions Harmattan.

Dinh Xuan Nguyen.
1961 *Apport français dans la littérature vietnamienne, 1651-1945.* Saigon: Imprimerie Xa-hoi.

Duiker, W. J.
1981 *The communist road to power in Vietnam.* Boulder: Westview Press.
1983 *Vietnam: nation in revolution.* Boulder: Westview Press.
1986 *Vietnam since the fall of Saigon.* 2nd edn. Athens, Ohio: Ohio University Press. (First edition, 1980).

Duong Dinh Khue
1966 *Les chefs d'oeuvre de la littérature vietnamienne.* Saigon: Kim Lai An Quan.
1976 *La littérature populaire vietnamienne.* Bruxelles: Thanh-long.

Duong Dinh Khue and N. Louis-Hénard
1978 "Aperçu sur la poésie vietnamienne de la décade pré-révolutionnaire." *BEFEO* 65, 2: 431-492.

Durand, M. and Nguyan Tran Huan
1985 *An introduction to Vietnamese literature.* New York: Columbia University Press. (Translation of 1969 French edition).

Emeneau, M. B.
1951 *Studies in Vietnamese (Annamese) grammar.* Berkeley; Los Angeles: University of California Press.

Gaspardone, E.
1934 "Bibliographie annamite." *BEFEO* 34: 1-173.

Gouin, A.
1957 *Dictionnaire vietnamien, chinois, français.* Saigon: Imprimerie d'Extreme-Orient.

Guimary, D. L.
1982 "South Vietnam: before 1975." In J. A. Lent, ed. *Newspapers in Asia: contemporary trends and problems.* Hong Kong: Heinemann, pp. 368-385.

Ha Van Tan
1980 "Nouvelles recherches préhistoriques et protohistoriques au Vietnam." *BEFEO* 68: 113-154.

Hoang Ngoc Thanh
1973 "*Quoc ngu* and the development of modern Vietnamese literature." In W. F. Vella, ed. *Aspects of Vietnamese history*. Honolulu: University Press of Hawaii, pp. 191-236. (Asian Studies at Hawaii, No. 8).

Hodgkin, T.
1981 *Vietnam: the revolutionary path*. London: Macmillan.

Hooker, M. B.
1978 *A concise legal history of South-East Asia*. Oxford: Clarendon Press.

Huard, P. and M. Durand
1975 *Connaissance du Vietnam*. New York: AMS Press. (Reprint of the 1954 Paris edition).

Hue, G.
1971 *Tu-dien Viet-Hoa-Phap. Dictionnaire vietnamien-chinois-français*. Saigon: Khai-tri. (Reprint of 1937 Imprimerie Trung Hoa edition).

Huffman, F. E.
1986 *Bibliography and index of mainland Southeast Asian languages and linguistics*. New Haven; London: Yale University Press.

Huynh Khac Dung
1970 *Hat boi: théatre traditionnel du Vietnam*. Saigon: Kim Lai An Quan.

Huynh Kim Khanh
1982 *Vietnamese communism, 1925-1945*. Ithaca, N.Y.: Cornell University Press.

Huynh Sanh Thong (ed. and trans.)
1979 *The heritage of Vietnamese poetry*. New Haven: Yale University Press.

Huynh Sanh Thong (trans.)
1986 *The song of a soldiers's wife (Chinh Phu Ngam)*. New Haven: Yale University Center for International and Area Studies.

Huynh Van Tong.
1973 *Lich su bao chi Viet-nam tu khoi den 1930 (History of Vietnamese newspapers from origins to 1930)*. Saigon: Tri Dang.

Isoart, P.
1969 *Le Viet-nam*. Paris: A. Colin.

Jenner, P. N.
1973 *Southeast Asian literature in translation: a preliminary bibliography*. Honolulu: University of Hawaii Press.

Jones, R. B. and Huynh Sanh Thong
1979 *Spoken Vietnamese*. Ithaca, New York: Spoken Language Services.

Karow, O.
1972 *Vietnamesisch-Deutches Wörterbuch*. Wiesbaden: Harrassowitz.

Langlet, P.
1970 "La tradition vietnamienne: un état national au sein de la civilisation chinoise, d'après la traduction des 33e et 34e chapitres du Kham dinh Viet su thong giam cuong muc." *BSEI* 45, 2-3: 2-18.
1985 *L'ancienne historiographie d'état au Vietnam: Kham dinh Viet su thong gian cuong muc. Texte et commentaire du Miroir complet de l'histoire Viet établi par ordre imperial (1856-1884) chapitres 36 et 37 (1722-1735)*. 2 vols. Paris: EFEO. (Collection de textes et documents sur l'Indochine, 14).

Le Thanh Khoi
1955 *Le Vietnam: histoire et civilisation*. Paris: Editions de Minuit.
1982 *Histoire du Vietnam des origines à 1858*. Paris: Sudestasie.

Le Van Duc and Le Ngoc Tru
1970 *Tu dien Viet Nam* (Vietnamese dictionary). 2 vols. Saigon: Khai Tri.

Le Van Ly
1960 *Le parler vietnamien: sa structure phonologique morphologique fonctionnelle*. Saigon: Bo Quoc-gia, Giao-duc, Vien Khao-co.

LeBar, F. M., G. C. Hickey and J. K. Musgrave
1964 *Ethnic groups of mainland Southeast Asia*. New Haven: HRAF Press.

Legay, R. and Tran Van Tot
1967 "Essai de bibliographie pratique sur les populations montagnards du Sud-Vietnam (1935-1966)." *BSEI* 3: 242-299.

Marr, D. G.
1971 *Vietnamese anticolonialism, 1855-1925*. Berkeley: University of California Press.
1979 "Vietnamese historical reassessment, 1900-1944." In A.J.S. Reid and D.G. Marr, eds. *Perceptions of the past in Southeast Asia*, Singapore:Heinemann pp. 313-339.
1981 *Vietnamese tradition on trial, 1920-1945*. Berkeley: University of California Press.

Mole, R. L.
1970 *The montagnards of South Vietnam: a study of nine tribes*. Rutland, Vt.; Tokyo: Charles E. Tuttle.

Moon, B. E.
1979 *Periodicals for South-East Asian studies: a union catalogue of holdings in British and selected European libraries*. London: Mansell.

Nguyen Dinh Hoa
1959 "Chu Nom: the demotic system of writing in Vietnam." *JAOS* 79: 270-274.

1963 *Read Vietnamese: a graded course in written Vietnamese.* Saigon: Vietnamese-American Association.
1971 *Vietnamese-English student dictionary.* Rev. ed. Carbondale: Southern Illinois University Press.
1974 *Colloquial Vietnamese.* Rev. ed. Carbondale: Southern Illinois University Press.
1980 *Hoa's essential English-Vietnamese dictionary: Tu-dien Anh-Viet.* Carbondale: Asia books.
1987 "Vietnam." In B. Comrie, ed. *The world's major languages.* London: Croom Helm, pp. 777-796.

Nguyen Du
1983 *The Tale of Kieu: a bilingual edition of Truyen Kieu, by Nguyen Du.* (Translated by Huynh Sanh Thong). New Haven: Yale University Press.

Nguyen Khac Kham
1976 "Vietnamese national language and modern Vietnamese literature." *East Asian Cultural Studies* (Tokyo), 15: 170-194.

Nguyen Khac Vien and Huu Ngoc
1982 *Vietnamese literature.* Hanoi: Foreign Languages Publishing House.

Nguyen Ngoc Bich
1975 *A thousand years of Vietnamese poetry.* New York: Knopf.

Nguyen Ngoc Huy
1980 "Les codes des Le: 'Quoc Trieu Hinh Luat' ou lois pénales de la dynastie nationale." *BEFEO* 67: 147-220.

Nguyen Ngoc Huy and Ta Van Tai.
1986 *The Vietnamese texts.* In M. B. Hooker, ed. *Laws of South-East Asia, Vol 1: The pre-modern texts.* Singapore, Butterworth, pp. 435-495; bibliography, pp. 555-565.
1987 *The Le Code. Law in traditional Vietnam: a comparative Sino-Vietnamese legal study with historical-judicial analysis and annotations.* 3 vols. Athens: Ohio University Press.

Nguyen Phu Phong.
1975 *Le vietnamien fondamental.* Paris: Editions Klincksieck.
1976 *Le syntagme verbal en vietnamien.* The Hague: Mouton.

Nguyen Phong Khanh.
1977 *Vietnamese legal materials, 1954-1975: a select annotated bibliography.* Washington D.C.: Library of Congress.

Nguyen Quang Xy and Vu Van Kinh.
1971 *Tu-dien chu nom. (Dictionary of Vietnamese in demotic script).* Saigon: Bo Giao-duc Trung-tam Hoc-lieu.

Nguyen The Anh
1967 *Bibliography critique sur les relations entre le Viet-Nam et l'Occident.* Paris: Maisonneuve et Larose.
1968, 1972-73 "Les publications de documents historiques dans la République du Vietnam depuis 1955." *BSEI* 43, 1:51-60, 47, 4:760-762; and 48, 1:143-150.

Nguyen Tien Lang
1974 "Panorama de la poésie contemporaine vietnamienne." In P. B. Lafont and D. Lombard, eds. *Littératures contemporaines de l'Asie du sud-est.* Paris: Asiathèque, pp. 99-110. (Colloque du XXIXe Congrès International des Orientalistes).

Nguyen Tran Huan
1974 "Panorama du roman vietnamien contemporaine (1905-1972)." In P. B. Lafont and D. Lombard, eds. *Littératures contemporaines de l'Asie du sud-est.* Paris: Asiathèque, pp. 111-124. (Colloque du XXIXe Congrès International des Orientalistes).
1981 "The literature of Vietnam, 1954-1973." In Tham Seong Chee, ed. Essays on literature and society in Southeast Asia. Singapore: Heinemann, pp. 321-345.

Nguyen Trong Binh, Nguyen Linh and Bui Viet Nghi
1976 *Ban doi chieu am duong lich 2,000 nam va nien bieu lich su (Comparative table of the lunar and solar calendars over 2000 years and historical chronology).* Hanoi: Khoa Hoc Xa Hoi.

Nguyen Van Canh
1983 *Vietnam under communism, 1975-1982.* Stanford: Hoover Institution Press.

Nguyen Van Khon
1962 *English-Vietnamese dictionary: Anh-Viet tu-dien.* Saigon: Khai Tri.
1966 *Vietnamese-English dictionary: Viet-Anh tu-dien.* Saigon: Khai Tri.

Nguyen Viet Chuoc
1974 *Luoc su bao chi Viet-nam* (An outline of the history of Vietnamese newspapers). Saigon: Nam Som.

Nunn, G. R. and Do Van Anh
1972 *Vietnamese, Cambodian and Laotian newspapers: an international union list.* Tapei: Chinese Materials and Research Aids Service Center.

Oger, H. J.
1909 *Introduction générale à l'étude de la technique du peuple annamite.* Paris: Geuthner.

Oliver V. L.
1976 *Cao dai spiritism, a study of religion in Vietnamese society.* Leiden: Brill.

Pham The Ngu
1972   *Viet-Nam van hoc su gian hoc tan bien (A new history of Vietnamese literature)*. 3 vols. 2nd edn. Saigon: Quoc-hoc tung thu. (First edition 1961-1965).

Pham Thi Ngoan
1973   "Introduction au Nam-Phong 1917-1934." *BSEI* 48, 2-3: 167-502.

Phan Ke Binh
1975-1980 *Viet-Nam phong tuc: moeurs et coutumes du Vietnam*. 2 vols. Paris: EFEO. (Collection de textes et documents sur l'Indochine, No.11).

Phan Thien Chau
1977   *Vietnamese communism, a research bibliography*. 2nd edn., Westport, Conn.; London: Greenwood Press. (First edition, 1975.)

Philastre, P.
1876   *Le Code Annamite*. 2 vols. Paris: Ernest Leroux.

Pike, D.
1978   *History of Vietnamese communism*. Stanford: Hoover Institution Press.

Pozner, P.
1980   "Le problème des chroniques vietnamiennes: origine et influences étrangères." *BEFEO* 67: 275-302.

Rageau, C,
1979   *Catalogue du fonds indochinois de la Bibliothèque Nationale. Vol.1: Livres imprimés en quoc ngu, 1922-1954*. Paris: Bibliothèque Nationale.

Rony, A. K.
1982   *Vietnamese holdings in the Library of Congress: a bibliography*. Washington, D.C.: Library of Congress.
1987   *Vietnamese holdings in the Library of Congress, Supplement 1979-85: a bibliography*. Washington D.C.: Library of Congress.

Schrock, J. L., et al.
1972   *Minority groups in North Vietnam*. Washington, D.C.: U.S. Government Printing Office.

Smith, R. B.
1967   "Sino-Vietnamese sources for the Nguyen period, an introduction." *BSOAS* 30: 600-621.
1971   *Viet-Nam and the West*. Ithaca, N.Y.: Cornell University Press. (First edition, London 1968).
1983- *An international history of the Vietnam war*. (4 volumes planned). London: Macmillan.

Sugnet, C. L. and J. T. Hickey
1983   *Vietnam war bibliography: selected from Cornell University's Echols collection*. Lexington, Mass.; Toronto: Lexington Books.

Taylor, K. W.
1983 *The birth of Vietnam*. Berkeley: University of California Press.

Thanh Nghi
1979 *Phap-Viet tan tu dien minh-hoa: nouveau dictionnaire francais-vietnamien*. Paris: Sudestasie.

Thompson, L. C.
1965 *A Vietnamese grammar*. Seattle: University of Washington Press.

Thompson, L. C. and Nguyen Duc Hiep
1952 *A Vietnamese reader*. Seattle: University of Washington Press.

Thompson, L. C. and D. D. Thomas
1967 "Vietnam." In T. A. Sebeok, ed. *Current trends in linguistics, Vol II: linguistics in East Asia and South-East Asia*. The Hague: Mouton, pp. 815-846.

Tran Van Dinh
1982 "Vietnam after 1975." In J. A. Lent, ed. *Newspapers in Asia: contemporary trends and problems*. Hong Kong: Heinemann, pp. 386-393.

Tran Van Giap
1938 "Les chapitres bibliographiques de Le Quy Don et de Phan Huy Chu." *BSEI* 13, 1: 1-217.
1972 *Luoc truyen cac tac qia Vietnam. (Brief biographies of Vietnamese authors)*. 2 vols. Hanoi: Khoa Hoc Xa Hoi.
1984 *Tim hieu kho sach Han Nom. (A study of Vietnamese works written in Chinese and demotic characters)*. Volume 1. Hanoi: Van Hoa. (First edition, 1970).

Truong Van Chinh
1970 *Structure de la langue vietnamienne*. Paris: Imprimerie Nationale, Libraire Orientaliste Paul Geuthner.

Truong Vinh Ky, P.
1884 *Grand dictionnaire annamite-français-annamite*. Saigon: Imprimerie de la Mission.

Turley, W. S.
1986 *The second Indochina war: a short political and military history*. Boulder: Westview Press.

Van Tan and Nguyen Van Dam
1977 *Tu dien tieng Viet (Vietnamese language dictionary)* Hanoi: Khoa Hoc Xa Hoi.

Vo Long The
1971 "Traductions et études vietnamiennes récentes." *BSEI* 46, 3: 389-395.

Vo Phan Thanh Giao Trinh
1975   *Ca dao: Vietnamese popular songs.* Brussels: Editions Thanh-long.

Vo Phien
1987   *Literature in South Vietnam (1954-1975).* (Translated by Huynh Sanh Thong). New Haven: Yale University Center for Southeast Asia Studies.

Werner, J. S.
1981   *Peasant politics and religious sectarianism: peasant and priest in the Cao Dai in Vietnam.* New Haven: Yale University Southeast Asia Studies.

Whitfield, D. J.
1973   *Historical and cultural dictionary of Vietnam.* Metuchen, N.J.: Scarecrow Press.

Whitmore, J. K.
1970   "Vietnamese historical sources for the reign of Le Thanh Tong (1460-1497)," and, "A note on the location of source materials for early Vietnamese history." *Journal of Asian Studies* 29: 373-394, and 657-662.

Wolters, O. W.
1979   "Historians and emperors in Vietnam and China: comments arising out of Le Van Huu's History, presented at the Tran court in 1272." In A. J. S. Reid and D. G. Marr, eds. *Perceptions of the past in Southeast Asia.* Singapore: Heinemann, pp. 69-89.

Woodside, A.
1976   *Community and revolution in modern Vietnam.* Boston: Houghton Mifflin.
1982   "Conceptions of change and of human responsibility for change in late traditional Vietnam." In D. K. Wyatt and A. Woodside, eds. *Moral order and the question of change: essays on Southeast Asian thought.* New Haven: Yale University Southeast Asia Studies, pp. 104-150.

Yamamoto, T.
1953   "List of Annamese books in the Bibliothèque Nationale (Paris)." *Toyo Gakuho* 36, 1: 87-107.

Yeager, J. A.
1987   *The Vietnamese novel in French: a literary response to colonialism.* Hanover: University Press of New England.

Zhang Huang
1968   *Combined chronological table of European and Asian dates: Ou Ya Jizuan Hebiao.* Tokyo: Dai-en Bookstore. (Reprint of original edition, Shanghai: Tu-shan-wan-ci-mutang, 1904).

Zucchelli, F.
1968   *Contes populaires du Vietnam d'autrefois.* Paris: Conconnier.

Malaysia

Fragmented, divided not only by the South China sea but by the independent Sultanate of Brunei, the Federation of Malaysia includes a number of territories on the Malay Peninsula and in Borneo which were once ruled by, or under the protection of, the United Kingdom. Peninsular or West Malaysia, called Malaya until 1963, achieved independence in 1957. It comprises first Penang and Melaka (Malacca), which were once part of the colony of the Straits Settlements and, secondly, the Malay sultanates or rajaships of Kelantan, Trengganu, Pahang, Johor, Negri Sembilan, Selangor, Perak, Kedah and Perlis. These Sultanates, often based on a single river, are located in the lowland regions on either side of the central mountain range. In 1963 the Malayan federation was expanded to incorporate Singapore (the third of the old Straits Settlements) and also the East Malaysian states of Sabah and Sarawak in Borneo. Brunei, which lies between the two Bornean states, did not join the Federation although it had been under British protection. Singapore left the Federation in 1965 to become an independent state.

The population of Malaysia is 16,100,000 (1986). Approximately 51% of the population is Malay, some 33% Chinese, and about 11% Indian. Islam is the state religion of Malaysia and its adherents include both the Malay community and a small proportion of the non-Malays. The national language is Malay, which is also the language of education and government. Several Chinese dialects and Indian languages are spoken and English is still widely used.

Malaysian and Indonesian history overlaps because the geographical boundaries of the countries are a product of a 19th century agreement between the Dutch and British colonial powers. Thus, the earliest known Malay polities were not on the Peninsula but in Sumatra, in present-day Indonesia. Seventh-century inscriptions in a Malay dialect tell of a state which may have been known as Srivijaya. It was a centre for Buddhist studies and a great trading entrepot and lasted for many centuries. By the time the powerful peninsular state of Melaka flourished, in the 15th century, Islam was firmly established among the Malays. Although Hindu and Buddhist elements are even now to be found in both court and village Malay culture, the rulers and people from the Melaka period onwards began increasingly to orient themselves towards the Muslim world.

In political terms the Malays never achieved a great deal of unity. For brief periods polities such as Melaka (until its conquest by the Portuguese in 1511) and Johor (which flourished in the 16th and 17th centuries) encompassed numerous little principalities on the Peninsula, in Sumatra and in other parts of the archipelago. In the early 16th century, the Brunei empire extended over the whole island of Borneo and into the southern Philippine islands. In general, however, the Malay world consisted of a multiplicity of rival kingdoms, each having its period of glory. Deli, in east Sumatra, was prominent in the 17th century; Trengganu, on the east coast of the Peninsula, in the 18th, and Pahang; which borders on Trengganu, was a place of considerable prosperity early in the 19th century. These rival polities competed with one another for trade and subjects: occasionally one ruler conquered another.

South-East Asia

If the Malay world was fragmented from a political point of view there was, nevertheless, a marked unity in the culture of the Malays. The Malay language was the *lingua franca* of the archipelago and the Malay-speaking peoples, scattered over a vast region from Sumatra to eastern Indonesia, shared a common culture characterized by a style of dress, a body of custom and etiquette and a literary tradition.

From the 16th century onwards, Europeans began to play an active role in the commercial and political life of the archipelago. It was only in the 19th century, however, that European influence made a serious impact on the culture and style of life of the Malays. From that time Western education competed with Islamic teachings (coming from India and the Middle East) for Malay attention.

By the 1820s, Penang, Melaka and Singapore were all British-ruled and

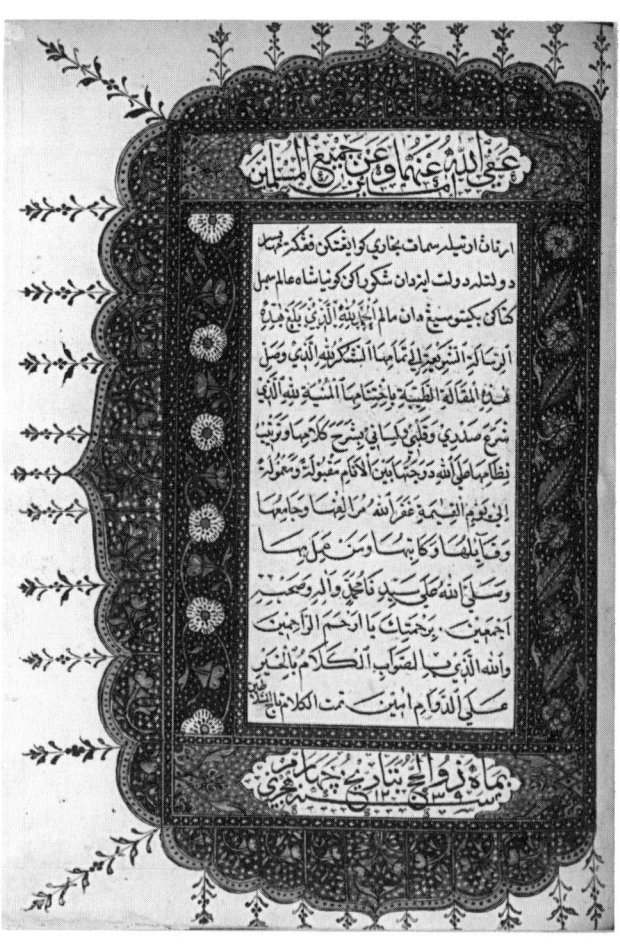

Illuminated page from 1824 manuscript of Taj as-Salatin

formed political and cultural enclaves within the Malay world. It was in these settlements that Malay culture was both challenged and fertilized by new streams of thought coming from the Muslim world and Europe. It was from Singapore and Penang also that the British began to exercise increasing political sway over the Malay kingdoms on the Peninsula. Beginning in the 1870s the different Sultans signed treaties with the British authorities which brought their states, in varying degrees, within the administrative and economic framework of the British empire.

In retrospect, the colonial period was brief, but European influence on Malay life did not cease with the obtaining of independence in 1957. Malaysia's government and legal structures, economic system, living styles and cultural life, continue to draw heavily from modern Europe as well as from Islam and the other earlier civilizations encountered.

One of the most important developments in the history of modern Malaysia was the immigration of large numbers of Chinese and Indians, particularly from the 19th century onwards, mainly to work in the tin mines and rubber plantations of the Peninsula. By the early 20th century they formed the majority of the population in a number of states and were able to dominate much of the economic life of British Malaya. The presence of these immigrant groups has influenced every aspect of Malaysian life. It has made Malaysia a plural society par excellence. Malaysia also contains many non-Malay indigenous peoples. These groups, many of whom have not adopted Islam, tend to live in the interior of the peninsula and form the majority of the population of East Malaysia. Some of these indigenous peoples, for instance the Iban of Sarawak, possess a considerable oral literature.

For bibliographies, see **Brown** (1986), **Karni** (1981), **Pelzer** (1971), **Perpustakaan Universiti Kebangsaan Malaysia** (1977) and **Roff** (1979). **Ding Choo Ming** (1981, 1982, 1984) gives a bibliography of bibliographies on Malaysia. For a bibliography and biographies of the British in Malaya, see **Heussler** (1981). The articles in **Lent** and **Mulliner** (1986) provide a survey of Malaysian studies and bibliography. A useful, if sometimes outdated introduction to Malaysia is **Wang Gungwu** (1964); see also **Bunge** (1985) and **Milne** and **Mauzy** (1986). The development of Malay culture is discussed in **Winstedt** (1981). On Malaysian history, see **Andaya** (1982), **Gullick** (1981, 1987), **Turnbull** (1980), and **Winstedt** (1962).

Dating Systems

A variety of dating systems have been used in Malaysia over the centuries. In recent centuries, however, the Islamic and Christian (Gregorian) calendars have prevailed. The Islamic (*Hijrah*) era came to Malaysia with Islam; it is used, for instance, on the 14th century Trengganu stone. The majority of dated Malay manuscripts bear *Hijrah* dates.

With the extension of European influence in the archipelago the Christian calendar has been adopted for many purposes. Publication dates of books and newspapers are frequently given in AD dates.

For the formula for conversion of the Islamic era into AD, see **Lewis** (1954). For conversion tables, see **Cattenoz** (1961). The days of the week given in

Freeman-Grenville (1963) are not reliable. For quick reference tables giving only the western dates for the first day of each Muslim year, see **Hazard** (1952) and **Philips** (1963).

Language

Malay (*Bahasa Kebangsaan* or the 'national language' to use its official title) is an Austronesian language (see Indonesia section). For many centuries it has been the *lingua franca* of the archipelago.

A basic form of Malay was used in commercial transactions; the language of the royal courts and that used in the dissemination of Islam was more complex. In modern Malaysia communication at the colloquial level is still carried on in a simplified Malay and the language of literature and government is more elaborate. It must be emphasised that the Malay language was used for centuries on both sides of the Melaka straits, and is the parent of modern Indonesian; furthermore, traditional Malay literature is as much part of the cultural inheritance of Indonesia as of Malaysia. For the sake of convenience, however, Malay language materials are discussed principally in the Malaysian section. The written Malay language both in the past and present remains reasonably uniform.

The main external influences on Malay (in chronological order) are Sanskrit, Arabic (and Persian) and English. Sanskrit influence appears first in Malay inscriptions dating from the 7th century. Sanskrit has enriched the vocabulary of Malay in the spheres of religion, ideas and statecraft.

Arabic began to influence Malay by the 14th century, after the establishment of Islam. In that century appeared the first Islamic Malay inscription (known as the Trengganu Stone) written in an Arabic script. Besides Arabic influence on Malay syntax, many Arabic loan words are found in Malay. Some of these (for example *adat, sebab, hal*) have been completely assimilated, but of the three thousand or so loan words from Arabic found in Malay most are used only in technical (usually religious) contexts.

From the 19th century onwards, both the lexicon and syntax of Malay were increasingly affected by European influence in the fields of technology, government and culture. Although the influence of Sanskrit and Arabic was exerted throughout the Malaysian/Indonesia area, for later European influence it is necessary to look separately at the modern states of Malaysia and Indonesia. Just as modern Malay owes much to English, so *Bahasa Indonesia* has been influenced by the Dutch. Very little has been published regarding European influence on Malay. What is probably the first compilation of European loan words in Indonesian and traditional Malay was published in 1983.

Baba Malay is a dialect of Malay spoken by the long-established Chinese communities of Penang and Melaka. It is characterized by 'mispronounciation' of its Malay elements and by its loan vocabulary from Chinese, particularly from Hokkien. Many Baba speakers, although of Chinese descent, do not speak a Chinese dialect; for communication outside their community they often use English.

For a description of the Malay language, see **Prentice** (1987). **Teeuw** (1959) provides a history of the language, while **Teeuw** (1961) gives a critical survey of language studies, and also lists studies of dialects of spoken Malay. On the language in Malay inscriptions, see **Casparis** (1975); on Sanskrit influence on Malay, see **Gonda** (1973); on Arabic influence in Malay, see, **Ronkel** (1899), and **Skinner** (1966) and for further references to research in this field and for a list of Arabic loan words, see **Jones** (1978); on European loan words, see **Grijns** (1983). A discussion of the separate development of Bahasa Malaysia and Bahasa Indonesia can be found in **Prentice** (1986). For a study of changing newspaper language, see **Mohd. Taib bin Osman** (1966). On Baba Malay, see **Tan Chee-Beng** (1980).

Major dictionaries for modern Malay are: Malay-Malay, **Iskandar** (1986); Malay-English and Malay-Malay, **Awang Sudjai Hairul** and **Yosoff Khan** (1977); Malay-German, **Karow** and **Hilgers-Hesse** (1978); English-Malay, **Winstedt** (1965). For classical Malay: Malay-English (in Jawi), **Wilkinson** (1901/1985), and in romanization, **Wilkinson**(1959), **Winstedt** (1971); Malay-Dutch (in Jawi), **Klinkert** (1916); Malay-French (in Jawi), **Favre** (1875). Among the teaching materials are: on grammar, **Asmah** and **Subbiah** (1968), **Payne** (1970), and **Winstedt** (1913); on spoken Malay, **Dyen** (1971), **King** (1960) and, as a tape course, **Wan Omar Rusdi** (1977); on written Malay, **King** (1964), and for the Jawi script, **Lewis** (1954).

Script

Very few examples survive of Malay written in its earliest script, the Pallava script from India (see Indonesia section). With the diffusion of Islam, a new script of Arabic derivation came into use. It is known in Malay as *Jawi* but in Indonesian as *Huruf Arab* or *Huruf Melayu*. This script employs all 28 characters of the Arabic alphabet, even though several of these letters are needed only for the spelling of Arabic loan-words. In addition, the needs of Malay phonology necessitated the creation of five additional letters to represent sounds not found in Arabic: for c, for ng; for p; for g; for ny. They are, in fact, adaptations of Arabic letters by adding more dots. The vowel signs *fatha*, *kasra* and *damma* are seldom used except in religious texts; the Malay names of these vowel signs (*baris di atas,* 'line above', *baris di bawah*, 'line below' and *baris di hadapan*, 'line in front', respectively) are reminiscent of the equivalent terms in Persian.

For about five centuries virtually all Malay writings were in the *Jawi* script. During most of this period the art of writing — and reading — appears to have been confined to circles of literacy associated with religion and the courts of the rulers.

In Malaysia, the use of the *Jawi* script was predominant until after the end of World War II, when it declined in favour of the romanized script. However, it is still taught in schools and retains a certain degree of usage. Romanized script was first introduced in the 17th century by Christian missionaries. The romanized spelling of Malay and Indonesian was based respectively on English and Dutch orthography and tends to emphasise the dissimilarity of the two. On 27 June 1972 agreement was reached on a new unified spelling to be used both in Indonesia and Malaysia and in August 1972 the agreement was implemented in both countries. The letters which functioned identically in the two orthographies have been retained in the new spelling and where usage differed the following changes were made:

Former Malay Spelling	Bahasa Indonesian Spelling	New Agreed Symbol
ch	tj	c
j	dj	j
y	j	y
ny	nj	ny
kh	ch	kh
gh	g	gh
sh	sj	sy

The agreed new symbols for the vowels are a,e,i,o and u. Thus, except in reading for material practice, there is no differentiation between the symbol for é *taling* ('long e') and e *pepet* ('short e'). The spellings for dipthongs (ai, au, oi) were retained.

For tables of Jawi script, see **Holle** (1882). For a comprehensive study of Jawi, see **Lewis** (1954). **Abdul Razak Abdul Hamid** and **Mokhtar Mohd. Dom** (1977) provide a course for learning Jawi script based on a popular televised series.

Manuscripts

The tradition of writing Malay manuscripts may have been begun in the 14th century at the time Islam was becoming established. Manuscripts are particularly important because they contain almost all the material for the study of what is called traditional Malay literature. The geographical area in which the tradition was practised extends beyond the territory of modern Malaysia to the (largely) coastal areas of Sumatra, Java, Kalimantan and other Indonesian islands. The earliest extant Malay manuscripts date from about 1600 AD. Nearly all are written in the Jawi script and pagination usually goes in the opposite direction from that of Western books.

Some Malay manuscripts are written on paper of local make, 'Chinese' paper; but the majority are on paper of European manufacture. Little is known about the inks used; sometimes they are of carbon black but usually blueish or brownish and sometimes introductory words or quotations from Arabic are highlighted in red. Around the middle of the 19th century acid inks were used which led to a later deterioration of the manuscript paper. Manuscripts are often bound in embossed leather, sometimes with Middle Eastern patterning. More recent manuscripts are in school exercise books or folded official stationery. Manuscripts are seldom attractively decorated in the Arabic and Persian tradition; in most the calligraphy and layout are plain. This may be because Malay manuscripts were less important as a written literary tradition than as the written record of what was essentially an oral tradition.

If manuscripts are dated the date is generally incorporated in a colophon immediately after the text. The *Hijrah* era is most frequently used. The date will, in general, be that of the completion or copying, not of the original composition. It is not uncommon, however, for a copyist simply to copy the date of the model he is following. Another indication of the date of manuscripts is the watermark. Watermarks are found on some of the European paper on which most Malay manuscripts are written. Despite the introduction of printing, the Malay manuscript tradition persisted on a small scale. In Brunei, for instance, it survived well into the 20th century.

For general discussion of Malay manuscripts, see **Ismail Hussein** (1966), **Jones** (1974), **Kratz** (1981) and **Sweeney** (1980). **Chambert-Loir** (1980) provides a survey of manuscript collections in which he calculates there are approximately 1650 Malay manuscripts in Leiden, 1000 in Jakarta, 600 in Britain and 200 in Malaysia. There are probably another thousand manuscripts in Aceh, North Sumatra. A more recent survey of collections can be found in **Ding Choo Ming** (1987), but it is impossible to give to any degree of accuracy the number of Malay manuscripts extant. There is probably an inestimable number of Malay manuscripts still in private hands and in other small collections in Malaysia,

The Government Gazette, printed by Bone in Penang, 1806

Brunei and Indonesia. For manuscript collections not listed in **Chambert-Loir** (1980), see **Abu Hassan Sham** (1974), **Ali Hj. Wan Mamat** (1985), **Ellen, Hooker** and **Milner** (1981), **Harun Mat Piah** and **Ismail Hamid** (1983), **Hussainmiya** (1978), **Jones** (1979), **Josselin de Jong** (1980), **Jumsari Jusuf** (1980), **Kratz** (1980), **Matheson** (1985), **Miller** (1982), **Ricklefs** and **Voorhoeve** (1977, 1982) and **Santa Maria** (1980). See also the references in the Indonesia section. **Ibrahim bin Ismail** (1981) discusses bibliographical control of Malay manuscripts.

Printing and Development of the Press

Christian missionaries were the first to print in Malay. A Malay version of the Gospel according to St. Matthew in roman characters, was printed for the Dutch East India Company in 1629. The whole Bible was published in romanised Malay in Amsterdam in 1731-33, and in Jawi script progressively between 1744 and 1758 in Batavia. A revision of the Jawi version was printed in Calcutta by the Serampore Mission Press in 1821. In Malaysia itself, the London Missionary Society (which established its first Malaysian mission in Melaka in 1815 and withdrew from the region in 1847) published not only Bibles and catechisms but also a Malay periodical and arithmetic book and some language-learning aides. The ten commandments were published in Malay by the Melakan missionaries in 1817; in Singapore, from 1823, C.H.Thomsen of the London Missionary Society printed government documents in Malay as well as missionary materials. The Society's Penang Mission began to publish in Malay in 1834. The first printing in English in Malaysia was pioneered by A.B.Bone who from 1806 to 1815 printed a newspaper, the *Government Gazette* (the title soon changed to *Prince of Wales Island Gazette*) in Penang; in 1807 Bone also printed *A Rough Sketch...of the Malay Language*.

Abdullah bin Abdul Kadir, often referred to as Munshi Abdullah, was the first Malay writer to have his work published. (Abdullah's writings are briefly discussed in the literature section). Abdullah was employed for many years by the missionaries of the London and other missionary societies, participating in the preparation of a new Malay Bible and of classical Malay texts (which were used in the instruction of students of Malay). A recension of the Malay Annals, the *Sejarah Melayu*, edited principally by Abdullah, was printed about 1831. Abdullah's own account of his journey up the east coast of the Peninsula, the *Pelayaran Abdullah*, appeared in 1838 and the *Hikayat Abdullah*, the autobiography of Abdullah, in 1849.

When the London Missionary Society withdrew from Melaka, Benjamin Peach Keasberry continued to run the printing establishment at Singapore which was known as the 'Mission Press'. It was at this press that Abdullah's work was printed. At Keasberry's death in 1875, John Fraser and D.C. Neave bought the press which survived until 1942.

A number of other presses were also in operation in the late 19th and early 20th centuries. Thus, in 1878, one of Abdullah's sons, Muhammed Ibrahim Munshi, published a pamphlet called *Pemimpin Johor*. This signalled the beginning of a lithographic press output in the form of literary compositions, translations, etc. Another printing press was to be found at the cultural and religious centre of Penyengat (part of the Riau-Lingga Sultanate which was located close to Singapore and within present day Indonesia). This press published Muslim and Malay literature and after 1911 it was moved to Singapore and became known as the Al-Ahmadiah Press. Around this time Penyengat scholars left Riau and Lingga to establish in Singapore the Muslim journal, *Al-Iman*. A third press was set up in the 1890s by the Methodist Mission at Singapore. Its publications included not only Christian literature but classical Malay texts and (after 1859) a monthly magazine. The Methodist Publishing House became the Malay Publishing House (M.P.H.) in 1928.

All these presses were located in Malaysia but printing of religious works also took place in the Middle East and India. During the 1880s Malay publications concerned with Islam reached Malaysia from Bombay and Mecca, where a printing press had been established with a Malay section in 1884.

The 1880s also saw the beginning of a published literature by and for the Straits' born Chinese community in what is popularly referred to as 'Baba Malay'. This literature flourished until around 1939. It consists mainly of translations of Chinese classical stories into 'Baba Malay'. But there were also some original works of fiction and several local compositions of *pantun*.

The colonial Government had begun to publish Malay writings in the late 1880s and played an increasingly important role in the early 20th century. In 1924 the 'Translation Bureau' was established at Sultan Idris Teachers Training College in the state of Perak. Text-books were published on a wide variety of topics and a 'Malaya Home Library Series' included translations from Shakespeare, Sherlock Holmes and the Arabian Nights. The 'Translation Bureau' was influenced by the Dutch publishing bureau, *Balai Pustaka*, in Indonesia.

Since *merdeka* (independence) the *Dewan Bahasa dan Pustaka*, the Malaysian Government's language and literature agency, has been an important influence on publishing. Set up in 1956, it published some 475 titles in its first ten years, including both translations and original Malay works. The latter included poetry as well as classical and modern verse. *Dewan Bahasa dan Pustaka* continues today to be the most prolific publisher of Malay literature, though private firms, such as Teks Publishing, Fajar Bakti, Heinemann, Eastern Universities Press, Pustaka Nasional and Utusan, contribute to the total output of contemporary literature. Malay writing from Brunei is almost wholly published by the *Dewan Bahasa dan Pustaka Brunei*. Not all publishing has been based in Singapore or Kuala Lumpur. The Asasiyyah Press, for instance, was established in Kelantan in 1929, the Jamiliah Press of Muar, Johor, was very prolific in the 1930s and, more recently, Pustaka Aman of Kelantan has been responsible for publishing a considerable volume of Malay literature.

Periodicals

The first Malay periodical the *Malay Magazine*, was published by the London Missionary Society. It appeared in 1821 and some issues are extant. Not until 1877 did the first Malay newspaper, *Jawi Peranakan* appear. It was established by an association of Muslims who, like Abdullah, were part Malay and part South Indian by descent. *Jawi Peranakan* is the name given to that community. Betweeen 1876 and 1905 at least seventeen periodicals were published, most of them sponsored and edited by *Jawi Peranakan*. In 1907 *Utusan Melayu*, which became an important Malay daily, began under the editorship of Eunos B. Abdullah. The major Malay newspapers today are *Utusan Melayu* (published in both Jawi and romanized editions) and *Berita Harian*.

Early printing and missionary publications are described in **Byrd** (1970). On the London Missionary Society's printing activities, see **O'Sullivan** (1984); also **Ibrahim bin Ismail** (1982). Malay translations of the Bible are listed and described in **Darlow** and **Moule** (1963). On Bone, see **Bloomfield** (1980). **Hutton** (1978) gives an account of the Europeans and Americans involved in printing. **Zain al-'Abidin bin Ahmad** (1940) and **Roff** (1967) describe lithographic publishing activity. **Hill** (1955) discusses the printing of Abdullah's writings. On Muslim scholars and publishing, see **Hamidy** (1983), and **Matheson** (1984); also **Roff** (1967); **Zain al 'Abidin bin Ahmad** (1940) has details on the Asasiyyah Press in Kelantan. On Baba Malay publications, see **Lombard-Salmon** (1977). On late 19th and early 20th century publishing industry, see **Proudfoot** (1986); on post-independence publishing activity, see **Dewan Bahasa dan Pustaka** (1967). The publications of the National Library of Malaysia (Perpustakaan Negara Malaysia) have contributed considerably to bringing 20th century Malay literature under improved bibliographic control. **Roff** (1972) analyses the development of Malay newspaper publishing and lists collections of Malay newspapers and their locations; **Proudfoot** (1985) supplements **Roff's** (1972) bibliography. On the *Malay Magazine*, see **Ibrahim bin Ismail** (1980). Also on the Malay press, see **Iskandar Haji Ahmad** (1973), **Nik Ahmad bin Haji Nik Hassan** (1963) and **Shahnon Ahmad** (1981); **Lent** (1982) provides a general survey of newspapers in Malaysia. **Lombard-Salmon** (1977) discusses Malay language newspapers published for the Chinese community. **Chen Mong Hock** (1967) describes early Chinese newspapers in Singapore.

Literature

Apart from the inscriptions written on copper or stone, some in Old Malay, the earliest extant Malay writings date from about 1600 A.D. The categorisation of Malay literature is still under debate. Malay has been written both in poetic and in prose form. The poetic genres include the *pantun* and the *syair*. A *pantun* consists of four lines, rhymed a b a b, the first two of which are said either to prepare lines three and four phonetically by means of an alluding sound, or to allude in a symbolic way to the essence of the last two lines.

Pantun are usually of a proverbial nature. In the past, they were not generally written down by Malays but rather recorded by European scholars. The *syair*, with its final rhyme scheme a a a a, can achieve epic length. *Syair* sometimes express the feelings of a mystic or lover; they also narrate historical and legendary events.

The variety of prose genres includes *kitab*, didactic Islamic literature usually translated or adapted from an Arabic original; *adab*, stories of the prophet Mohammed and of Muslim saints and heroes; and *hikayat*, some of which have many of the characteristics of chronicles, others having more in common with European epics and romance. The best known Malay 'chronicle' is the Malay Annals, the *Sejarah Melayu* (or more correctly, the *Sulalatu's Salatin*); *Hikayat Hang Tuah* is the most famous 'romance'. The 19th century text *Tuhfat al-Nafis* is also an important work.

Pre-modern Malay literature was often written anonymously; in some cases the author's name is given; more frequently, the copyist is named at the end of the manuscript. It cannot be assumed that the copyist played no role in the composition of a text. Especially in the case of *hikayat* he frequently adapted a text to his own needs. Malay texts often exist in many recensions. The distinction between Malay oral and written literature is not always clear. *Hikayat*, for example, were sometimes memorised and often read aloud. European and modern Malay scholars, on the other hand, have recorded in writing a wide range of oral literature. The historical development of pre-modern Malay literature (including both Indian and Islamic influence) is discussed briefly in the Indonesia section.

Munshi Abdullah is usually regarded as the first modern Malay author, although his work did not inspire a new literary movement in the 19th century. Although Abdullah wrote in a style often reminiscent of the best classical Malay writings, his works are modern in that they value realism, assert explicitly a personal view, criticise assumptions underlying Malay political and social behaviour and celebrate such Western values as the freedom of the individual. Abdullah's most quoted work is his autobiography, the *Hikayat Abdullah*. Abdullah's writings had markedly little influence on Malay literature during the remainder of the 19th century.

Pre-modern texts continued to be copied (though often at the request of Europeans) and some new *hikayat*, for instance, were composed well into the 20th century. One obvious reflection of Abdullah's concerns is to be found in the writing of his son, Muhammed Ibrahim, who wrote an account of a journey to the West Coast states, the *Hikayat Pelayaran Muhammed Ibrahim*.

Novels and short stories concerned with modern social and moral problems began to appear in the 1920s, apparently as a reaction to Western and Middle-Eastern cultural influences. The first such novel in a Malayan setting was *Kawan Benar* by Ahmad bin Mohd. Rashid Talu. At roughly the same time an increasing number of short stories were published in popular magazines. Common themes were forced marriage and the moral evils of urban life. Some of the main writers were Syed Sheikh Al-Hady Abdul Rahim Kajai and Ishak Hj. Muhammad. Another group of writers, connected with Sultan Idris Training College, Tanjung Malim, were inspired by contemporary Indonesian literature. Prominent among these authors was Harun Aminurrashid.

After World War II, the '50 Generation (*Asas '50*) were an influential group, consisting of Malay writers mainly based in Singapore. The novel has continued to be a popular form until the present day. Novel-writing competitions run by *Dewan Bahasa dan Pustaka* (established in 1956) encouraged the emergence of new writers. Principal novelists included A. Samad Said, Ibrahim Omar, Abdullah Hussain, Azizi Hji Abdullah and Shahnon Ahmad. Short story output has expanded greatly. In topic the stories have developed from nationalism to realistic social comment, followed by a trend towards the more personal themes. Some of the main writers have been Keris Mas, Baha Zain, Arena Wati, Awam-il-Sarkam and Anwar Ridhwan. In poetry, the free-form *sajak*, which began to emerge during the Japanese occupation, has ousted the traditional forms (*pantun* and *syair*) which predominated in pre-war verse. As in the novel and short story, social criticism has been the prevalent aim. Among the leading poets have been Masuri S.N., Usman Awang (Tongkat Warrant), A. Samad Said, A. Latiff Mohidin, Suhaimi Hj. Muhammad, Noor S.I., Dharmawijaya, Hadzraimi A. R. and Muhammad Haji Salleh. Much drama has been performed on stage, radio and television, but little is published and this form has less public impact than the printed media.

Legal Literature

The best known texts are the laws of Melaka, Pahang, Perak and Kedah. In essence they share similar characteristics to the legal literature described as Malayo-Muslim in the Indonesia section. The most famous and the exemplar for the others is the *Undang-Undang Melaka*. A slightly distinct class of law text is the Negri Sembilan 'Laws of Sungei Ujong', which is essentially a written verson of oral law preserved in the form of traditional sayings. A final class of texts are the manuscripts produced in British Borneo (now Sabah and Sarawak) under government aegis and consisting of rationalizings of local customs — often with an Islamic element — for administrative/judicial use.

Inscriptions are examined in **Casparis** (1975). The *pantun* is discussed in **Braasem** (1954) and **Overbeck** (1922). On the *syair,* see **Koster** and **Maier** (1982), **Muhammad Naguib al-Attas** (1968, 1971), **Sweeney** (1971), **Teeuw** (1966), and **Thomas** (1979). **Braginsky** (1975) deals with the problems of Malay versification in a broader way. On Islamic literature, see **Ismail Hamid** (1982), and on *hikayat* and the Malay chronicles, see **Bausani** (1979), **Bottoms** (1962, 1965) **Brakel** (1975), **Josselin de Jong** (1964), and **Winstedt** (1969). For some recent discussions of *hikayat* literature, see **Errington** (1979), and **Milner** (1982). For the role of the copyist, see **Iskandar** (1968), **Kratz** (1981), and **Voorhoeve** (1964). For a translation of the 19th century text, *Tuhfat al-Nafis*, see **Matheson** and **Andaya** (1982). For general studies of traditional Malay literature, see **Hooykaas** (1952), **Liaw Yock Fang** (1975), **Mohd. Taib bin Osman** (1976), **Sweeney** (1980) and **Winstedt** (1969). For an interesting survey of studies on traditional Malay literature, see **Ismail Hussein** (1966; reprinted with added bibliography in 1974).

The problems and methods of modern collecting of oral literature in Malaysia (and Indonesia) are discussed in **Rosidi** (1973), and **Sweeney** (1972, 1973, 1976); **Sweeney** (1987) discusses the relations between oral and written traditions. For general discussions of Malay folk literature, see **Brakel** (1976), **Hooykaas** (1952), **Wilkinson** (1907), and **Winstedt** (1969). Collections of *pantun* and proverbs are listed in the bibliography by **Deakin** (1978) and in **Teeuw** (1961): the indexes of such journals as *JMBRAS*, *BKI* and *TBG* should also be consulted under the headings 'folk lore', *pantun* and *letterkunde*. Two bibliographies that deal with printed editions of traditional Malay literature and works about that literature are **Ismail Hussein** (1978 a/b). **Chambert-Loir** (1975) provides a bibliography of translations of traditional Malay literature into Western languages.

Abdullah's links with earlier Malay literature are discussed in **Skinner** (1978). Biographical details of Abdullah are given in **Milner** (1980) and **Traill** (1979, 1981, 1982) provides further discussion. On Mohammed Ibrahim, see **Sweeney** and **Phillips** (1975). **Zain al 'Abidin bin Ahmad** (1940, 1941) discusses late 19th century developments and Malay literature of the pre-World War II period. Modern poetry is discussed in **Muhammed Haji Salleh** (1975, 1977). **Maimunah Mohd. Tahir** (1987) provides an overview of the development of modern Malay literature in its political and social context; see also the discussion in **Banks** (1987) which also includes a bibliography of novels and other Malay literary works and in **Tan Chin Kwang** (1986); **Tham Seong Chee** (1975, 1981 a/b) examines political aspects and influences. General discussions of modern Malay literature are also to be found in **Abu Bakar Hamid** (1975), **Anwar Ridhwan** (1976), **Li Chuan Siu** (1970, 1972, 1975), **Mohd. Taib bin Osman** (1976), **Yahaya Ismail** (1967-68, 1975) and **Zaini-Lajoubert** (1980).

For bibliographical information on studies of modern Malay literature, see **Jabatan Pengajian Melayu** (1976) and **Perpustakaan Universiti Kebangsaan Malaysia** (1977); see also the bibliography by **Deakin** (1978) for citations on all aspects of literature. A bibliography of modern Malay literature is found in **Safian Hussain** (1985), while Malay novels for 1925-42 are listed in **Abu Bakar Hamid** (1972) and for 1920-80 in **Ding Choo Ming** (1980), who also includes short stories and dramas. Short stories of the 1950s are listed in **Ismail Dahaman** (1968) and **Ding Choo Ming** (1985) lists short stories for the period 1980-84. Biographies and bibliographies of 63 writers are found in **Ilias Zaidi** (1976); see also **Baharuddin Zainal** (1981, 1985). Lastly, on legal literature, see **Hooker** (1986) who surveys law texts of the region and gives a detailed bibliography. In addition, for the *Undang-undang Melaka,* see **Liaw Yock Fang** (1976); also **Hooker** (1968); on the laws of Negri Sembilan, see **Winstedt** and **Josselin de Jong** (1954).

Bibliography

Abdul Razak Abdul Hamid, Haji and Haji Mokhtar Mohd. Dom
1977   *Belajar tulisan Jawi: learn Jawi.* Petaling Jaya: Fajar Bakti.

Abu Bakar Hamid
1972   "Bibliografi novel-novel Melayu 1925-1942." *Nusantara* 2:261-8.

Abu Hassan Sham
1974   "Naskhah-naskhah Melayu di Muzium Sarawak." *Dewan Bahasa* July: 336-342.

Ali Hj. Wan Mamat
1985   *Katalog manuskrip Melayu di Belanda.* Kuala Lumpur: Perpustakaan Negara Malaysia.

Andaya, B.W. and L.Y. Andaya
1982   *A history of Malaysia.* London: Macmillan.

Anwar Ridhawan
1976   *Disekitar pemikiran kesusastraan Malaysia 1952-1972.* Kuala Lumpur: Dewan Bahasa Pustaka.

Asmah Haji Omar
1982   *Language and society in Malaysia.* Kuala Lumpur: Dewan Bahasa dan Pustaka.

Asmah Haji Omar and Rama Subbiah
1968   *An introduction to Malay grammar.* Kuala Lumpur: Dewan Bahasa dan Pustaka, Kementerian Pelajaran Malaysia.

Awang Sudjai Hairul and Yusoff Khan
1977 *Kamus lengkap*. Petaling Jaya: Pustaka Zaman.

Baharuddin Zainal
1981 *Wajah*. Kuala Lumpur: Dewan Bahasa dan Pustaka.
1985 *A biography of Malaysian writers*. Kuala Lumpur: Dewan Bahasa dan Pustaka.

Banks, D. J.
1987 *From class to culture: social conscience in Malay novels since independence*. New Haven: Yale Center for International and Area Studies. (Southeast Asian Studies Program, Monograph No. 29).

Bausani, A.
1979 *Notes on the structure of the classical Malay hikayat*. Melbourne: Monash University. (Centre of Southeast Asian Studies Working Paper, No. 16).

Bloomfield, B. C.
1980 "A.B. Bone and the beginning of printing in Malaysia." *IOLR Report for the year 1979*, pp. 7-33.

Bottoms, J. C.
1962 "Malay historical works." In K. Tregonning, ed. *Malaysian historical sources*. Singapore: University of Singapore, pp. 36-62.
1965 "Some Malay historical sources: a bibliographical note." In Soedjatmoko, ed. *An introduction to Indonesian historiography*. Ithaca: Cornell University Press, pp. 156-193.

Braasem, W. A.
1954 *Moderne Indonesische Literatuur*. Amsterdam: Van der Peet.

Braginsky, V. Y.
1975 "Some remarks on the structure of the 'Sya'ir Perahu' by Hamzah Fansuri." *BKI* 131: 409-426.

Brakel, L. F.
1975 *The Hikayat Muhammad Hanafiyyah: a medieval Muslim-Malay romance*. The Hague: Nijhoff.
1976 Die Volksliteraturen Indonesiens. In H. Kähler, ed. *Handbuch der Orientalistik*. Dritte Abteilung, 3: *Literaturen*, 1. Leiden; Köln: Brill.

Brown, Ian and Rajeswary Ampalavanar
1986 *Malaysia*. Oxford: Clio Press. (World Bibliographical Series, Volume 12).

Bunge, F. M. (ed.)
1984 *Malaysia: a country study*. Washington D.C.: US Government Printing Office. (American University, Foreign Area Studies).

Byrd, C. K.
1970 *Early printing in the Straits Settlements 1806-1858.* Singapore: Singapore National Library.

Casparis, J. G. de.
1975 *Indonesian paleography: a history of writing in Indonesian from the beginnings to c.AD 1500.* London: Brill.

Cattenoz, H. G.
1961 *Tables de concordance des ères chrétienne et hegirienne.* Rabat: Editions techniques Nord-africaines.

Chambert-Loir, H.
1974 "La sauvegarde des littératures régionales Indonesiennes." *Archipel* 7:175-98.
1975 "Bibliographie de la littérature malaise en traduction." *BEFEO* 42: 395-439.
1980 "Catalogue des catalogues de manuscrits malais." *Archipel* 20: 45-70.

Chen Mong Hock
1967 *Early Chinese newspapers in Singapore 1881-1912.* Singapore: Singapore National University.

Darlow, T. H. and H. F. Moule
1963 *Historical catalogue of the printed editions of Holy Scripture in the Library of the British and Foreign Bible Society.* New York: Kraus. (Originally published 1903-11).

Deakin, C., et al.
1978 *Indonesian reading list.* 3rd edn. London: Indonesia Circle.

Dewan Bahasa dan Pustaka
1967 *Dewan Bahasa dan Pustaka in ten years: a general outline of its first ten-year progress and achievement.* Kuala Lumpur: Dewan Bahasa dan Pustaka.

Ding Choo Ming
1980 *A bibliography of Malay creative writings: vol 1, Brunei, Malaysia, Singapore 1920-1980* Bangi: Universiti Kebangsaan Malaysia.
1981 *A bibliography of bibliographies on Malaysia.* Petaling Jaya: Hexagon Elite Publications.
1982 "A bibliography of bibliographies on Malaysia: supplement I." *SEARMG Newsletter* 23 1-18.
1984 "A bibliography of bibliographies on Malaysia: supplement II." *SEARMG Newsletter* 26: 1-13.
1985 "Bibliography of Malay short stories, 1980-1984: supplement I." *SEARMG Newsletter* 28: 1-38.
1987 "Access to Malay manuscripts." *BKI* 143, 4: 425-467.

Dyen, I.
1971 *Spoken Malay.* New York: Holt.

Ellen, R. F., M. B. Hooker and A. C. Milner
1981 "The Hervey Malay Collection in the Wellcome Institute." *JMBRAS* 54, 1: 82-92.

Errington, S.
1979 "Some comments on style in the meanings of the past." *JAS* 38, 2: 231-44.

Favre, P.
1875 *Dictionnaire malais-français.* 2 vols. Vienna: Imprimerie Imperiale et Royale.

Freeman-Grenville, G. S. P.
1963 *The Muslim and Christian calendars.* London: Oxford University Press.

Gonda, J.
1973 *Sanskrit in Indonesia.* 2nd edition. New Delhi: International Academy of Indian Culture.

Grijns, C. D., et al.
1983 *European loan words in Indonesian: a checklist of words of European origin in Bahasa Indonesia and traditional Malay.* Leiden: KITLV. (Indonesian Etymological project, 5).

Gullick, J. M.
1981 *Malaysia.* London: Benn.
1987 *Malay society in the late nineteenth century: the beginnings of change.* Singapore; Oxford: Oxford University Press.

Hamidy, U. U.
1983 "Kegiatan percetakan Riau seabad berselang." *Optimis* 36: 71-73.

Harun Mat Piah and Ismail Hamid
1983 "Koleksi manuskrip-manuskrip Melayu di Brunei: satu maklumat awal." *Sari* 1, 2: 103-123.

Hazard, H. W.
1952 *Atlas of Islamic history.* Princeton: Princeton University Press.

Heussler, R.
1981 *British Malaya: a bibliographical and biographical compendium.* New York; London: Garland Publishing.

Hilgers-Hesse, I., and O. Karow
1978 *Indonesisch-Deutsches Wörterbuch.* Wiesbaden: Harrassowitz.

Hill, A. H., ed.
1955 "The Hikayat Abdullah." *JMBRAS* 28, 3:5-354.

Holle, K.F.
1882 *Tabel van oud-en Nieuw-Indische alphabetten: Bijdrage tot de paleographie van Nederlandsch-Indie*. Batavia: W. Bruining and Co.

Hooker, M. B.
1968 "The Malayan legal digests." *JMBRAS* 41, 1:157-170.
1986 " The law texts of Muslim South-East Asia." In M. B. Hooker, ed. *Laws of South-East Asia, vol 1: the pre-modern texts*. Singapore: Butterworth, pp. 347-433; bibliography, pp. 539-554.

Hooykaas, C.
1937 *Over Maleische literatuur*. Leiden: Brill.
1952 *Literatuur in Maleis en Indonesische*. Groningen; Jakarta: Wolters.

Hussainmiya, B. A.
1978 "Malay manuscripts in Sri Lanka." *Indonesia Circle* 17:39-40.

Hutton, P.
1978 *Make what I can sell: the story of Jack Chia-MPH*. Singapore: Jack Chia-MPH.

Ibrahim bin Ismail
1980 "In quest of the *Malay magazine* (1821-22)." *Indonesia Circle* 21: 45-49.
1981 "Malay manuscripts: some major contributions to their bibliographical control." *SEARMG Newsletter* 20:1-10.
1982 "Missionary printing in Malacca, 1815-1843." *Libri* 32, 3: 177-206.

Ilias Zaidi
1976 *Biografi penulis dan karya*. Kuala Lumpur: Fargoes.

Iskandar, Teuku
1968 "Some aspects concerning the work of copyists of Malay historical writings." *Peninjau Sejarah* 3,2.
1986 *Kamus Dewan*. 3rd ed. Kuala Lumpur: Dewan Bahasa dan Pustaka. (1st published 1970).

Iskandar Haji Ahmad
1973 *Persuratkhabaran Melayu 1876-1968*. Kuala Lumpur: Dewan Bahasa dan Pustaka.

Ismail Dahaman
1968 *Bibliografi cherpen Melayu 1951-1957*. Kuala Lumpur: Dewan Bahasa dan Pustaka.

Ismail Hamid
1982 *Arabic and Islamic literary tradition with reference to Malay Islamic literature*. Kuala Lumpur: Utusan Publications.

Ismail Hussein
1966 "The study of traditional Malay literature." JMBRAS 39, 2:1-22.
1974 *The study of traditional Malay literature, with a selected bibliography*. Kuala Lumpur: Dewan Bahasa dan Pustaka.
1978a *Bibliografi teks cetakan sastera tradisi Melayu*. Kuala Lumpur.
1978b *Bibliografi sastera Melayu*. Kuala Lumpur.

Jabatan Pengajian Melayu
1976 *Latihan ilmiah dan thesis pengajian Melayu*. Kuala Lumpur: Universiti Malaya.

Jones, R. A.
1974 "More light on Malay manuscripts." *Archipel* 8:45-58.
1978 *Arabic loan words in Indonesian: a check-list of words of Arabic and Persian origin in Bahasa Indonesia and traditional Malay, in the reformed spelling*. London: Indonesian Etymological Project, 3.
1979 "Six undescribed Malay manuscripts: a preliminary note." *Indonesia Circle* 19: 26-31.

Josselin de Jong, P. E. de
1964 "The character of the Malay annals." In J. Bastin and R. Roolvink, eds. *Malaysian and Indonesian studies: essays presented to Sir Richard Winstedt on his eighty-fifth birthday*. Oxford: Oxford University Press, pp. 235-241.
1980 "Privately owned Malay manuscripts in Malaya." *Indonesia Circle* 21: 24-31.

Jumsari Jusuf, et al., (ed.)
1980 *Katalog koleksi naskah Maluku*. Jakarta.

Karni, R. S.
1980 *Bibliography of Malaysia and Singapore*. Kuala Lumpur: Penerbit Universiti Malaya.

Karow, O. and I. Hilgers-Hesse.
1978 *Indonesisch-Deutsches Wörterbuch*. Wiesbaden: Harrassowitz.

King, E. S.
1960 *Speak Malay!* London: University of London Press.
1964 *Write Malay!* London: University of London Press.

Klinkert, A. C.
1916 *Nieuw maleish-nederlandsch woordenboek met arabisch Karakter, naar de beste en laatste bronnen bewerkt*. Leiden: E.J. Brill.

Koster, G. L. and H. Maier
1982 "Variation within identity in the *Syair Ken Tambuhan*." *Indonesia Circle* 29: 3-17.

Kratz, E. U.
1974 "The origins and development of Malay and Indonesian literature." *SEALG Newsletter* 21: 1-11.
1980 "A brief description of the Malay manuscripts of the 'Overbeck Collection' at the Museum Pusat, Jakarta" *JMBRAS* 53, 1: 90-106.
1981 "The editing of Malay manuscripts and textual criticism." *BKI* 137: 229-293.

Lent, J. A.
1982 "Malaysia." in J. A. Lent, ed. *Newspapers in Asia: contemporary trends and problems*. Singapore: Heinemann Educational Books, pp. 252-266.

Lent, J. A. and K. Mulliner (eds.)
1986 *Malaysian studies: archaeology, historiography, geography and bibliography*. DeKalb: Northern Illinois Center for Southeast Asian Studies, Occasional Papers.

Lewis, M.B.
1954 *A handbook of Malay script*. London: Macmillan.

Li Chuan Siu
1970 *A bird's eye view of the development of modern Malay literature*. Kuala Lumpur: Pustaka Antara.
1972 *Ikhtisar sejarah kesusasteraan Melayu baru 1830-1945*. Kuala Lumpur: Pustaka Antara.
1975 *An introduction to the promotion and development of modern Malay literature 1942-62*. Yogkakarta: Penerbitan Yayasan Kanisius.

Liaw Yock Fang
1975 *Sejarah kesusasteraan Melayu klassik*. Singapore: Pustaka Nasional.
1976 *Undang-Undang Melaka: the laws of Melaka*. The Hague: Nijhoff.

Lombard-Salmon, C.
1977 "Writings in romanized Malay by the Chinese of Malaya: a preliminary inquiry." *Kertas-kertas pengajian Tionghoa: papers on Chinese studies* (University of Malaya), 1,: 69-95.

Maimunah Mohd. Tahir, Ungku
1987 *Modern Malay literary culture: a historical perspective*. Singapore: Institute of Southeast Asian Studies.

Matheson, V.
1984 "Questions arising from a nineteenth-century Riau *Syair*." *RIMA* 17, 1.
1985 "Kisah pelayaran ke Riau: journey to Riau, 1984." *Indonesia Circle* 36: 3-22.

Matheson, V. and B. W. Andaya
1982 *The precious gift: Tuhfat al-Nafis*. KualaLumpur: Oxford University Press.

Miller, G.
1982 *Indonesian and Malayan traditional manuscripts held in public collections in Australia*. Canberra: The Library: Australian National University. (Bibliographical Series, 2).

Milne, R.S. and D.K. Mauzy
1986 *Malaysia: tradition, modernity and Islam*. Boulder: Westview Press.

Milner, A.C.
1980 "A missionary source for a biography of Munshi Abdullah" *JMBRAS* 53, 1: 111-119.
1982 *Kerajaan: Malay political culture on the eve of colonial rule*. Tucson: The University of Arizona. Press for the Association of Asian Studies. (Monograph XL).

Mohd. Taib bin Osman
1964 *Modern Malay literature*. Kuala Lumpur: Dewan Bahasa dan Pustaka.
1966 *The language of the editorials in Malay vernacular newspapers up to 1941: a study in the development of the Malay language in meeting new needs*. Kuala Lumpur: Dewan Bahasa dan Pustaka.
1976 "Classical and modern Malay literature" in H. Kähler, ed. *Handbuch der Orientalistick*. Dritte Abteilung, 3: *Literaturen*, 1.

Muhammed Haji Salleh
1975 "Recent trends in Malay-Indonesian poetry." *Sari Terbitan Tak Berkala*. Bangi: Universiti Kebangsaan Malaysia. Institut Bahasa Kesusastraan dan Kebudayaan Melayu.
1977 *Tradition and change in contemporary Malay-Indonesian poetry*. Kuala Lumpur: National University of Malaysia.

Muhammad Naguib al-Attas
1968 *The origin of the Malay sha'ir*. Kuala Lumpur: Dewan Bahasa dan Pustaka.
1971 *Concluding postscript to the origin of the Malay sha'ir*. Kuala Lumpur: Dewan Bahasa dan Pustaka.

Nik Ahmad bin Haji Nik Hassan
1963 "The Malay press." *JMBRAS* 36, 1:37-78.

O'Sullivan, L.
1984 "The London Missionary Society: a written record of missionaries and printing presses in the Straits Settlements 1815-1847." *JMBRAS* 57, 2: 61-104.

Overbeck, H.
1922 "The Malay pantun." *JMBRAS* 85: 4-28.

Payne, E.M.F.
1970 *Basic syntactic structure in standard Malay.* Kuala Lumpur: Dewan Bahasa dan Pustaka; Kementerian Pelajaran Malaysia.

Pelzer, K.J.
1971 *West Malaysia and Singapore: a selected bibliography.* New Haven: HRAF Press.

Perpustakaan Universiti Kebangsaan Malaysia.
1977 *Kajian-kajian bahasa dan kesusastraan Melayu.* Kuala Lumpur: Universiti Kebangsaan Malaysia. (Bibliografi kebudayaan Melayu, Vol. 4).

Philips, C.H.
1963 *Handbook of oriental history.* London: Royal Historical Society.

Prentice, D.J.
1986 "Lexicography and colonialism: a Southeast Asian case-study." In C.M.S. Hellwig and S. Robson, eds. *A man of Indonesian letters: essays in honour of Professor A. Teeuw.* Dordrecht: Foris. (Verhandelingen van het KITLV 121).
1987 "Malay (Indonesian and Malaysian)." in B. Comrie, ed. *The world's major languages.* London; Sydney: Croom Helm, pp. 913-935.

Proudfoot, I.
1985 "Pre-war Malay periodicals: notes to Roff's bibliography drawn from government gazettes." *Kekal Abadi* 4,4: 1-28.
1986 "A formative period in Malay book publishing." *JMBRAS* 59, 2: 101-132.

Ricklefs, M.C. and P. Voorhoeve
1977 *Indonesian manuscripts in Great Britain.* London: Oxford University Press. (London Oriental Bibliographies No. 5).
1982 "Indonesian manuscripts in Great Britain. Addenda et corrigenda." *BSOAS* 45, 2: 300-322.

Roff, W.R.
1967 *The origins of Malay nationalism.* Kuala Lumpur: University of Malaya Press.
1972 *Bibliography of Malay and Arabic periodicals published in the Straits settlements and peninsular Malay States 1876-1941.* London: Oxford University Press.
1979 *Southeast Asian research tools: Malaysia, Singapore, Brunei.* Honolulu: University of Hawaii. (Southeast Asia Paper No. 16, Part IV).

Ronkel, Ph. S. van
1899 "Over invloed der Arabische syntaxis op de Maleische." *TBG* 41: 498-528.

Rosidi, Ajip.
1973 "My experiences in recording '*pantun Sunda*'." *Indonesia* 16: 105-111.

Safian Hussain, Siti Aisah Murad and Fadzil Agussallim
1985 *Bibliografi sastera Melayu moden 1925-1980*. Kuala Lumpur: Dewan Bahasa dan Pustaka.

Santa Maria, L.
1980 "A la recherche de manuscrits malais en Italie." *Archipel* 20: 79-86.

Shahnon Ahmad
1981 *Kesusasteraan dan Etika Islam*. Kuala Lumpur: Fajar Bakti.

Skinner, C.
1966 "The influence of Arabic upon modern Malay." *Intisari* 2, 1: 34-47.
1978 "Transitional Malay literature: Part 1, Ahmad Rijaluddin and Munshi Abdullah." *BKI* 134,4: 466-487.

Sweeney, A.
1971 "Some observations on the Malay Sha'ir." *JMBRAS* 44, 1: 52-70.
1972 "Some suggestions on the collecting of oral literature, with special reference to West Malaysia." *Federation Museums Journal* 17: 61-72.
1973 "Professional Malay story-telling: some questions of style and presentation." *JMBRAS* 46, 2: 1-53.
1976 "The Pak Pandir cycle of tales." *JMBRAS* 49, 1:15-88.
1980 *Authors and audiences in traditional Malay literature*. Berkeley: Center for South and Southeast Asian Studies, University of California, monograph series No. 20.
1987 *A full hearing: orality and literacy in the Malay world*. Berkeley; London: University of California Press.

Sweeney, A. and N. G. Phillips
1975 *The voyages of Mohammed Ibrahim Munshi*. Kuala Lumpur: Oxford University Press.

Tan Chee-beng
1980 "Baba Malay Dialect." *JMBRAS* 53, 1:150-166.

Tan Chin Kwang
1986 "The 'missing link' in modern Malay literary history: a study of the influence of social and educational backgrounds on literary development." *Archipel* 31: 97-115.

Teeuw, A.
1959 "A history of the Malay language." BKI 115: 138-156.
1961 *A critical survey of studies on Malay and Bahasa Indonesia*. The Hague: Nijhoff.
1966 "The Malay sha'ir: problems of origin and tradition." *BKI* 122: 429-446.

Tham Seong Chee
1975 "Literary response and the social process — an analysis of cultural and political beliefs among Malay writers." *Southeast Asian Journal of Social Science.* 3, 1: 85-106.
1981a "The politics of literary development in Malaysia." In Tham Seong Chee, ed. *Essays on literature and society in Southeast Asia.* Singapore: Singapore University Press, pp. 216-252.
1981b "Literary response and the social process: an analysis of the cultural and political beliefs among Malay writers." In Tham Seong Chee, ed. *Essays on literature and society in Southeast Asia.* Singapore: Singapore University Press, pp. 253-286.

Thomas, P.L.
1979 "Syair and Pantun prosody." *Indonesia* 27: 51-63.

Traill, H.F. O'B.
1979 "An Indian protagonist of the Malay language — Abdullah Munshi, his race and mother tongue." *JMBRAS* 53, 2: 67-83.
1981 "Aspects of Abdullah Munshi." *JMBRAS* 52,3:35-56.
1982 "The lost manuscript of Hikayat Abdullah Munshi." *JMBRAS* 55, 2: 126-134.

Turnbull, C.M.
1980 *A short history of Malaysia, Singapore and Brunei.* Melbourne: Cassell.

Voorhoeve, P.
1964 "A Malay scriptorium." In J. Bastin and R. Roolvink, eds. *Malaysian and Indonesian studies: essays presented to Sir Richard Winstedt on his eighty-fifth birthday.* Oxford: Oxford University Press, pp. 256-266.
1980 "List of Malay MSS which were formerly kept at the General Secretariat in Batavia." *Archipel* 20: 71-78.

Wan Omar Rasdi, Hasan Muhammad Ali and Asmah Haji Omar
1977 *Kursus permulian Bahasa Malaysia.* Kuala Lumpur: Dewan Bahasa dan Pustaka.

Wang Gungwu
1964 *Malaysia: a survey.* Melbourne: Cheshire.

Wilkinson, R.J.
1901 *A Malay-English dictionary.* 2 vols. Singapore.
1907 *Malay literature.* Kuala Lumpur: F.M.S. Government Press.
1959 *A Malay-English dictionary (romanized).* 2 vols. London: Macmillan.
1985 *Kamus Jawi-Melayu-Inggeris: a classic Jawi-Malay-English dictionary.* Melaka: Baharudinjoha. (Facsimile Reprint of Wilkinson 1901.)

Winstedt, R.O.
1913 *Malay Grammar.* Oxford: Claredon.
1962 *History of Malaysia.* Singapore: Marican.

1965 *An unabridged English-Malay dictionary.* 4th edn. Kuala Lumpur. Marican.
1969 *A history of classical Malay literature.* Kuala Lumpur: Oxford University Press.
1971 *An unabridged Malay-English dictionary.* Kuala Lumpur: Marican.
1981 *The Malays: a cultural history.* (Revised by Tham Seong Chee). Singapore: Graham Brash.

Winstedt, R.O. and P.E. de Josselin de Jong
1954 "Undang-undang Sungei Ujong." *JMBRAS* 29, 3: 22-59.

Yahaya Ismail
1967-8 *Kesusasteraan moden dalam esei dan keritek.* 2 vols. Singapore: Pustaka Nasional.
1976 *Sejarah sastra melayu moden.* Kuala Lumpur: Fajar Bakti.

Zain al-'Abidin bin Ahmad
1940 "Modern developments." *JMBRAS* 17, 3: 142-162.
1941 "Recent Malay literature." *JMBRAS* 19, 1:1-20.

Zaini-Lajoubert, M.
1980 "Les grandes étapes de la littérature malaise moderne." *Archipel* 19: 181-192.

Indonesia

The Republic of Indonesia, formerly the Netherlands East Indies, comprises a large part of the archipelago extending from the mainland of South-East Asia to New Guinea. The population of Indonesia is approximately 170,000,000 and includes more than 350 different ethnic groups. Each one has its own identity, history and language. In private and in informal situations, the various regional languages such as Javanese, the Batak languages of Sumatra and the Toraja of Sulawesi continue to be used as well as the national language, Indonesian (*Bahasa Indonesia*). Approximately half of the population is Javanese. The western part of Java, however, is inhabited by Sundanese (the next largest ethnic group) and parts of east Java (as well as the island of Madura) contain the Madurese. The island of Java has tended to dominate the archipelago both culturally and politically.

Islam is the majority religion in Indonesia, but there exist important Hindu and Christian minorities. A number of external cultural influences have made themselves felt in Indonesia. Just as in other parts of South-East Asia, Indian political and religious ideas contributed to the development of small kingdoms from the beginning of the Christian era. The earliest Indianized kingdoms so far discovered were located in eastern Borneo and West Java and date from the 5th century. Not long afterwards the Malay kingdom of Srivijaya, based in southern Sumatra, began to dominate the western archipelago and achieved renown as a centre of Sanskrit Buddhist studies.

From the early 8th until the early 10th century Java was the site of a highly sophisticated Indianized culture. Products of this culture are the famous temples, the Buddhist Borobodur and the Hindu Prambanan. In the following centuries the political centre of Java shifted to East Java, where the empire of Majapahit arose in the 13th century. Majapahit exercised a strong cultural influence on the surrounding islands during the next two hundred years. During this period Javanese culture became firmly established in the island of Bali.

Another external influence on Indonesia was Islam, which reached the archipelago in the 13th century, probably via South India. Having promoted the establishment of Muslim states in northern Sumatra, Islam spread slowly along the various trade routes. By the end of the 15th century the new religion became dominant in port towns, such as Gresik and Demak, on Java's north coast. From there it gradually gained influence in the interior and in regions to the east of Java. Bali, however, remained staunchly Hindu and it was for this reason that the island was able to preserve the literature (in the form of palm leaf manuscripts) of pre-Islamic Java.

Europeans were first attracted to the archipelago by the spice of the Moluccas. The Portuguese arrived at the beginning of the 16th century; the Dutch followed almost a century later. During the 17th and early 18th centuries the Dutch East India Company (the Vereenigde Oostindische Compagnie or V.O.C.) came to control an increasing amount of territory in Java. Finally, in 1749, the ruler of the central Javanese kingdom of Mataram acknowledged the sovereignty of the Dutch. The revolt which followed split the kingdom in two.

The two halves, Surakarta and Yogyakarta, which survived until the end of the colonial era, remain the principal centres of Javanese culture up to the present day.

The V.O.C. was wound up in 1799 and the Dutch state took over its possessions. In the 19th century the Dutch extended their control in other parts of the archipelago. Dutch authority was established in Sumatra, in the southern part of Borneo and in the eastern archipelago. At times the Dutch were in competition with British imperial expansion. It was the agreements between the two European powers, particularly the Anglo-Dutch treaty of 1824, which determined the territorial limits of British Malaya and of the Dutch East Indies and therefore of the modern states of Malaysia and Indonesia. From 1830 the Dutch authorities introduced the 'cultuurstelsel' (culture system) which was designed to bring the government steady and continuous profits by enforcing cultivation and delivery of export crops such as sugar and coffee. In 1860 the system and corruption of Dutch rule was denounced in the novel *Max Havelaar*, written under the pseudonym Multatuli by a former colonial official Edouard Douwes Dekkar. A more liberal policy began to take effect and the culture system was gradually dismantled. From the beginning of the 20th century the Dutch began to implement an 'ethical policy' which emphasized the welfare and education of Indonesians. An early Javanese champion of women's education and emancipation was Raden Adjeng Kartini whose letters were published in 1911 under the title *Door duisternis tot licht* (Through darkness to light) and subsequently in an English edition under the title *Letters of a Javanese princess*.

1908 saw the formation of *Budi Utomo* ('High Endeavour'), a Javanese association of officials and intellectuals. Other political/nationalist groups followed. From 1912 the nationalist organization *Sarekat Islam* spread rapidly throughout rural areas, becoming increasingly radical and factionalised. It competed and clashed with the *Parti Kommunis Indonesia* (Indonesian Communist Party, PKI) which, following an abortive rebellion against Dutch rule in 1925-26, was destroyed, only re-emerging some twenty years later.

Dutch colonial rule in Indonesia effectively came to an end in 1942, when Japanese forces occupied the country during World War II. After the Japanese surrender, Indonesian nationalists proclaimed independence on 17th August 1945, marking the start of a five-year armed struggle against the returning Dutch forces. Hostilities finally ceased in 1949, when Indonesia began the task of nation-building under its first president, Sukarno. Following an unsuccessful attempted Communist coup in 1965, the New Order government of General Suharto came to power.

For bibliographies of Indonesia, see **Deakin** (1978), **Kennedy** (1965) and **Lan Hiang Char** (1979). Since 1970, the Koninklijk Instituut voor Taal-, Land- en Volkenkunde, Leiden, has issued *Excerpta Indonesica* which provides summaries of scholarly books and articles published on Indonesia. For a bibliography of Islam in Indonesia, see **Boland** and **Farjon** (1983). For ethnography, see **LeBar** (1972). For Indonesian culture and art, see **Holt** (1980). For general histories of Indonesia, see **Legge** (1980), **Peacock** (1973), **Soebadio** and **Sarvaas** (1978), **Ricklefs** (1981) and **Vlekke** (1959). **Coolhaas** (1980) surveys studies of Dutch colonial history.

Dating systems

The era used in early Java, and in Bali today, is the *Saka* era (=AD 78). The Javanese calendar (*taun Jawa*), as used at present, however, follows a different system introduced in 1625 and requires a conversion table. The Islamic (*Hijrah*) era (see Malaysia section) is not in common use in Indonesia. At present the Western calendar is most commonly used, although elements of indigenous calendrical systems are still employed for specific purposes.

Calendrical systems are discussed in **Casparis** (1978), **Pigeaud** (1967-80, vol. 1), **Ricklefs** (1978) and **Soebardi** (1965). **Pigeaud** (1938) contains conversion tables for Javanese dates.

Languages

Malay was proclaimed the national language (*Bahasa Indonesia*) of Indonesia by the All Indonesian Youth Congress at Jakarta in 1928 and was adopted by the independent Indonesian state. The characteristics and history of the Malay language and of *Bahasa Indonesia* (which began to follow its own line of development) are discussed briefly in the Malaysia language section.

Although most Indonesians speak *Bahasa Indonesia,* an estimated two to four hundred languages also continue to be spoken in Indonesia and written literature is still produced in some of them. The majority of these languages belong to the large Austronesian language family. Among the exceptions are languages in Irian Jaya (Western New Guinea) and other parts of Eastern Indonesia. The study of Austronesian languages is perhaps next in importance to that of the Indo-European and Semitic language families; however Austronesian linguistics is hampered by a scarcity of reliable descriptions of individual languages.

The major vernaculars in Indonesia (in geographical order), with extremely rough estimates in millions of speakers (based mainly on the 1971 census), are as follows: - North Sumatra: Acehnese (2) and Toba Batak (2.5); West Sumatra: Minangkabau (3); West Java: Sundanese (20); Central and East Java: Javanese (65); Madura and East Java: Madurese (5); Bali: Balinese (2.5); Lombok: Sasak (2).

Javanese

Javanese is an Austronesian language and its closest relatives are the other languages of western Indonesia (including Sulawesi). One of the chief features of Javanese is a highly developed system of polite language and an honorific vocabulary, the so-called '*ngoko-krama* phenomenon'. This is also a feature of neighbouring languages such as Sundanese, Madurese and Balinese, where it is probably attributable to Javanese influence.

Especially in literary language, Javanese displays a large number of loans from Sanskrit. The literary idiom of the *kakawin* (Sanskrit-inspired poetry) and *prawa* (prose) is termed old Javanese, while the language of the *kidung* (indigenous poetry) and certain other prose works is called middle Javanese. The latter reflects a more modern form of the language, probably current in the

14th and 15th centuries. Finally, any work written in Java from the 16th century onwards, from after the establishment of Islam in Java, is called Modern Javanese. Modern Javanese includes, therefore, not only the 'classical' language of the 18th century court literature but also the short story of the present day.

Javanese is the language of the shadow theatre (*wayang*), as well as other forms of modern dramas such as the *ketoprak* and *ludrug*. Functioning as a cultural language and as the language of daily life for a substantial population group, Javanese has exercised an influence on the national language and on many regional languages. But *Bahasa Indonesia* is also having an effect on Javanese, especially among the more sophisticated town-dwellers.

Standard Javanese is found in Solo (Surakarta) and Yogyakarta. Beyond these areas Javanese is marked by a number of regional dialects which linguists are still analysing. Variations can be found on a small scale, from village to village and there are also socially determined speech variations, ranging from the court (*kraton*) down to the village (*desa*).

A bibliographical survey of the languages of Indonesia and of developments in Indonesian and Austronesian linguistics is to be found in **Uhlenbeck** (1971). Bibliographical monographs exist on the languages of Sumatra (**Voorhoeve** 1955), Borneo (**Cense** and **Uhlenbeck** 1958), on Malay and *Bahasa Indonesia* (**Teeuw** 1961) and on the languages of Java and Madura (**Uhlenbeck** 1964). *Bahasa Indonesia* is described in **Prentice** (1987) and the development of *Bahasa Indonesia* as the national language is discussed in **Kentjono** (1976). For further references to *Bahasa Indonesia*, see Malaysia section.

For Indonesian, major dictionaries are: Indonesian-Indonesian, **Abdul Chaer** (1976), **Iskander** (1970), **Poerwadarminta** (1976); Indonesian-English, **Echols** and **Shadily** (1963), **Schmidgall-Tellings** and **Stevens** (1981); English-Indonesian, **Echols and Shadily** (1975); Indonesian-Dutch, **Poerwadarminta** and **Teeuw** (1952); Indonesian-French, **Labrousse** (1984); French-Indonesian, **Soemargono** and **Labrousse** (1969); Indonesian-German, **Karow** and **Hilgers-Hesse** (1978).

Dictionaries of other Indonesian languages are: Minangkabau-Dutch, **Van der Toorn** (1891); Old Javanese-English, **Wojowasito** (1980), **Zoetmulder** (1982); Javanese-German, **Herrfurth** (1972); Javanese-English, **Horne** (1974); Javanese-Dutch, **Pigeaud** (1938); Sundanese-Dutch, **Coolsma** (1913); Sundanese-Indonesian, **Satjadibrata** (1956); Balinese-Indonesian, **Kamus** (1978); Indonesian-Balinese, **Kamus** (1975); Balinese-English, **Barber** (1979); Toba Batak-German, **Warneck** (1977); Buginese-Dutch, **Matthes** (1874); Acehnese-Dutch, **Djajadiningrat** (1934); Makasarese-Dutch, **Cense** and **Abdoerrahim** (1979).

Among the teaching and other language materials are: on Indonesian grammar, **Labrousse** (1978), **Kähler** (1956), **MacDonald** (1976), **Sarumpaet** and **Mackie** (1966), **Sarumpaet** (1972) and **Wolff** (1980); Indonesian language courses with tapes are **Johns** (1977, 1981) **Pollard** and **Jones** (1972) and **Wolff** (1971); another course is **Wolff** (1984, 1986); a reader is **Sarumpaet** and **Hendrata** (1986-87); on Javanese, **Horne** (1961, 1963), **Ras** (1977) and on old Javanese, **Zoetmulder** and **Poedjawijatna** (1954). On Buginese, **Sirk** (1983).

Scripts

Although it is possible that Indonesia produced autochthonous writing systems, three types of script imported from abroad have played the most important role in the history of Indonesian writing. They are: scripts of the syllabic type deriving from Indian scripts; Arabic script and the roman script. The use of each of these scripts in Indonesia is connected with international movements of trade and religion which have influenced cultural life in various parts of the archipelago.

The oldest inscriptions found in Indonesia are those of Kutai in East Kalimantan, which date from around 400 AD. They are written in the so-called 'early Pallava script', a pre-Nagari script of South Indian type of the 5th to the 9th century AD. The language of the inscriptions is Sanskrit. Other Sanskrit inscriptions in early Pallava script have been found in West Java.

A more recent script, called 'later Pallava', is used in the Northern Javanese inscriptions of Tuk Mas (7th century) and Canggal (732 AD) and in the old Malay Srivijaya inscriptions of 683, 684 and 686 AD found in the South Sumatra region. The Batak alphabet of Northern Sumatra and the Rejang, Kerinchi and Lampung scripts of South Sumatra are believed to derive from this 'later Pallava' or 'Old Malay' script of South Sumatra. It also appears to have influenced the Makassar and Bugis scripts of South Sulawesi and the script of Bima and Sumbawa. These different scripts would, of course, have been influenced by the nature of the writing materials used in particular areas (for example, bark cloth, wood, bamboo, horn or palm leaf) and by the phonological systems of the languages concerned. In the course of time, therefore, considerable differences arose between the various scripts.

The Old Javanese or Kawi script may not derive directly from the later Pallava script: Kawi shows characteristics of its own, suggesting that it was essentially used for writing on palm leaf. The earliest dated inscription in the early Kawi script is a Sanskrit text of 760 AD from Malang, East Java. The earliest example of a text in the Old Javanese language is the inscription of Sukabumi of 804 AD. A 'later Kawi' script associated with East Java and derived from the early Kawi script is used mainly in inscriptions of the Kediri period (925-1250 AD). A later variant is the Majapahit script (ca. 1250-1450 AD), which is the script used in the oldest extant Javanese manuscripts. The so-called Melayu script, represented by 14th century inscriptions found in Central Sumatra, may be considered a variant of the Majapahit script.

The precursor to the modern Balinese script (a rounded form of the Javanese) evolved during the late Majapahit period and reached Bali and Lombok where it supplanted older scripts as a vehicle for the Old-Javanese literary inheritance preserved in these islands. In Java's north coastal towns, different styles of writing continued in use, one beside the other, over several centuries. From this rather complex situation the modern Balinese and modern Javanese scripts emerged, probably through patronage of the royal courts, as dominant writing styles for Bali and Java.

The modern Balinese script is still used for old Javanese as well as Balinese texts, but literacy in this script has been steadily declining in Bali in recent years. Similarly, in Java, the modern Javanese script was taught in schools and used in printing presses till World War II, but has now practically fallen into disuse.

The Arabic script, which was introduced into Indonesia with Islam, is of a totally different character. It is described in the Malaysia section. The oldest inscriptions using Arabic script are in tomb stones (possibly imported) found in North Sumatra and East Java. From the 14th century onwards, however, this script has been used for texts in Indonesian languages, such as Malay, Acehnese and Minangkabau. It has also been used for Javanese and Sundanese, but only in religious circles. It proved to be especially ill-suited to Javanese and, in order to avoid reading errors, was often written with vowel signs. The name *pegon*, meaning 'foreign', given to this script by the Javanese, shows that it was never fully accepted.

Phonetic changes in Acehnese and, to a lesser degree, in Minangkabau made reading gradually more difficult, because of the fixed spelling. In modern Indonesian, the Arabic script is now seldom used except in the religious sphere. A spelling system for Acehnese in the latin alphabet was set up by Snouck Hurgronje.

The roman script was introduced by Europeans in the 17th century. It was encouraged by scholars such as H. N. van der Tuuk and officers of the colonial administration who sometimes asked their scribes to make transcriptions in roman characters of indigenous manuscripts. The use of roman characters gained ground from about 1920 with the spread of western-type schooling, economic progress and the nationalist movement which stressed the need for social and cultural innovation. The rise of modern literature in Indonesian/Malay also contributed to the popularity of the roman script.

The roman script was used in colonial times in elementary schools for texts in the regional languages, with the exception of Javanese, Sundanese, Madurese and Balinese.

In the first decade of the 20th century Ch. A. van Ophuysen was assigned the task of designing a uniform spelling system for use in all the Malay language publications of the Dutch colonial government. The system adopted was based on the phonetic value of the roman characters. The van Ophuysen spelling was used until 1947 when the Indonesian government introduced the Suwandi system. The most important change was the replacement of the symbol oe by u. The spelling reforms of 1972, aiming at a uniform spelling for Indonesia and Malaysia, are described in the Malaysia section. The new uniform spelling, enforced by the central government, is taught in schools and used by the mass media. For the regional languages, spelling systems along similar lines have been set up. Reading of texts written in the old scripts will soon be restricted to a small number of specialists.

On early Indonesian writing, see **Casparis** (1975). On the development of scripts, see **Nimpoeno** (1936), **Noordenbos** (1941) and **Pigeaud** (1967-80). On Acehnese, see **Hurgronje** (1893) and **Langen** (1889). The new spelling systems for Balinese, Javanese and Sundanese are described in *Pedoman Ejaan...*(1976).

Manuscripts

Manuscripts in Indonesian languages are found mainly in various collections in Indonesia, Malaysia, Brunei, the United Kingdom, Germany, Denmark, Italy and the Netherlands. In most cases, these collections have been described in manuscript catalogues. Above all, see the extensive bibliography in **Ricklefs** and **Voorhoeve** (1977, 1982). See also: **Behrend** (1988), **Chambert-Loir** (1980a/b), **Girardet** (1983), **Hinzler** (1986-87), **Manik** (1975), **Mudjanattistomo** (1971), **Naerssen, Pigeaud, Voorhoeve** (1977), **Overbeck** (1926), **Pigeaud** (1967-80, 1975), **Pigeaud** and **Voorhoeve** (1985), **Poerbatjaraka, Vooerhoeve, Hooykaas** (1950) and **Voorhoeve** (1971, 1975, 1977,1980). There is a revised and augmented new edition (stencilled) of **Ronkel** (1908) in Indonesian by **Sutaarga** (1972). A new catalogue in English of the Malay manuscripts preserved in the library of the University of Leiden is in preparation. Many manuscript catalogues give useful introductions to literature and chronology, etc. For further details and catalogues of Malay manuscripts, see Malaysia section.

Printing and Development of the Press

The first printing in Indonesia was in 1659. Only the Dutch title and printer of the work, however, is known. The first surviving evidence of the V.O.C.'s printing activity is a peace treaty which Speelman concluded with the King of Makassar in 1668. It is a booklet of fourteen pages and is badly printed. No printer's name is given. Later in the same year, the Company contracted with H. Brants to print all types of material of which a number of regulations regarding the salaries of notaries, attorneys and other officials have survived. The Company made use of contract printers until 1718, the last being Andreas Loderus, who printed a compendium of Malay dictionaries. In that year, the Company installed its own press. Printing was mostly of administrative material such as the *Naamboek*, a yearly list of the Company's servants, but the Company press also published works for the Bataviaasch Genootschap van Kunsten en Wetenschappen.

The first press to use Arabic type was the Native or Malay Press, attached to the Seminarium Theologicum at Batavia. This press published a catechism in Malay in 1746. Leydecker's Old Testament translation (in Arabic characters) and Ferreira d'Almeida's Portuguese Old Testament translation were also published before the press was incorporated into the Company's press in 1755. The Arabic types used for the printing of the Bible in Jawi in Batavia (between 1744-58) were donated in 1742 to the Church of Batavia by the Wetstein brothers of Amsterdam.

In the 19th century, presses were established by missionaries: for example, by Medhurst at Batavia, Kam at Ambon and by Heimering at Kupang. A notable private press was that of a civil servant, H. J. Domis, who was Resident of Semarang and Pasuruan in the 1820s. This press printed a Dutch-Javanese dictionary.

In the second half of the 19th century the great influx of Europeans and the extension of education made it profitable to set up commercial printing and publishing houses to provide books and newspapers both in Dutch and in the main Indonesian languages. Management and ownership of such enterprises generally remained in European, Indo-European and Chinese hands. Before World War I one of the few important Indonesian enterprises was the lithograph press, run by Sayyid Oesman, which produced a large number of Arabic and Malay booklets between 1875 and 1914.

In the 20th century the government was especially active. The publishing bureau or *Volkslectuur* (*Balai Pustaka*), established in 1908, provided a growing number of Indonesian readers with literature in several languages. Although *Balai Pustaka* still exists today it has ceased to play a key role on propagating new and modern literature. Important publishers which emerged in the post-independence period were Gunung Agung, Pembangunan and Nusantara (in Bukit Tinggi in Sumatra). The *Lembaga Kebudayaan Rakyat* (People's Cultural Institute, LEKRA) also ran its own publishing company in the 1960s.

In recent times one of the leading publishers has been Dunia Pustaka Jaya, which reprints old books as well as launching new authors. University presses have begun to publish works of academic value. The University of Indonesia Press and the Gadjah Mada University Press are leaders in this field and publish in both Indonesian and English. Lurid, popular pulp fiction has a wide market. Two representative publishers of this market are Cypress and Kresno in Jakarta. Other important publishers are Gramedia (fiction and non-fiction), Sinar Harapan, Bharatara, Djambatan and the Catholic Nusa Indah Press in Ende, Flores. Two leading publishers of Islamic works are Bulan Bintang in Jakarta and Mizan in Bandung.

Newspapers and Periodicals

Difficult relationships between government and journalists have influenced the development of the indigenous-language press up to the present day. The first attempts to establish newspapers in *pasar* Malay and Javanese were made in the mid-1850s (Javanese-character *Bromartni*, published in Surakarta; and the Malay *Soerat Kabar Bahasa Melajoe* in Surabaya) and were followed by some twenty other papers in the next half-century (the most successful being *Selompret Melajoe* in Semarang which ran from 1860 to 1911, *Bintang Timoer* in Surabaya from 1862 to 1887 and *Bintang Barat* in Batavia from 1869 to 1899). All these papers were owned and published by Dutchmen and since strict regulations forbade criticizing government policy their task was to provide a mixed audience of Dutch, Chinese and Indonesian readers with day-to-day local news, information about international events and advertisments.

In the first quarter of the 20th century, with literacy spreading and the press laws somewhat relaxed, newspapers in Javanese and Malay became more widespread, but now they were owned and run not by the Dutch but by Indonesians. Though circulation was generally small, often only a few hundred copies per issue, many cities possessed a number of papers. The failure rate for these papers was high, both because they were poorly funded and managed and because many had clear political connections and thus were subject to government suppression. The best known and most influential among them were *Darmokondo* (published in Javanese by *Budi Utomo* in Solo from 1904 to 1939), *Oetoesan Hindia* (Malay; leftist *Sarekat Islam*, later PKI; Semarang,

1914-26). Another development was the publication of newspapers in Malay by Chinese firms; the most noteworthy among these was *Sin Po* (Batavia, 1910-42). In 1918 the Netherlands Indies government began to publish summaries of the contents of the non-Dutch press; this *Overzicht van de inlandsche en maleisch-chinese pers* continued until 1940.

In the late 1920s a number of developments influenced the press. The suppression of Communist uprisings in 1926-27 ushered in a new period of harsher police and government supervisions. The determination to adopt local Malay as Indonesian, the language of nationalism, brought both a gradual refinement to the language itself and a symbolic importance to the use of it in communication. And the development of splits within the secular nationalist movement meant a critical and divided press, with papers attacking each other as frequently as they attacked the Dutch. Important publications were the daily *Bintang Timoer* (Batavia, 1926-1936), the daily *Pemandangan* (Batavia, 1933-58), the quarterly *Daulat Rakjat* (Batavia, 1931-34), the BPI-Parindra daily *Soeara Oemoem* (Surabaya, 1931-42), and the Muhammadiyah daily *Adil* (Surakarta, 1933-42). A lively local press existed in Medan, where throughout the 1930s the nationalist dailies *Sinar Deli* and *Pewarta Deli* crossed swords with the Dutch press and government, with local Islamic publications and with

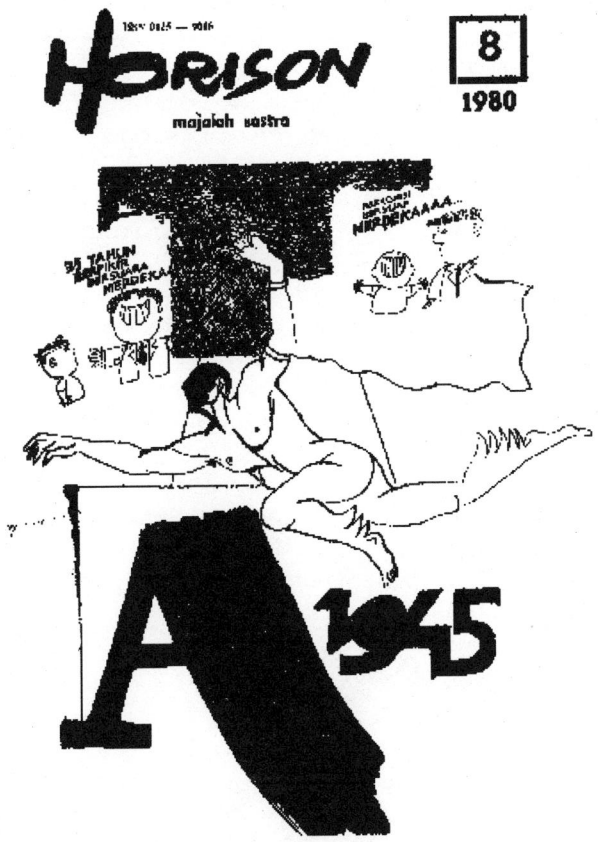

Horison literary magazine,
issue commemorating 35 years of independence

each other. In 1937 an Indonesian-language press service, *Antara*, was established; it has endured and is now an official organ. Under the Japanese, only a few newspapers were permitted to publish and they were monitored closely. Most important was *Asia Raja* in Jakarta; others included *Sinar Baroe* in Semarang and *Soeara Asia* in Surabaya.

With the end of World War II and the proclamation of independence, Indonesian publications proliferated both in those areas which fell under the Dutch and in the new Republic's territory. *Berita Indonesia*, which continued to be published in Jakarta, even after the Dutch took over that city, is a major source for the revolutionary period; *Kedaulatan Rakjat* and *Nasional* were produced in the Republican capital of Yogyakarta. In the 1950s, the first years of complete independence, the Indonesian press was at its most liberated and interesting. The Jakarta-based dailies of the major parties (PNI's *Suluh Indonesia,* PSI's *Pedoman,* PKI's *Harian Rakjat,* Masyumi's *Abadi* and NU's *Duta Masjarakat*) dominated the scene, sharing the limelight a little with such Jakarta independents as *Merdeka* and *Indonesia Raja*. Newspapers in other cities continued to publish, but even such stalwarts as Medan's *Waspada* and Yogyakarta's *Kedaulatan Rakjat* were being eclipsed by the capital-based press. With the turn towards Guided Democracy in the late 1950s, the period of political freedom ended and papers and parties Sukarno deemed to be antirevolutionary were proscribed.

After the rise of the New Order in 1966, a period of freedom ensued, but in the 1970s the government gradually banned certain topics, investigative methods and newspapers. In this new era, the outstanding papers are the Jakarta dailies *Kompas* and *Sinar Harapan*. Other important Jakarta newspapers are *Merdeka* and the popular *Pos Kota*, while outside Jakarta only *Surabaya Post* aspires to be more than popular press. The founding in 1971 of the lively and innovative weekly news magazine *Tempo* is a highlight of that period. The intellectual journals of opinion *Prisma* and *Optimis* and the quality woman's magazine *Femina*, are also popular and informative. The Islamic journals *Panji Masyarakat, Kiblat* and others have retained their regularity and respectable circulations for many years.

For details on printing and publishing, see **Chijs** (1875-1903), **Graaf** (1969), **Kimman** (1981), **Kratz** (1979), **Ockeloen** (1966), **Zubaidah** (1972). In addition, **Ahmat** (1984) provides a detailed study of the origins of the vernacular press in Indonesia. Also on various aspects of the press in Indonesia, see **Garis Besar** (1971), **Said** (1976) and **Soebagio** (1977). **Anderson** (1982) gives a profile of newspapers in the 1970s.

Bibliographical aids on current publications include the annual *Daftar Buku* published by the publishers' association, *Ikatan Penerbit Indonesia (IKAPI)*, which lists current publications. For catalogues of Indonesian serials, see **Hardjoprakoso** (1973), **Moon** (1979), **Nunn** (1971, 1977), **Reid** (1974) and **Santoso** (1981, 1982, 1983).

Literature

Most of the many hundreds of Indonesian languages have not produced a written literature. Oral literatures, however, are widspread and they have many features in common. Indonesian oral literature comprises both prose and poetry. The poetry frequently has a formal structure: for example, a feature of Bare'e poetry is that the line must consist of eight syllables, the verse of four lines. Rhyme is usually a feature: in the *kajori*, in the form aaaa or aabb; in the *bolingoni* the second pair of lines parallels the first, with variation in word order or the use of synonyms. *Bolingoni* are often harvest songs; *kajori* were sung on all possible occasions — as love ballads, welcoming and mourning songs, satirical songs etc. In general the words are improvised, although a number of songs have become popular and are repeated from generation to generation.

As regards both style and content, similar verse forms are found in all Indonesian languages. The best known example is the Malay *pantun* (see the Malaysia section). Indonesian folk literature includes not only these short, epigram-like verses, but much longer poetry. This poetry is similar in formal structure to the shorter forms. The litanies of the Bare'e priests, Timore death songs, the Dayak pregnancy songs, the mythological hymns of Nias and headhunting songs are primitive in the sense that they voice fundamental human emotions. This literature is very lively: although it is to a certain extent governed by tradition, the individual reciter was able to display his creative talent.

The dividing line between religious and secular literature is not clear. Riddles (in prose or poetry), for instance, sometimes fulfilled a religious function in Bare'e society. They were recited in particular during the rice growing, as a form of sympathetic magic: the solving of the riddle promoted the sprouting of the rice. But in other Indonesian societies riddles have a clearly profane character. Many Indonesian languages contain a sort of rhythmic prose, using short and pithy sentences in an almost poetic fashion. The Minangkabau rules of law, for instance, take this form.

Indonesian prose includes a great variety of subject matter and styles. Prose narratives were often presented orally. They sometimes lasted the whole night and must have been even more difficult to memorise than poetry. Although making use of ancient tales, these narratives owed much to the creativity of individual story-tellers. The genres and subject matter of Indonesian narrative literature are difficult to describe. Categories based on western literature (fairy tales, myths, legends, historical narratives, romantic and adventure stories) are seldom useful. A story that has a historical background, for instance, will develop into a myth and animal tales may develop into tales about men. In the course of a story, the animals may turn out to be humans or the humans animals.

The different literary traditions in Indonesia have influenced one another over time and foreign influences have come from many directions. Indian literature has been especially important. The animal tales provide a good example of the complexity of literary traditions. Perhaps the best known are the story cycles of the *kancil* or *pelandok*, the mousedeer, who by his cleverness escapes all sorts of dangers and manipulates even the mightiest of animals. From early times these story cycles were influenced by India, at first probably

South-East Asia

by oral adaptation of individual tales, later by the introduction of written literature. Of particular importance was the *Panchatantra*, the ancient Indian story collection, in which animal tales were told to the ignorant sons of kings to instruct them in the principles of politics. In creating the mousedeer cycle, Indonesians adapted the Indian stories to their own literary tastes.

Batak birch bark manuscript

The absence of a clear distinction between folk and written literature is indicated by the fact that folk literature (such as the mousedeer cycle) swarms with motifs and material which appear to derive from foreign written works. Many Batak and Dayak tales also show signs of Indian influence. For instance, there exists a Malay oral tale which, although clearly the Indian *Ramayana*, has been adapted to the Malay narrative tradition: it described heroes and heroines, scenery, clothes and weapons in a Malay fashion. In much written literature, on the other hand, all sorts of ancient indigenous material is to be found alongside elements of foreign origin. The indigenous material is often well hidden beneath Sanskrit names. The work of the anthropologist Rassers has been especially important in drawing the attention of western philologists to features which are peculiar to the Indonesian literary tradition.

Rassers' particular concern was the Panji tale. He discerned in this text — which is known in a form dating from no earlier than the 14th century — a variety of old Javanese motifs. Although Rassers' interpretation of this tale as a totemic initiation rite (influenced also by moon mythology motifs) has been rejected, his work encouraged a better understanding of all sorts of Indonesian literature. Especially in relation to the so-called historical literature of Indonesia and in the Japanese *wayang* literature, researchers such as Berg and Pigeaud have sought anthroplogical interpretations based on Indonesian culture.

Indian influence is clearest in Old Javanese literature. It covers principally the period 900-1500, but the writing of literature which followed Indian models probably took place even earlier. An inscription of 856 AD from Java, for instance, shows how refined the application of rules of Sanskrit verse had already become in Old Javanese. By far the majority of extant texts, however date from after 1000 AD. The period was of great importance for the later cultural and literary development of Java. It witnessed an evidently systematic translation of Sankrit works into Old Javanese prose. The great epics, the *Mahabharata* and the *Ramayana* and some of the *purana* (lexicons, grammars and didactic texts) were translated and edited for Javanese needs. As a result of this work, there developed a Javanese prose style which can be seen also in original Old Javanese writings. Examples of these original writings are the *Tantu Panggelaran* and the *Korawasrama*.

Aesthetically, the most interesting genre of Javanese literature is the *kavya*, called *kakawin* in Javanese. The adaptation of this Indian genre was not easily achieved. A complicated and rich metrical structure that is determined by differences between long and short vowels had to be introduced. This poetry was developed to technical and artistic perfection. The subject matter of the *kakawin* seems to have been borrowed almost entirely from India. It includes epic matter, in particular sections from the *Mahabharata,* and stories from more specifically Buddhist literature. The fact that the precise Indian source of the *kakawin* has never been ascertained indicates that the old Javanese did not merely borrow but adapted the Indian subject matter.

The function of the *kakawin* literature has received considerable attention. It is certainly court literature: rulers were sometimes invoked in the text as patrons. But Zoetmulder has noted that the texts themselves give priority to another function. The literature is a form of yoga, a sort of mystical exercise. Poetry was the search for literary beauty and the way to reach oneness with the Godhead. It was a form of mystical worship and the poets therefore called their works temples to which the Godhead descended in order to meet them.

The 14th century *Nagarakertagama* is exceptional among the *kakawin*. It is not made up of mythological matter, but, as the poet himself explains, was 'a description of the land' — that is, of Majapahit, the Javanese kingdom of that time. When the first manuscript of the *Nagarakertagama* was discovered in 1894 it was considered to be an important source of historical knowledge. Another 'historical' work (in prose) is the *Paraton*, the Book of Kings. In such texts as the *Calon Arang*, or the many 'historical' *kidung* of late Old Javanese or Balinese origin, a historical background or nucleus can also be identified, but the mythological or legendary character is much stronger.

In modern Javanese literature, which began after the coming of Islam to Java but did not flourish until after 1700 AD, there are many lengthy works of more or less historical character called *babad*. The best known of these is the *Babad Tanah Jawi*, in which the history, or rather the bringing under cultivation, (*babad* means literally 'bring under cultivation') of the island is related from the beginning of Creation.

In this historical literature Indian and Muslim traditions are fused with indigenous traditions and the ruler and dynasty hold a completely central position. Much work has been done regarding the interpretation of historical texts and the Javanese conception of history by C.C. Berg who argues that this literature is a type of mythology produced by court poets as a form of literary magic; it is therefore fundamentally unreliable as a source for historical study. Such conclusions led Berg to an excessive re-evaluation of both Javanese literature and history, but his work has established the importance of interpreting Javanese literature in the context of Javanese culture. A product of this approach is the discovery that the break between Old and Modern Javanese literature is more apparent than real. Javanese historical literature demands admiration as literature. It is sometimes written as poetry, sometimes as prose. The distinction is not essential for the Javanese.

Texts containing historical material are found in many other parts of Indonesia. Some of these texts are mere genealogies, others are elaborate mythological/legendary/historical/anecdotal accounts. The masterpiece of Malay literature, the *Sejarah Melayu* (see Malaysia section), contains all these elements. Other texts are more homogeneous. The *Hikayat Aceh,* for instance, is a typical king-book, in which the history of the greatest Sultan of Aceh (in North Sumatra), Iskander Muda (1607-1636), is told in accordance with Indo-Persian literary forms. The *Hikayat Hang Tuah,* on the other hand, is a myth portraying the Malay subject and is a suitable companion to the many king-books.

There is much other literature in Indonesia, but a great deal of it is based directly on Indian, Persian and Arabic models. The great story cycle, the *Hikayat Bayan Budiman,* the *Thousand and One Nights,* the history of the seven or ten viziers, the Muslim version of the tale of Alexander the Great and the stories and legends of the Prophet himself and of his contemporaries (the *Hikayat Amir Hamzah* is the most popular), have all found their way to the archipelago and contributed to the Indonesian literary repertoire. They are found not only in direct translations but as revisions which have been more or less assimilated to local tastes.

Muslim religious literature, which ranged from purely dogmatic and legal to mystical and devotional writings, also assumed a largely Indonesian character. The most important contribution to Indonesian literature and to the whole spiritual life of Islam in the following centuries was made by a number of writers at the court of Aceh in the first half of the 17th century. Inspired by the famous mystics Ibn-al-Arabi and Jalal al-Din Rumi, these writers produced a rich mystical literature written in a lively and characteristic Malay form. The foremost authors were Hamzah Fansuri and Nuruddin ar-Raniri. Mysticism also flourished in Java in both an extreme pantheistic form as well as within the orthodox conception of Islam. The *Serat Centhini,* for instance, a poetical work of 3000 pages presented as a travel account of two people, contains a sort of encyclopaedia of Javanese culture. It is saturated with mystical speculation and experience.

The 19th century was to some extent a transitional period in the emergence of modern literature. The Javanese writer Ranggawarsita, although still rooted in the traditions of Javanese culture, was clearly influenced by contact with the West. In the Malay world the work of Raja Ali Haji, although adhering to traditional values, presents innovation in form and content. The new era is more easily detected in the writings of Abdullah (see Malaysia section).

The second half of the 19th century witnessed the growth of a literary culture closely linked with the emerging vernacular press. Sensational news stories sometimes provided the subject for stories which were told or retold or re-composed in poetic form as *syair*, such as the celebrated *Nyai Dasima* murder case. This literature, written in Low Malay, flourished in Eurasian and Chinese urban communities. However, the real modernization of Indonesian literature probably commenced early in the 20th century and was related to political developments. It originated in student groups in the 1920s which were influenced by the emerging nationalism and sought artistic expression for the new ideals. The Malay language became the language of that literary expression and was proclaimed the language of the Indonesian people, *Bahasa Indonesia*, in 1928.

Before World War II Sumatrans made a particular contribution to the new literature. In 1922 Muhammad Yamin was the first to publish a volume of poems. He produced another volume in 1928 and his works demonstrate a development from a local Sumatran to a national Indonesian poet that is characteristic of the period. Other poets were Rustam Effendi and the theosophist Sanusi Pane. Meanwhile prose also developed. It was encouraged by Balai Pustaka, the government popular literature bureau which offered publication possibilities and an audience to Indonesian writers. Many of the novelists were Minangkabau, from West Sumatra; this was no accident as their language is close to Malay and their matrilineal social organization led to a particularly severe clash between traditional and modern ideas. Marah Rusli was one of the first of these writers with his popular novel *Sitti Nurbaya*; Abdul Muis, Nur St. Iskander and many others followed, most of them with variants on the same theme.

A more conscious reflection on the cultural worth of the past and its ideals for the future developed in the 1930s. The monthly journal *Pudjangga Baru*, under the inspiring but controversial editorship of St. Takdir Alisjahbana, gave expression to these concerns. Takdir drew his inspiration from the dynamism of the west, while Sanusi Pane looked towards the cultural heritage of the east and the writings of Tagore. *Pudjangga Baru* also undertook the publishing of the first Indonesian psychological novel, *Belenggu,* by Armijn Pane which had been rejected by Balai Pustaka on the grounds of alleged immorality. To this group belonged also the greatest pre-war poet, Amir Hamzah.

The Japanese occupation of the Netherlands Indies was a momentous event. That an Asian power could bring to an end 350 years of Dutch colonial presence in Indonesia was a revelation to Indonesians. Nationalism which had been suppressed and weakened in the 1930s revived during the war years. Although little was published from 1942 to 1945 due to harsh Japanese censorship, the foundations were laid for the literary and political revolution of 1945. The poets and writers who came to the fore were called the *Angkatan 45*, the generation of 1945, epitomised by the figure of Chairil Anwar. The ideals of this group are most succinctly expressed in the *Gelanggang* Testimony of 1950 which proclaimed 'we are the heirs of world culture.' For this generation, humanism and human dignity were the great ideals.

The influence of the Dutch novelists E. Marsman and G. Slauerhoff on the form and content of this literature is unmistakable, but other western writers were also read. The young writers of the *Angkatan 45* participated in world literature and their style was a radical departure from the sentimentality, reflection and word-play prevalent in pre-war literature: the *Angkatan 45* were fierce, direct and raw. Idrus pioneered the 'new simplicity' style of this modern prose with his seminal short stories, of which the most famous is *Surabaya*. The capabilities of Indonesian prose were further developed in the writings of Pramoedya Ananta Toer.

In the post-war years Indonesian writers were confronted with the ideological conflicts which increasingly dominated Indonesia's internal politics in the 1959-65 period. The literary scene became increasingly polarised along political lines, with the central debate being between advocates of universal humanism and social realism. As the communist cultural organization LEKRA became ideologically stronger, literature was forced into a social-realist harness. After 1965, the fall of President Sukarno, the eclipse of the Indonesian Communist Party (PKI) and the imprisonment of many writers associated with LEKRA, there developed a variegated literary life. It was expressed in newspapers and general weeklies rather than in strictly literary magazines. Only *Horison*, which was established in 1966, was able to maintain itself as a literary journal. The cultural monthlies, *Budaya Jaya* (now defunct) and *Basis*, also deserve mention. The most important publisher of literary work after 1970 was Pustaka Jaya, under the direction of Ajip Rosidi, who was himself one of the most important writers and literary historians of post-1955 Indonesia. A remarkable feature of the period is the popularity of so-called 'pop novels' for which there seems to be an insatiable market.

Important poets are Rendra, Subagio Sastrowardojo and, of a younger generation, Goenawan Mohamad, Sapardi Djoko Damono, Abdul Hadi W.M. and Sutardji Calzoum Bachri. Of the prose writers, the novelist Nh. Dini, the journalist Mochtar Lubis, Achdiat Karta Mihardja, Umar Kayam and Budi Darma deserve mention. Iwan Simatupang, Putu Wijaya, Danarto and Linus Suryadi are more revolutionary in literary style. Since 1980, the historical novels of Pramoedya Ananta Toer and Y.B. Mangunwijaya testify to a re-evaluation of Indonesian historical consciousness

The stage is very important in Indonesia but especially in recent times it has developed into an independent art form in which the written text plays a subordinate role. There is also very little drama published. Although literary criticism has not developed to a great extent in Indonesia, mention must be made of H.B. Jassin who has done much to document modern Indonesian literature. He built up the Pusat Dokumentasi Sastra H.B. Jassin, an essential source of material for every researcher on Indonesian literature. Other critics deserving mention include the creative writers mentioned above and Boen S. Oemarjati, Jakob Sumardjo, Dami N. Toda, Bakri Siregar and Arief Budiman. Post-war Javanese literature, though not so important from a literary point of view, deserves attention for sociological reasons.

Legal Literature

The legal literature of Indonesia is complex but may be classified as follows: (1) laws of Java and Bali; (2) Malayo-Muslim laws (mainly Sumatra and the outer islands, but also Java); (3) local recensions of the classical Islamic lawbooks of the Middle East; and (4) oral law (*adat*).

1. Java and Bali

The earliest surviving evidence of law is contained in epigraphy and consists of tax and land charters of the 14th century and *jayapattra* (*jayasong*) of the 10th-18th centuries. The latter are directly based on the Indian model and their function was to demonstrate that an article in law had been settled. They contained a statement of argument by both parties, the evidence, the law text (*smrti*) applied and the decision of the judge authenticated by seal. *Jayappatra* of the later period departed somewhat from the original model. The second and main source of Javanese/Balinese legal literature is the law text, known generally as *Agama*. It does not follow or refer to the Indian form, as do the Burmese and Thai, but it does incorporate significant elements of Sanskrit technical usage as well as some Indian content. The earliest date for an *Agama* manuscript is 1811 AD, but from internal evidence an *Agama* tradition can be located in the 16th century with possible earlier connections. The third source for Javanese/Balinese law is the *pepakem* ('lawbook') dating from the 18th century, a number of which are known. They appear to have been guides or *compendia* for *jaksa* (collegiate tribunals) use in legal administration. Their content is wholly indigenous in contrast to the *Agama* literature.

2. Malayo-Muslim laws

These consist of law texts (*undang-undang*) and are found in Aceh, Minangkabau, the west and south of Sumatra as well as in the Celebes and the southern Philippines (for Malayan versions, see Malaysia section) as well as more generally in the Malay-Muslim communities of the Indonesian archipelago. Characteristically they are concerned with the definition of sovereignty, the relation between the Islamic ethic and indigenous prescription and with detailed prescriptions relating to property (both movable and immovable) and personal relations.

3. Classical Islamic Lawbooks

The major works are found in local translations or in the original Arabic with glosses in all the main languages of Indonesia. Perhaps the most prominant are the *Tuhfat al-Muhtaj, Al-Risalah, Fath Al-Wahhab* and the *Minhaj at-Talibin*.

4. Oral Law

The *adat* (customary law) literature began to be seriously produced in written form in the mid-19th century. It was designed by the Dutch government for practical administrative and judicial use and this conditioned both its form and content. *Adat* writings, in Indonesian translation, continue to be widely used in the courts of the Republic of Indonesia.

Bibliographic information regarding oral literature of Indonesia can be found in **Cense** and **Uhlenbeck** (1958), **Teeuw** (1961), **Uhlenbeck** (1964) and **Voorhoeve** (1955). Thorough surveys of Indonesian oral literature are rare. Among the exceptions are the surveys of the Batak literature of North Sumatra (**Voorhoeve**, 1927); Nias literature (**Steinhart**, 1937, 1954); the Dayak literature of Borneo (**Dunselman**, 1955, 1959); the Bare'e literature of the Torajas of Central Sulawesi (**Adriani**, 1914); the Totemboan literature of Minahasa in North Sulawesi (**Schwartz**, 1907); the literature of Timor (**Middelkoop**, 1949, 1963); and the oral poetry of the Minangkabau of West Sumatra (**Phillips**, 1981).

On the *panji* tales, see **Rassers** (1922, 1959); **Maxwell** (1886) discusses a Malay adaptation of the *Ramayana*. For interpretations of historical and *wayang* literature, see **Berg** (1927, 1938, 1951, 1961, 1965) and **Pigeaud** (1938, 1967-80); on some *babad* traditions, see **Kumar** (1976) and for a discussion of the *Babad Tanah Java* and interpretations of it to date, see **Ras** (1986).

A general survey (in Russian) and extensive bibliography of Indonesian literature is **Parnickel** (1980). Malay literature is discussed in **Winstedt** (1969). For old and modern Javanese literature, see **Pigeaud** (1967-80, especially vol. 1) and **Zoetmulder** (1974). Balinese literature is discussed in **Hooykaas** (1979). On the antecedents of modern Indonesian literature, see **Sykorsky** (1980) and **Watson** (1971). An anthology of *peranakan* literature is found in **Toer** (1982), while a bibliography and discussion of literature in Malay by the Chinese of Indonesia is found in **Salmon** (1981). **Teeuw** (1979) is a major study of Indonesian literature. On aspects of modern Indonesian literature, see also **Hill** (1984), **Johns** (1959), **Kähler** (1976), **Kratz** (1979, 1982), **Oermarjati** (1978, 1981) and **Tham Seong Chee** (1981); also the articles in **Chambert-Loir** (1980c). See also bibliographical references in **Deakin** (1978). On Sumatran contributions to Indonesian literature, see **Freidus** (1977). **Ras** (1979) discusses the emergence of modern Javanese literature and gives an anthology and survey of post-war Javanese literature. A good amount of modern Indonesian literature has been translated into English; see particularly **Aveling** (1974b, 1976, 1978, 1985b) and further bibliographical references therein. On modern Indonesian poetry, see **Aveling** (1974a and 1985a). LEKRA and its publications are discussed in **Foulcher** (1986). For a history of Dutch colonial literature, see **Nieuwenhuys** (1982).

Lastly, on Javanese law and the law texts of Java and Bali, see **Hoadley** and **Hooker** (1981, 1986); on Muslim law texts, see **Hooker** (1984, 1986); on customary law, see **Hooker** (1978), **Ter Haar** (1948) and **Vollenhoeven** (1918-33); on Dutch colonial law, see **Hooker** (1975).

Balinese palm leaf manuscript illustrating the Bagus Umbara story

Bibliography

Abdul Chaer
1976 *Kamus dialek Melayu Jakarta - bahasa Indonesia.* Ende: Penerbit Nusa Indah.

Adriani, N. and A. C. Kruyt
1914 *De Bare'e Sprekende Toradja's van Midden Celebes III.* Taal-en Letterkundige Schets der Bare'e taal en overzicht van het Taalgebied: Celebes zuid Halmahera. Batavia: Landsdrukkerij.

Ahmat bin Adam
1984 *The vernacular press and the emergence of modern Indonesian consciousness* (1855-1913). Ph.D. thesis. SOAS, University of London.

Anderson, M. H.
1982 "Indonesia." In J. A. Lent, ed. *Newspapers in Asia: contemporary trends and problems.* Hong Kong: Heinemann Asia, pp. 193-218.

Aveling, Harry
1974a *A thematic history of Indonesian poetry, 1920 to 1974.* DeKalb: Center for Southeast Asian Studies, Northern Illinois University (Special Report, no. 9).

Aveling, Harry (ed. and trans.)
1974b *Man and society in the works of the Indonesian playwright Utuy Tatang Sontani.* Honolulu: Southeast Asian Studies Program, University of Hawaii. (Southeast Asia Paper, no 13).
1976 *From Surabaya to Armageddon: Indonesian short stories.* Singapore: Heinemann Educational Books.
1978 *Gestapu: Indonesian short stories on the abortive Communist coup of 30 September 1965.* Honolulu: Southeast Asian Studies Program, University of Hawaii. (Southeast Asian Studies Paper, no. 6).
1985a *Contemporary Indonesian poetry.* St. Lucia: University of Queensland Press. (2nd edn.)

Aveling, Harry (trans.)
1985b *Crossing the border: five Indonesian short stories by Danarto and Pramoedya Ananata Toer.* Clayton, Victoria: Monash University, Centre of Southeast Asian Studies. (Working Paper no. 38).

Barber, C. C.
1979 *A Balinese-English dictionary.* 2 vols. Aberdeen: University of Aberdeen. (Aberdeen University library, Occasional Publications, No. 2).

Behrend, T. E.
1988 "Small collections of Javanese manuscripts in Indonesia." *Archipel* 35: 23-42.

Berg, C. C.
1927 *De middlejavaansche historische traditie.* Santport: C. A. Mees.
1938 "Javaansche geschiedschriving." In F. W. Stapel, ed. *Geschiedenis van Nederlandsche Indie,* vol 2. Amsterdam: Joost van den Vondel.
1951 *De evolutie der Javaanse geschiedschrijving.* Amsterdam: Noord-Hollanse uitgevers Maatschappij.
1961 "Javanese historiography - a synopsis of its evolution." In D. G. E. Hall, ed. *Historians of South East Asia.* London: Oxford University Press, pp. 13-23.
1965 "The Javanese picture of the past." In Soejatmoko, ed. *An introduction to Indonesian historiography.* Ithaca: Cornell University Press, pp. 87-118.

Boland, B. J. and I. Farjon
1983 *Islam in Indonesia: a bibliographical survey.* Dordrecht: Foris Publications (KITLV Bibliographical series, 14).

Casparis, J. G. de
1975 *Indonesian paleography: a history of writing in Indonesia from the beginnings to c. A.D. 1500.* Leiden; Köln: Brill (*Handbuch der Orientalistik.* Dritte Abteilung: *Indonesien, Malaysia und die Philippinen,* ed. H. Kähler. 4, 1).
1978 *Indonesian chronology.* Leiden; Köln: Brill. (*Handbuch der Orientalistik.* Dritte Abteilung, 1,1).

Cense, A. A. and Abdoerrahim
1979 *Makkassaars-Nederlands Woordenboek.* s' Gravenhage: Nijhoff.

Cense, A. A. and E. M. Uhlenbeck
1958 *Critical survey of studies on the languages of Borneo.* s' Gravenhage: Nijhoff. (KITLV Bibliographical series, 2).

Chambert-Loir, H.
1980a "Catalogue des catalogues de manuscrits malais." *Archipel* 20: 45-69.
1980b "Les manuscrits malais de Bale, Lund, Singapour et Paris." *Archipel* 20: 87-98.

Chambert-Loir, H. (ed.)
1980c *Sastra: introduction à la littérature indonésienne contemporaine.* Paris: Association Archipel. (Cahier d'Archipel, 11).

Chijs, J. A. van der
1875-1903 *Proeve eener Nederlandsch Indische bibliographie, 1659-1870.* Batavia: Bruining & Wijt. (Verhandelingen van het Bataviaasch Genootschap van Kunsten en Wetenschappen. Deel 37, 39, 55).

Coolhaas, W. P.
1980 *A critical survey of Dutch colonial history.* (2nd edn., revised by G. J. Schuttle). The Hague: Nijhoff (KITLV Bibliographical Series, 4).

Coolsma, S.
1913 *Soendaneesch-Hollandsche Woordenboek.* Leiden: A. W. Sitjhoff.

Deakin, C., et al.
1978 *Indonesian reading list.* 3rd edn. London: Indonesia Circle.

Dunselman, P. D.
1955 *Kana sera: zang der zwangerschap.* The Hague: Nijhoff. (Verhande lingen van het KITLV, Deel 17).
1959 *Uit de literatuur der Mualung-Dajaks.* The Hague: Nijhoff. (KITLV).

Djajadiningrat, H.
1934 *Atjesch-Nederlandsch Woordenboek.* 2 vols. Batavia: Landsdrukkerij.

Echols, J. M., and H. Shadily
1963 *An Indonesian-English dictionary.* Ithaca: Cornell University Press.
1975 *An English-Indonesian dictionary.* Ithaca: Cornell University Press.

Foulcher, K.
1986 *Social commitment in literature and the arts: the Indonesian "Institute of People's Culture" 1950-1965.* Clayton, Victoria: Monash University, Centre of Southeast Asian Studies.

Freidus, A.J.
1977 *Sumatran contributions to the development of Indonesian literature, 1920-1942.* Honolulu: University of Hawaii Press. (Asian Studies at Hawaii, No.19).

Garis Besar
1971 *Garis besar perkembangan pers Indonesia.* Jakarta: Serikat Penerbit Suratkabar.

Girardet, N.
1983 *Descriptive catalogue of the Javanese manuscripts and printed books in the main libraries of Surakarta and Yogyakarta.* Wiesbaden: Franz Steiner. (Schriftenreihe des Südasien-Instituts der Universität Heidelburg 30).

Graaf, H. J. de
1969 *The spread of printing: Eastern hemisphere: Indonesia.* Amsterdam: Vangendt; New York: A. Schram.

Hardjoprakoso, M.
1973 *Katalogus surat kabar: koleksi Perpustakaan Museum Pusat 1810-1973.* Jakarta: Museum Pusat, Department P & K.

Herrfurth, H.
1972 *Djawanisch-Deutsches Wörterbuch.* Leipzig: VEB Verlag Enzyklopädie.

Hill, D. T.
1984 *Who's left? Indonesian literature in the early 1980s*. Clayton, Victoria: Monash University. (Working Paper No. 33).

Hinzler, H. I. R.
1986-87 *Catalogue of Balinese manuscripts in the library of the University of Leiden and other collections in the Netherlands*. 2 vols. Leiden: Brill. (Codices Manuscripti Bibliothecae Universitatis Leidensis, 23).

Hoadley, M. C. and M. B. Hooker
1981 *An introduction to Javanese law*. Tuscon: University of Arizona Press, for the American Association of Asian Studies.
1986 "The law texts of Java and Bali." In M.B. Hooker, ed. *Laws of South-East Asia. Vol. 1: the pre-modern texts*. Singapore: Butterworth, pp. 241-346; bibliog. pp. 533-538.

Holle, K. F.
1882 *Tabel van oud-en nieuw-Indische alphabetten: Bijdrage tot de palaeographie van Nederlansch-Indie*. Batavia: Bruining & Co.

Holt, C.
1967 *Art in Indonesia: continuities and change*. Ithaca: Cornell University Press.

Hooker, M. B.
1975 *Legal pluralism: an introduction to colonial and neo-colonial laws*. Oxford: Clarendon Press.
1978 *Adat law in modern Indonesia*. Kuala Lumpur: Oxford University Press.
1984 *Islamic law in South-East Asia*. Kuala Lumpur: Oxford University Press.
1986 "The law texts of Muslim South-East Asia." In M. B. Hooker, ed. *The laws of South-East Asia. Vol. I: the pre-modern texts*. Singapore: Butterworth, pp. 347-433; bibliog. pp.539-554.

Hooykaas, C.
1979 *Introduction à la littérature balinaise*. Paris: Archipel. (Cahier d'Archipel 8).

Horne, E. C.
1961 *Beginning Javanese*. New Haven; London: Yale University. (Yale Linguistic Series, 3).
1963 *Intermediate Javanese*. New Haven; London: Yale University. (Yale Linguistics Series, 4).
1974 *Javanese-English dictionary*. New Haven; London: Yale University Press.

Hurgronje, C. S.
1893 "Studien over de Atjehsche Klank-en Schriftleer." *TBG* 35: 346-442.

Iskander, T.
1970 *Kamus Dewan*. Kuala Lumpur: Dewan Bahasa dan Pustaka.

Johns, A. H.
1959 "The novel as a guide to Indonesian social history." *Bijdragen tot de Taal-, Land-, en Volkenkunde van Nederlandisch Indie* 115: 232-248.

Johns, Y.
1977 *Bahasa Indonesia langkah baru: a new approach*. Canberra: Australian National University Press.
1981 *Bahasa Indonesia: Book 2, langkah baru: a new approach*. Canberra: Australian National University Press.

Kähler, H.
1956 *Grammatik der Bahasa Indonesia*. Wiesbaden: Harrassowitz. (Porto Linguarum Orientalium; neue Serie 2).

Kähler, H. (ed.)
1976 *Indonesien, Malaysia und die Philippinen unter Einschluss der Kap-malaien in Südafrika*. Leiden; Köln: Brill. (*Handbuch der Orientalistik*, Dritte Abteilung, 3, 1: *Literaturen*).

Kamus
1975 *Kamus Indonesia-Bali*. Jakarta: Pusat Pembinan dan Pengembangan Bahasa.
1978 *Kamus Bali-Indonesia*. Denpasar: Panitia Penyusun Kamus Bali-Indonesia.

Karow, O. and J. Hilgers-Hesse
1978 *Indonesich-Deutsches Wörterbuch*. Wiesbaden: Harrassowitz.

Kennedy, R.
1965 *Bibliography of Indonesian peoples and cultures*. New Haven: HRAF Press.

Kentjono, D.
1976 "Introduction to the development of Bahasa Indonesia." *East Asian Cultural Studies* 15: 143-168.

Kimman, E.
1981 *Indonesian publishing*. Baarn: Hollandia.

Kratz, E. U.
1979 "The origins and development of Malay and Indonesian literature." *SEALG Newsletter* 21: 1-11.

1982 "The Indonesian short story after 1945." In J. H. C. S. Davidson and H. Cordell, eds. *The short story in South East Asia*, London: School of Oriental and African Studies, pp. 139-166.

Kumar, A.
1976 *Surapati man and legend: a study of three babad traditions*. Leiden: Brill. (Australian National University Centre of Oriental Studies, Oriental Monograph Series, No. 20).

Labrousse, P.
1978 *Méthode d'indonésian*. 2 vols. Paris: Archipel/Asiathèque. (Cahier d'Archipel, 3 & 4).
1984 *Indonésien-français: dictionnaire général*. Paris: Association Archipel.

Lan Hiang Char
1979 *Southeast Asia research tools: Indonesia*. Honolulu: University of Hawaii. (Southeast Asia Paper No.16, part II).

Langen, K. F. H. van
1889 *Handleiding voor de Beoefening der Atjehsche Taal*. 's Gravenhage: Nijhoff.

LeBar, F.
1972 *Ethnic groups of insular Southeast Asia. Vol. 1: Indonesia, Andaman Island and Madagascar*. New Haven: HRAF Press.

Legge, J. D.
1980 *Indonesia*. Sydney: Prentice-Hall.

Lombard, D.
1976 *Introduction à l'indonésien*. Paris: SECMI Publications Orientalistes de France. (Cahier d'Archipel, 1).

MacDonald, R. R.
1976 *Indonesian reference grammar*. Ithaca: Cornell University Southeast Asia Program.

Manik, L.
1973 *Batak-Handschriften*. Wiesbaden: Franz Steiner. (Verzeichnis der Orientalischen Handschriften in Deutschland , Band XXVIII).

Matthes, B.
1874 *Boegineesch-Hollandsch Woordenboek, met Hollandsch-Boegineesch Woordenlijst*. 's Gravenhage: Nijhoff.

Maxwell, W. E.
1886 "Penglipor Lara Sri Rama: a Malay fairy tale founded on the Ramayana." *JSBRAS* 17:1-84, 87-115.

Middelkoop, P.
1949 *Een studie van het timoreesche Doodenritueel.* Batavia: (Verhandelingen van het Bataviaasch Genootschap van Kunsten en Wetenschappen, Deel 76).
1963 *Headhunting in Timor and its historical implications: introduction and texts.* 3 vols. Sydney: University of Sydney. (Oceania Linguistic Monograph no. 8, a, b, c).

Moon, B. E.
1979 *Periodicals for South-East Asian studies: a union catalogue of holdings in British and selected European libraries.* London: Mansell.

Mudjanattistomo, R. M.
1971 *Katalogus manuskrip Kraton Jogjakarta.* Jogjakarta: Lembaga Bahasa Nasional, Tjabang 11.

Naerssen, F. H. van, Th. G. Th. Pigeaud and P. Voorhoeve
1977 *Catalogue of Indonesian manuscripts. Part 2: Old Javanese charters, Javanese, Malay and Lampung manuscripts, Maas Lange's Balinese letters and official letters in Indonesian languages.* Copenhagen: the Royal Library. (Catalogue of Oriental Manuscripts, Xylographs etc. in Danish Collections, vol 4, part 2).

Nieuwenhuys, R.
1982 *Mirror of the Indies: a history of Dutch colonial literature.* Amhurst: University of Massachusetts Press.

Nimpoeno, Raden S.
1936 *Tjarakan (het Javaanse Alphabet).* Groningen & Batavia.

Noordenbos, C.
1941 *Klanken Teken van het Javaans.* Batavia: J. B. Wolters.

Nunn, G. R.
1971 *Indonesian newspapers: an international union list.* Taipei: Chinese Materials and Research Aids Service Center.
1977 *Southeast Asian periodicals: an international union list.* London: Mansell.

Ockeloen, C.
1966 *Catalogus van boeken en tijdschriften uitgegeven in Nederlandsch Oost-Indie van 1870-1937.* Amsterdam: Swets and Zeitlinger.

Oemarjati, B. S.
1978 "Development of modern Indonesian literature." In H. Soebadio and C. A. du M. Sarvaas, eds. *Dynamics of Indonesian history.* Amsterdam; New York; Oxford: North Holland Publishing Company.
1981 "Isteri, Cinta and Arjuna: Indonesian literature at the crossroad." In Tham Seong Chee, ed. *Essays on literature and society in Southeast Asia.* Singapore: Singapore University Press, pp. 82-96.

Overbeck, H.
1926 "Malay manuscripts in public libraries in Germany." *JMBRAS* 4, 2: 233-259.

Parnickel, B. B.
1980 *Vvedenie v literaturnuju Istoriju Nvsantary.* Moskva: IX-XIX vv. Izdatel'stvo 'NAVKA', Glavnaja hedakciaja vostocnej literatury.

Peacock, J. L.
1973 *Indonesia: an anthropological perspective.* Pacific Palisades: Goodyear.

Pedoman Ejaan
1976 *Pedoman Ejaan Bahasa daerah Bali, Jawa, dan Sunda yang disempurnakan.* Jakarta: Pusat Pembinaan dan Pengembangan Bahasa, Departemen Pendidikan dan Kebudayaan.

Phillips, N.
1981 *Sijobang: sung narrative poetry of West Sumatra.* London: Cambridge University Press.

Pigeaud, Th. G. Th.
1938 *Javaans-Nederlands Handwoordenboek.* Batavia: Wolters.
1967-80 *Literature of Java: catalogue raisonné of Javanese manuscripts in the library of the University of Leiden and other public collections in the Nederlands.* 4 vols. The Hague: Nijhoff. (Vol. 4 published as supplement by Leiden University Press. [Bibliotheca Universitas Leidensis Codices Manuscripti, XX]).
1975 *Javanese and Balinese manuscripts.* Wiesbaden: Franz Steiner. (Verzeichnis der Orientalischen Handschriften in Deutschland, Band XXXI).

Pigeaud, Th. G. Th. and P. Voorhoeve
1985 *Handschriften aus Indonesien (Bali, Java and Sumatra).* Wiesbaden: Franz Steiner. (Verzeichnis der Orientalischen Handschriften in Deutschland, Band XXVII, 2).

Poerbatjaraka, R. M. Ng., P. Voorhoeve and C. Hooykaas
1950 *Indonesische Handschriften. Lembaga Kebudajaan Indonesia "Koninklijk Bataviaasch Genootschap van Kunsten en Wetenschappen."* Bandung: A. C. Nix.

Poerwadarminta, W. J. S. and A. Teeuw
1952 *Indonesisch-Nederlands Woordenboek.* Groningen: J. B. Wolters.

Poerwadarminta, W. J. S.
1976 *Kamus Umum bahasa Indonesia.* Jakarta: Balai Pustaka.

Pollard, T. and R. A. Jones
1972 *Mindopak: minimal Indonesian for practical use.* London: Australian Union of Students.

Prentice, D. J.
1987 "Malay (Indonesian and Malaysian)." In B. Comrie, ed. *The world's major languages.* London; Sydney: Croom Helm, pp. 913-935.

Ras, J. J.
1977 *Elementair Javaans.* Leiden: Vakgroep Indonesische Taal- en Culturen.
1979 *Javanese literature since independence: an anthology.* The Hague: Nijhoff. (VKITLV, 88).
1986 "The Babad Tanah Jawi and its reliability: questions of content, structure and function." In C. D. Grijns and S. O. Robson, eds. *Cultural contact and textual interpretation.* Dordrecht: Foris, pp. 246-273. (KITLV, 115).

Rassers, W. H.
1922 *De Pandji-Roman.* Leiden; Antwerp: Akademisch Proefschrift.
1959 *Panji, the cultural hero: a structural study of religon in Java.* The Hague; Nijhoff. (KITLV Translation Series, 3).

Reid, A. J. S., et al.
1974 *Indonesian serials 1942-1950 in Yogyakarta libraries with a list of government publications in the Perpustakaan Negara, Yogyakarta.* Canberra: Australian National University Press.

Ricklefs, M. C.
1978 *Modern Javanese historical tradition: a study of an original Kartasura chronicle and related materials.* London: SOAS.
1981 *A history of modern Indonesia.* London: Macmillan.

Ricklefs, M. C. and P. Voorhoeve
1977 *Indonesian manuscripts in Great Britain.* Oxford: Oxford University Press. (London Oriental Bibliographies, vol. 5).
1982 "Indonesian manuscripts in Great Britain: addenda et corrigenda." *BSOAS* 45, 2: 300-322.

Ronkel, Ph. S. van
1908 "Catalogus der Maleische handschriften van het Koninklij Instituut voor Taal-, Land-, en Volkenkunde van Nederlandsch-Indie." *BKI* 60: 181-247.
1921 *Maleische en Minangkabausche Handschriften in de Leidensche Universiteits-Bibliotheek.* Leiden: Brill.

Said, H. M.
1976 *Sejarah pers di Sumatera Utara, dengan masyarakat yang dicer minkannya (1885-Maret 1942).* Medan: Waspada.

Salmon, Claudine
1981 *Literature in Malay by the Chinese of Indonesia*. Paris: Archipel. (Etudes insulindiennes-Archipel: 3).

Santoso, W., et al.
1981 *Katalog majalah terbitan Indonesia 1928-1941: Koleksi Perpustakaan Museum Nasional*. Jakarta: Perpustakaan Nasional.
1982 *Katalog majalah terbitan Indonesia 1942-1980: Koleksi Perpustakaan Museum Nasional*. Jakarta: Perpustakaan Nasional.
1983 *Katalog majalah terbitan Indonesia 1779-1927: Koleksi Perpustakaan Museum Nasional*. Jakarta: Perpustakaan Nasional.

Sarumpaet, J. P.
1972 *The structure of Bahasa Indonesia*. Box Hill, Vic: J. P. Sarumpaet.

Sarumpaet, J. P. and H. Hendrata
1986-87 *A modern reader in Bahasa Indonesia: books 1 and 2*. Box Hill, Victoria: n.p. (1st published 1968).

Sarumpaet, J. P. and J. A. C. Mackie
1966 *Introduction to Bahasa Indonesia*. Melbourne: Melbourne University Press.

Satjadibrata, R.
1956 *Kamoes Soenda-Indonesia*. Djakarta: Balai Poestaka, no. 1561.

Schwartz, J. A. T.
1907 *Totemboansch Teksten*. Leiden: Nijhoff.

Schmidgall-Tellings, A. Ed. and A. M. Stevens
1981 *Contemporary Indonesian-English dictionary*. Athens, Ohio: Ohio University Press.

Sirk, U.
1983 *The Buginese language*. (Translated from the Russian by E. H. Tsipan; edited by L. I. Shkarban). Moscow: Nauka, for Central Department of Oriental Literature. (Languages of Asia and Africa series).

Soebadio, H. and C. A. du M. Sarvaaas (eds.)
1978 *Dynamics of Indonesian history*. Amsterdam; New York; Oxford: North Holland Publishing Company.

Soebagio, I. N.
1977 *Sejarah pers Indonesia*. Jakarta: Dewan Pers.

Soebardi
1965 "Calendrical traditions in Indonesia." *Madjallah Ilmu-ilmu Sastra Indonesia III*, I: 49-61.

Soermargono, F. and P. Labrousse
1969 *Kamus dasar Perantjis-Indonesia.* Bandung: Ananta; distrib. Alliance Française.

Steinhart, W. L.
1937 *Niassche Teksten met Nederlandsche Vertaling en Aantekeningen.* (VBG, 73).
1954 *Niasse Teksten.* The Hague: Nijhoff. (KITLV).

Sutaarga, M. A.
1972 *Katalogus koleksi naskah Melayu Museum Pusat. Penyusun M. Amir Sutaarga, Jumsari Jusuf, Tuti Munawar, d.* Jakarta. (Stencilled).

Sykorsky, W. V.
1980 "Some additional remarks on the antecedents of modern Indonesian literature." *BKI* 136: 498-516.

Teeuw, A.
1961 *A critical survey of studies on Malay and Bahasa Indonesia.* The Hague: Nijhoff. (KITLV Bibliographical Series, 5).
1979 *Modern Indonesian literature.* 2 vols.(2nd edn.) The Hague: Nijhoff. (KITLV Translation Series, 10, 1 and 2).

Ter Haar, B.
1948 *Adat law in Indonesia.* New York: Institute of Pacific Relations.

Tham Seong Chee
1981 "The social and intellectual ideas of Indonesian writers, 1920-1942." In Tham Seong Chee, ed. *Essays on literature and society in Southeast Asia.* Singapore: Singapore University Press, pp. 97-124.

Toer, Pramoedya Ananta
1982 *Tempo doeloe: antologi sastra pra-Indonesia.* Jakarta: Hastra Mitra.

Toorn, J. L. van der
1891 *Minangkabausch-Maleisch-Nederlandsch Woordenboek.* 's Gravenhage: Nijhoff.

Uhlenbeck, E. M.
1964 *A critical survey of studies on the languages of Java and Madura.* 's Gravenhage: Nijhoff. (KITLV Bibliographical Series, 7).
1971 "Indonesia and Malaysia." In T. A. Sebeok, ed. *Current trends in linguistics, vol 8: Linguistics in Oceania.* The Hague; Paris: Mouton, pp. 55-111. (Also published in the same series, vol 2: *Linguistics in East Asia and South East Asia* (1967), pp. 847-898).

Vlekke, B. H. M.
1959 *Nusantara: a history of Indonesia.* The Hague: Van Hoeve.

Vollenhoven, C. van
1918-1933 *Het Adatrecht van Nederlandsche-Indie.* 6 vols. Leiden: Brill.

Voorhoeve, P.
1927   *Overzicht van de Volksverhalen der Bataks.* Leiden: (Dissertatie).
1955   *Critical survey of studies in the languages of Sumatra.* 's Gravenhage: Nijhoff. (KITLVBibliographical series 1).
1971   *Südsumatranische Handschriften.* Wiesbaden: Franz Steiner. (Verzeichnis der Orientalischen Handschriften in Deutschland, Band XXIX).
1975   *Catalogue of Indonesian manuscripts. Part 1: Batak manuscripts.* Copenhagen: The Royal Library. (Catalogue of Oriental Manuscripts, Xylographs, etc. in Danish Collections, vol 4, part 1).
1977   *Codices Batacici.* Leiden: Universitaire Pers.
1980   "Elio Modigliani's Batak books." *Archivio per l'Antropologia e la Etnologia* CIX-CX. Firenze: Stamperia Editoriale Parenti.

Warneck, J.
1977   *Toba Batak-Deutsches Wörterbuch.* 's Gravenhage: Nijhoff.

Watson, C. W.
1971   "Some preliminary remarks on the antecedents of modern Indonesian literature." *BKI* 127: 415-433.

Winstedt, R. O.
1969   *A history of classical Malay literature.* Kuala Lumpur: Oxford University Press.

Wojowasito, S.
1980   *A Kawi lexicon,* ed. R. F. Mills. Ann Arbor: Center for South and Southeast Asian Studies (Michigan Papers on South and Southeast Asia, No. 17).

Wolff, J. U.
1971   *Beginning Indonesian.* Ithaca: Cornell University, Southeast Asia Program.
1980   *Formal Indonesian.* Ithaca: Cornell University, Southeast Asia Program.

Wolff, J. U., Dede Oetomo and Daniel Feitkiewicz
1984;1986 *Beginning Indonesian through self instruction.* 3 vols. Ithaca: Cornell University, Southeast Asia Program.

Zoetmulder, P. J.
1974   *Kalangwan: a survey of Old Javanese literature.* The Hague: Nijhoff.
1982   *Old Javanese-English dictionary.* Leiden: Nijhoff. (KITLV).

Zoetmulder, P. J. and I. R. Poedjawijatna
1954   *Bahasa Parwa: Tata Bahasa Djawa kuno.* Djakarta: Obor.

Zubaidah, I. S. A.
1972   *Printing and publishing in Indonesia: 1602-1970.* (Ph.D. Thesis, Indiana University, 1972). Ann Arbor: University Microfilms.

The Philippines

The Republic of the Philippines is the official name of the Philippine Islands, an archipelago of over 7,000 islands with a population of just over 48,000,000 (1980 census). The population, largely of Malay origin, has retained its own culture and language despite almost 400 years of colonisation. Unlike much of South-East Asia, there is little indication of Hindu or Buddhist influence in the Philippines. Islam, however, spread to the region from the mid-15th century onwards and had the greatest impact in Mindanao and the Sulu Islands which today have a substantial Muslim minority. One lasting result of Spanish rule is that the majority of the population is Christian, predominantly Roman Catholic.

There are a number of ethnic groups in the Philippines. It has been suggested that there were successive waves of migration into the islands by land bridges and short sea passages, but it is difficult to establish such theories with any degree of certainty. Human remains have been found at Tabon which can be dated to 20,000 BC and archaeological evidence shows continuous human activity in the area. Social organization in the Philippines ranges from 20th century urban societies to people still living a stone-age way of life as hunter-gatherers. Some people still practice swidden agriculture, others wet-rice cultivation including the Ifugao and Bontoc on ancient and spectacular terraces in Luzon. For other groups, the sea is an important focus for economic and social activity. Many people nowadays work in plantation (hacienda) agriculture, industrial production and other urban employment. The Chinese community, established since before the beginning of Spanish rule, has always played an important part in the Philippines' economy and trading activities. Most Chinese have become Christians and intermarried with Filipino families.

Knowledge of the pre-Hispanic period of Philippines history is limited and much archaeological research remains to be done. No uncontested pre-Hispanic Philippine documents have been published and Philippine historians have turned to the records of neighbouring countries for possible references. The reconstruction of pre-Hispanic society and history poses many problems and is very much dependent on external sources, particularly the accounts of Spanish and other early European visitors to the islands. Filipino scholars have also increasingly drawn on oral tradition and anthropological research. The family genealogies, *Tarsilas*, of the Muslim rulers of Sulu and Magindanao provide some account of the pre-Hispanic period. Much has been made too of the *Maragtas*, an account of ten Bornean *datus* (chiefs) of whom it is related that they sailed to Panay in the 13th century.

The Spanish occupied and colonized the Philippines in the 16th century, although opposition to Spanish rule was never completely suppressed and the Muslim (Moro) Sultanates of Mindanao and Sulu resisted Spanish suzerainty until 1878. The Spanish ruled from Manila and the economy of the new colony depended for over 200 years on the Manila galleon which brought silver dollars from Mexico to purchase spices, Chinese silks, porcelain, jade, etc., in Manila to take back for sale in Mexico and Spain. Chinese settlers and merchants were key figures in this trade. Spanish officials, preoccupied with profiting from the galleon trade, did little to develop agriculture and industry. The *encomienda* system whereby the Spanish granted individuals (*encomendero*) rights to collect tributes or taxes from the local population failed to provide enough revenue for the colony and exposed the people to exploitation and abuse.

The Roman Catholic clergy were a critical element in the Spanish impact on the Philippines. Different religious orders (Augustinians, Franciscans, Jesuits, Dominicans and Recollects) were assigned different regions as missionary fields and rapidly brought about large scale conversion to Christianity, and the suppression of many local customs. The official administrative establishment relied greatly on the parish priests who spoke the local language and wielded much influence. In time, many controversies arose about the division between civil and ecclesiastical authority and, above all, about the appointment of Filipino priests. The religious orders amassed wealth and property, and they and the local Spanish priests came to be feared and hated for their power and abuses.

In the second half of the 19th century, the opening of the Philippines to world trade, the rise of an educated Filipino middle class (the *ilustrados*), and the influx of liberal administrators and ideas following the Spanish Revolution of 1868, culminated in increasing demands for equal rights for Filipinos, freedom of speech and assembly, and political and economic reforms. A revolution against the Spanish occurred in 1895-98. The execution by the Spanish in 1896 of the moderate nationalist, Jose Rizal, fuelled revolutionary fervour. But the revolutionary leadership of Bonifacio and Aguinaldo became disunited. In June 1898 Aguinaldo declared the Philippines an independent Republic, but following the outbreak of the Spanish-American War the Americans intervened and occupied the Philippines. In December 1898 Spain transferred sovereignty over the Philippines to the United States. In 1901 Aguinaldo abandoned guerrilla resistance and acknowledged allegiance to the United States. Under American rule, English language education replaced Spanish and the Filipinos were allowed many elements of self-government, with different political parties and leaders.

During the Japanese occupation of the Philippines in World War II, the Republic of the Philippines with Jose P. Laurel as President was set up by the Japanese. True independence was not attained, however, until after the American liberation of the Philippines and the inauguration of the independent Republic of the Philippines on July 4, 1946. Many problems faced the Philippines whose economy had been devastated by the war. Of the many guerrilla units that had operated against the Japanese, the Hukbalahap in particular continued armed resistance and agitation for land reform. Of the successive Philippines Presidents, Magsaysay and Macapagal had perhaps the best intentions and record for improving conditions for the Filipino masses. In 1969 President Marcos became the first President to be re-elected to office, but growing unrest and dissatisfaction led to the imposition of martial law in September 1972. The martial law period lasted until January 1981.

The assassination in August 1983 of opposition leader Benigno Aquino on his arrival at Manila airport, came as the climax of a growing tide of political violence and unleashed popular forces for change. The Presidential elections of 1986 resulted, after dramatic public demonstrations and defection of the military, in the exile of the Marcos family, and the swearing in as President of Corazon Aquino.

For bibliographies of the Philippines, see **Baradi** (1979) and the essays in **Hart** (1978, 1981) which also provide a survey of the state of Philippine studies. A general survey is **Bunge** (1984) and the three-volume study edited by **Haskins** (1982). **Steinberg** (1982) provides a good introduction to the modern Philippines and its history. On Philippines pre-history, see **Fox** (1979), **Jocano** (1975), and **Loofs** (1978). General histories of the Philippines are **Agoncillo** and **Guerrero** (1973), **Constantino** (1976), and **Phelan** (1959). On the Philippine revolution and nationalism, see **Agoncillo** (1956) and **Mahajani** (1971). For guides to source materials, archives, selections from the archives, translations of documents and a discussion of historiographical problems, see **Baradi** (1979), **Blair** and **Robertson** (1903-09), **Boxer** (1961), **Cruikshank** (1984), and **Scott** (1982, 1984); in addition **Larkin** (1979) and **May** (1987) discuss Philippine historiography and challenge traditional interpretations; see also the essays in **Stanley** (1984) reappraising the American period. On ethnic groups, see **LeBar** (1975), **Llamzon** (1978), and the bibliography by **Saito** (1972). On Muslim Filipinos, see **Gowing** (1974) and **Jocano** (1983), and the bibliographies by **Mashur** (1983) and **Tiamson** (1979). For the beginnings of Christianity in the Philippines, see **Sitoy** (1985). For works on law, including customary law, see the references in **Baradi** (1979, pp. 220-233), and **Fernandez** (1970). A survey of Philippine art and illustrative examples can be found in **Casal** (1981) and **Haskins** (1982, vol.3).

Language

The official national language of the Philippines is Pilipino, which is substantially based on Tagalog, the language spoken principally in Manila and the central provinces of Luzon. English is widely used as a *lingua franca* between speakers of different Philippine languages as well as in higher education and official and international communications. A bilingual (Pilipino and English) educational policy from primary to tertiary levels was instituted in 1974.

Spanish, the language of many written works in the colonial period, was by the end of Spanish rule spoken by only about 10% of the population and declined still further after the introduction of the American educational system. A creole language, Chavacaro, did, however, emerge and survives to this day (and indeed is the majority language in Zamboanga city). A revised national language, Filipino, which would be constructed from a number of Philippine languages rather than just Tagalog, was proposed in the 1973 constitution, but this has not yet progressed far.

It is generally agreed that the Philippine languages belong to the Western branch of Austronesian languages and fall into three large groups: Northern Philippine, Meso-Philippine, and Southern Philippine. There is some dispute about the attribution of languages to groups and sub-groups, as well as about the exact number of Philippine languages and dialects.

The 1975 census recorded 73 indigenous languages spoken as a first language by over 1,000 individuals in the Philippines. Eight Philippine languages are spoken by over 86% of the population, in the following proportions: Cebuano (Sebuano) 24.1%; Tagalog 21%; Ilocano 11.7%; Hiligaynon 10.4%; Bikol 7.8%; Waray-Waray 5.5%; Pampangan 3.2%; and Pangasinan 2.45%. Cebuano, Hiligaynon and Waray-Waray are very often referred to as Visayan, or Bisayan. The first four languages listed are also widely spoken as second languages and possess extensive bodies of written literature.

Tagalog is the most dominant language in the country by virtue of its position as the basis of Pilipino. It is the language of the Luzon region, in which Manila, the capital and political and communications centre of the country, is situated. A great many Tagalog films and television programmes are produced in Manila, as is most of the non-English literature of the country, including the popular Tagalog *komiks*.

On the development of the national language, see **Gonzalez** (1980). Descriptions of the languages of the Philippines, their consonantal and vowel systems and grammar together with bibliographical references are given in **Llamzon** (1978); see also **Constantino** (1971c), **Reid** (1981), and the bibliography by **Makarenko** (1981). **McFarland** (1981) provides a linguistic atlas and a description of the language groups. On the influence of Spanish on Tagalog, see **Bowen** (1971); **Lopez** (1944) lists English loan words and describes foreign language influences in general ; on Malay loan words in Tagalog, see **Wolff** (1976) who also comments on English and Spanish loan words.

Dictionaries of the major languages are: English-Tagalog, **Panganiban** (1965-66); Tagalog-English, **Panganiban** (1973). Cebuano-English, **Wolff** (1972), **Yap** (1971); English-Cebuano, **Cabonce** (1983). Ilokano-English, **Constantino** (1971a). Hiligaynon-English, **Motus** (1971). Bikol-English, **Mintz** and **Roasario Britanico** (1985). An etymological dictionary of the new language, Filipino, is being compiled by **Zorc** (1979-). Grammars are: for Tagalog, **Llamzon** (1976), **Ramos** and **Guzman** (1971), **Schachter** and **Otanes** (1972); for Cebuano, **Bunye** and **Yap** (1971a/b); for Ilokano, **Constantino** (1971b); for Hiligaynon, **Wolfendon** (1971). For additional references on grammars, dictionaries and teaching materials, see **Johnson** (1976) and **Reid** (1981).

Script

The existence of indigenous Philippine writing systems, syllabic scripts of Indic origin, is recorded in early Spanish accounts of the country. There are various theories about the history of these scripts, their transmission to the Philippines and the way they were used.

One theory favoured is that the scripts are in fact one script which evolved variations at the hands of different scribes. The script is thought to have come into the archipelago about 1000 AD, but the earliest datable writing is the Calatagan pot of about the 14th or 15th century AD. Writing in the Philippine syllabic script has been found on bamboo, palm leaves, tree bark and pottery but it does not appear to have been used for stone or copper plate inscriptions as it was in other countries of the region. The Spanish used the script in parallel texts, including the first book printed in the Philippines, but they rotated the characters ninety degrees. The Roman alphabet was brought to the Philippines by the Spanish and was increasingly used for all Philippine languages. Spanish orthography has gradually been changed by American influence. In the Southern Philippines, the Arabic script is also used.

For discussion and analysis of different theories concerning the indigenous syllabic scripts, and for examples, see **Francisco** (1973); also **Scott** (1984), and **Villamor** (1922).

Printing and Development of the Press

Printing was introduced to the Philippines by the Spanish. The earliest printed book was the *Doctrina Christiana*, printed in 1593 by the xylographic method. The bilingual (Tagalog and Spanish) text was printed on facing pages, with the Tagalog text in Philippine syllabic script. Between 1593 and 1648, 81 books (of which 24 were in Tagalog) were published by the printing presses of the various religious orders.

The majority of publications were grammars and dictionaries, together with catechisms and confessions in various Philippine languages (a Visayan catechism was published in 1610 and an Ilocano version in 1621).

Many early works were printed by Tomas Pinpin, regarded as the father of Philippines printing. Pinpin produced fourteen books on the presses of the Dominicans and Jesuits. He is credited with printing *Sucesos felices*, the first newsletter in the Philippines, in 1637 (with a second issue in 1639). In addition, *hojas volantes* (fly sheets) have been found dating back to 1799. They carried the title '*Al publico*' and acted as 'town criers' for the Spanish in the Philippines. The first newspaper, the Spanish language *Del Superior Gobierno*, began only in 1811. It was published to provide the Spanish colonists with information about events in Europe. There followed a number of short-lived newspapers. The strict censorship exercised by the Government and the Church was a great hindrance to newspaper publishing. But in the more liberal climate of the second half of the 19th century, newspaper publishing expanded. The first vernacular newspaper, *El Pasig*, began in 1862, and was published fortnightly in a bilingual Spanish and Tagalog edition. The first daily newspaper in Tagalog, *Diariong Tagalog*, was founded in 1882 by del Pilar, who a few years later in Spain with other intellectual exiles (the Propagandists), founded *La Solidaridad*. *El Icano*, a more nationalistic paper, began in 1889. In 1886 the first Cebu paper, *El Boletin de Cebu*, was started.

The Philippine press played an outstanding role in the revolution against Spain, but *La Solidaridad* (1889-95), considered the mouthpiece of the revolution, was published in Spain and smuggled into the Philippines. *La Independencia*, begun in 1898, was especially important. The secret revolutionary organization, the *Katipunan*, founded by Andres Bonifacio, used Tagalog for most of its communications and its paper, *Kalayaan*.

After the American occupation, numerous English newspapers emerged, but Spanish and indigenous language papers also continued. The Tagalog paper, *Liwayway*, for instance, was founded in 1922 and was an important outlet for Tagalog literature. The first American newspaper to appear continuously was the *Manila Times*, established in October 1898 and published under various owners until 1930. In September 1945, the *Manila Times* was the name chosen for the first English newspaper to be published after peace was restored.

In the post-independence period the Philippines press was relatively free from censorship. But the imposition of martial law by President Marcos in 1972 stopped the publication of many newspapers. The government controlled paper, the *Daily Express*, rapidly increased its circulation. Non-English publications such as *Balita ng Maynila* and *Liwayway*, which were owned by Marcos employees, also benefited in the martial law period.

As in other fields of writing, the English language press has presented a challenge to the vernacular press, but both have continued to exist side by side.

Taylor (1927) gives a history of the early Philippine press, and **Lent** (1982) covers the press in the 1970s. On newspapers and mass media in general, see also **Feliciano** and **Icban** (1967), and **Lent** (1971), and the bibliographies by **Jesus** (1976) and **Lent** (1975). **Saito** and **Mak** (1984) provide an international union list of Philippine newspapers.

Cover of Spanish language journal published Manila 1859-60

Literature

Although some of the population of the Philippines used writing prior to the arrival of the Spanish, they do not appear to have used it for literary purposes. Transmission of narrative was oral and this tradition is still alive in some areas. Several regional epics have been recorded and translated, but there is still work to be done in this field. Two epics are recorded from the Christian lowland groups, the Iloko *Lam-ang* and the Bikol *Handiong*; from the non-Christian groups of Luzon six are reported of which the best known are the Ifugao *Hudhud* and the Kalinga *Ullalim*; one epic has been recorded from the Visayas, the *Hinilawod*; several texts have been reported or partially recorded from groups on Mindanao, and among the Muslims of Mindanao at least five epics have been reported. Epics are metrical in form and are performed for an audience, sometimes accompanied by music. **E. A. Manuel** (1969) has provided a typological description which suggests the inner richness of the epic tradition. Another form of early indigenous literature is proverbs and riddles.

Some are quoted in a Tagalog-Spanish dictionary which, although published in 1754, was compiled in the course of the preceding century.

The Spanish brought new literary forms which, while retaining a Spanish or Spanish-derived name, were adapted and influenced by the absorption of indigenous elements. The replacement of indigenous belief systems by Christianity and the spread of literacy challenged oral literature and the old epic narrative. Creative changes took place in folk forms as foreign forms were syncretised. Yet, despite the influence of Spanish forms (and later of English/American writing), scholars have remarked upon the persistent presence of indigenous elements in the development of Tagalog literature. For example, in the first printed Tagalog literary work, a Christian poem published in *Memorial de la vida cristiana* (1605), the poetic structure and the imagery derive from pre-colonial traditions. The Spanish translated many works — particularly lives of the saints — into local languages. In 1712 Father Antonio de Borja's translation, *Barlaan at Josaphat*, was published. The story tells of the two saints' work in converting India to Christianity, but it has also been suggested that the ultimate source of the story is an account of the Buddha's youth.

Two narrative verse forms introduced by the Spanish became integral parts of the Filipino imagination. These were the metrical romance, *corrido* and the *pasyon*. The *pasyon* is an account of the life of Christ focusing on his suffering, crucifixion and resurrection. It is printed, but during Holy Week it may be read aloud or chanted (*pabasa*) and it may be dramatised on stage (*sinakulo* or passion play). The nine major linguistic groups of Luzon and Visayas possess versions of the *pasyon* — the oldest being Iloko from 1621 (although this is thought to be a translation of the work of St. Vincent Ferrer). The *pasyon* literature exemplifies the use of indigenous modes in the Christian cause. The most numerous versions of the *pasyon* are in Tagalog, commencing in 1704

Filipino rural life, 1860

with the *Ang Mahul na Pasion ni Jesu Christong Panginoon Natin* by Don Gaspar Aquino de Belen. This and later *pasyons* were extremely popular. Aquino de Belen's work was reprinted five times by 1760 and served as the basis for subsequent Tagalog *pasyons*. Aquino de Belen's work was the first written narrative poem in the history of Tagalog literature.

The *corrido* (in Pampangan *kuriru*) is also known as *buhay* and *historia* by the Tagalogs, while the counterpart of *buhay* among Ilokos is *panagbiag* and among Visays is *bida* or *vida*. These terms refer to an extended verse narrative of the life and adventures of a person, or group of persons, who are usually of the nobility. In Tagalog literature, a distinction came to be drawn between *corrido* and *awit*, the former written in octosyllabic, the latter in dodecasyllabic lines. Other distinctions have also been made, that *corrido* presents heroic characters with magical powers and is meant to be read aloud, whereas the *awit* does not employ the supernatural and is set to music. Introduced into the Philippines at the end of the 16th century, the themes of the *corrido* lie in a narrow and predictable vein, most conspicuously that of romantic love or religious-didactic themes. There are strong influences in the *corrido* and the *awit* from the European romance cycles, Spanish history, the Bible and other Christian sources. Both styles of verse narrative were prominent in the 18th and 19th centuries.

An important and transitional work is *Florante at Laura*, a narrative poem in the *awit* tradition, by Francisco Baltazar, better known as Balagtas (1788-1862). It was printed in 1838 by the Colegio de Santo Tomao, although there is no extant copy of this edition. In the course of the next hundred years, twenty-five Tagalog editions are known to have been published and it was also translated into other Philippine languages. *Florante at Laura* is considered a masterpiece of Tagalog literature. It broke new ground in the use of Tagalog as a literary medium and in the creative adaptation of narrative verse forms as a vehicle for socially relevant material. Balagtas used allegory, symbolism and veiled satire to conceal from the censors his condemnation of the evils of Spanish rule.

Glimpses of life can also be found in another literary form, the manuals of conduct. An example of this type of work is the anonymous *Lagda sa pagca maligdon sa tauong Bisaya,* first published in 1734 and republished in four more editions in the 19th century. This work is generally considered a landmark in Cebuano literature because of its immense popularity and the quality of its language.

Theatrical forms were also borrowed from the Spanish and the earliest known form is the *komedya* or *moro-moro* which was originally created by Spanish priests. The theme of the *komedya* was the defeat of the Muslims by Christian armies. Balagtas wrote over a hundred *komedya*, while his mentor, José de la Cruz (Huseng Sisiw) was another leading author of *komedya*. Towards the end of the 19th century the *zarzuela* or operetta was borrowed from Spain and given local life. It was seen as a refreshing departure from the *komedya* which it ousted and the earlier *zarzuela* reflected the political ferment of their age, but this form, too, gradually became stylized and static. With the introduction of the cinema and other new forms of entertainment in the 1920s the theatrical traditions of *zarzuela* declined in popularity.

The most famous Philippine novels are *Noli me Tangere* (1887) and *El*

Filibusterismo (1891), both written in Spanish by the Filipino nationalist, José Rizal, but not published in the Philippines until the American period. Rizal's novels are a powerful denunciation of the unjust social and political conditions of the Philippines under Spanish rule. Predating Rizal's first novel by two years is Pedro Alejandro Paterno's *Ninay: costumbres Filipinas*, published in Madrid in 1885. While lacking the powerful social realism and literary talent of Rizal's work, it is historically significant for its depiction of the life of the Tagalog nobility. The first Tagalog novel was Gabriel Beato Francisco's *Cababalaghan ni P. Brava*, serialized in the Tagalog paper *Ang Kapatid ng Bayan* in 1899. The turn of the century saw a spate of Tagalog novels and novels in other Philippine languages appeared within a decade. A much renowned Ilokano novel is Pena Grisalogo's *Mining Wenno Ayat Ai Cararua*, published in 1914.

One of the best known Tagalog authors of this early period was Lope K. Santos. His novel, *Banaag at Sikat* (1906) although full of romance contained a message of social agitation and has been cited as a source of inspiration of the Hukbalahap movement. Another work which combines romance with social criticism is Faustino Aguilar's *Ang Lihim ng Isang Puto* (1927). Later social realist novels include Antonio G. Sempio's *Punyal na Ginto* (1933). A much respected novel about World War II is Lazaro Francisco's *Sugat ng Alaala* (1949). The same author made trenchant criticism of post-war Filipino society in *Maganda Pa ang Daigdig*. Another work in this mode is *Pagkamulat ni Magdalena* (1958) by Alejandro G. Abodilla and Elpidio Kapulong. Much has been written with a focus on tenancy problems - see, for instance, Dominador Merasol's *Ginto ang Kayamangging Lupa* (1975-6). Such writings are, however, a minority in that the majority of Tagalog novels published are popular romances. To some extent, too, there has been a tendency to consider writing in English to be more significant and sophisticated. These views are challenged by **Reyes** (1982) in his examination of Tagalog novels from 1905-1975.

The short story developed more slowly than the novel. Beginning in the early years of the 20th century, short stories were published in newspapers and periodicals. A newspaper editor, Deogracias A. Rosario, is sometimes described as the father of the short story. The founding of the weekly magazine *Liwayway* did much to stimulate short story writing. Fresh literary influences contributed to the development of the genre during the war when the Japanese discouraged writing in English. Some authors who had formerly written in English introduced the style of Joyce, Hemingway and others to Tagalog writing. In the post-war decades many stories have been written on political themes.

In the field of free verse also, Japanese intervention led to an influx of new styles. Not only the Japanese *haiku*, but also the influence of such poets as Whitman, Sandburg and Cummings had an impact on free verse. The old Tagalog poetic form, the *tanoga*, also reappeared in the work of such authors as Alejandro G. Abadilla. Again, social criticism competed with romance as a central theme of modern poetry. Tagalog literature has also influenced that of other Philippine languages through translations. Regional literature is encouraged in many ways, by sponsorship of literary prizes and through publications in regional magazines and anthologies, but Tagalog still tends to predominate as a literary language.

In the 20th century the biggest challenge to Philippine vernacular literature has been the English language. Many Philippine authors chose English as their medium of expression and the first novel in English, Zoilo M. Galang's *A child of sorrow* was published in 1921. Many English language newspapers such as the *Free Press*, the *Graphic*, together with the monthly *Philippine Magazine* encouraged literary writing. The government established a Commonwealth Literary Award in 1939 and literary works displaying social consciousness and social realism won many prizes. English literature, like Spanish literature, had a productive influence on a variety of genres of indigenous literature. Much Philippine literature continues today to be written in English.

On the epic literature of the Philippines, see **Castro** (1983), **Galdon** (1980), **Manuel** (1958, 1969, 1975), **Maquiso** (1977), and **Realubit** (1983). **Pfeiffer** (1975) deals with the part played by music in epic performances. On riddles, see **Hart** (1964). On the stages of development of the *pasyon*, see **Tiongson** (1972), and on the importance of the *pasyon* from a non-literary perspective, see **Ileto** (1979). On *awit* and *corrido*, see **Eugenio** (1987). For bibliographical guidance and sources of Philippine literature, see **Baradi** (1979, pp. 241-256). A great deal has been written, not always of high quality, on all aspects of Philippine literature. **Bresnahan** (1976) and **Manuud** (1967) contain useful essays by, among others, Eugenio, Jocano and Lumbera. Two overall surveys of Philippine literature are **Castillo y Tuazon** and **Medina** (1972) and **Veloro, Enriquez** and **Alejandro** (1973). Other works of literary criticism and history are **Bernad** (1983), **Galdon** (1980), **Hosillos** (1984), **Lumbera** (1982, 1984), **Medina** (1981), **Mojares** (1983), and **San Juan** (1974) - many of these contain anthologies also. **Lumbera** (1968, 1969) examines Aquino de Belem's work and other Tagalog poetry. **Hernandez** (1976) covers the beginnings of modern drama. For the literatures of different language groups (including Tagalog), see also **Castro** (1981), **Eugenio** (1976), **Fernandez** (1978), **Foronda** (1976, 1978), **Luangco** (1982), **Mojares** (1975), **Realubit** (1983), **Reyes** (1982), **Zapanta-Manlapaz** (1981). On Philippine literature in English see **Abdul Majid** (1970) which includes a bibliography of publications 1921-66, and the essays in **Galdon** (1979); also, the article by **Bernad** (1981) which has an extensive bibliography and listing of anthologies.

Bibliography

Abdul Majid bin Nabi Baksh
1970 "The Philippine novel in English: a critical history." *Philippine social sciences and humanities review* 35, 1-2 (Mar - June): 1-193.

Agoncillo, Teodoro A.
1956 *The revolt of the masses: the story of Bonifacio and the Katipunan.* Quezon City: University of the Philippines Press.

Agoncillo, Teodoro A., and Milagros C. Guerrero
1973 *History of the Filipino people.* 4th edn., Quezon City: Garcia. (7th edn. published 1987 restores some portions cut from earlier editions).

Baradi, Edita R.
1979 *Southeast Asian research tools: the Philippines.* Honolulu: University of Hawaii. (Southeast Asia Paper No. 16, Part V).

Bernad, Miguel A.
1981 "Philippine literature in English: some sociological considerations." In Thom Seong Chee, ed. *Essays on literature and society in Southeast Asia.* Singapore: Singapore University Press, pp. 145-159.
1983 "Philippine literature: a two-fold renaissance." In M.A. Bernad, *Tradition and discontinuity: essays on Philippine history and culture.* Manila: National Book Store, pp. 3-26.

Blair, Emma H., and James A. Robertson (eds.)
1903-09 *The Philippine islands 1493-1898: explorations by early navigators.* Cleveland, Ohio: Clark. 55 vols. (Reprinted the Philippines, 1962).

Bowen, J. D.
1971 "Hispanic languages and influences in Oceania." In T. Sebeok, ed. *Current trends in linguistics.* Vol. 8: *Linguistics in Oceania.* The Hague: Mouton, pp. 938-952.

Boxer, C. R.
1961 "Some aspects of Spanish historical writing on the Philippines." In D. G. E. Hall, ed. *Historians of South East Asia.* London: Oxford University Press, pp. 200-212.

Bresnahan, Roger J. (ed.)
1976 *Literature and society: cross-cultural perspectives.* (Proceedings of the 11th American Studies Conference, Los Banos).

Bunge, F. (ed.)
1984 *Philippines: a country study.* Washington, D.C.: U.S. Govt. Printing. (American University, Foreign Area Studies, Area Handbooks Series).

Bunye, Maria Victoria R., and Elsa Paula Yap
1971a *Cebuano for beginners.* Honolulu: University of Hawaii Press. (PALI language texts: Philippines).
1971b *Cebuano grammar notes.* Honolulu: University of Hawaii Press. (PALI language texts: Philippines).

Cabonce, Rodolfo
1983 *An English-Cebuano Visayan dictionary.* Manila: Metro Manila.

Casal, Gabriel, et al.
1981 *The people and art of the Philippines.* Los Angeles: Museum of Cultural History, University of California, LA.

Castillo Y. Tuazon, Teofilo del and Buenaventura S. Medina
1972 *Philippine literature from ancient times to the present.* Quezon City: Teofilo del Castillo.

Castro, Jovita Ventura (ed.)
1983 *Epics of the Philippines.* (Quezon City): ASEAN Committee on Culture and Information. (Anthology of ASEAN Literatures: Philippines; 1).

Castro, Rosalinda Icban
1981 *Literature of the Pampangos.* Manila: University of the East Press.

Constantino, Ernesto A.
1971a *Ilokano dictionary.* Honolulu: University of Hawaii Press. (PALI language texts: Philippines).
1971b *Ilokano reference grammar.* Honolulu: University of Hawaii Press (PALI language texts: Philippines).
1971c "Tagalog and other major languages of the Philippines." In T.A. Sebeok, ed. *Current trends in linguistics, Vol. 8: Linguistics in Oceania.* The Hague: Mouton, pp. 112-154.

Constantino, Renato
1976 *A history of the Philippines: from Spanish colonization to the second world war.* New York: Monthly Review Press. (Published 1975 under title: *The Philippines: a past revisited*).

Cruikshank, Bruce
1984 *Filipiniana in Madrid: field notes on five major manuscript collections.* Honolulu: University of Hawaii Philippine Studies Program, Philippine Studies Program, (Philippine Studies Occasional Papers, 6).

Eugenio, Damiana L.
1976 "Tagalog literature." In R. J. Bresnahan, ed. *Literature and society: cross-cultural perspectives.* Los Banos.
1987 *Awit and corrido: Philippine metrical romances.* Manila: University of the Philippines Press.

Feliciano, Gloria D. and Crispulo J. Icban
1967 *Philippine mass media in perspective.* Quezon City: Capital.

Fernandez, Doreen G.
1978 *The Iloilo zarzuela, 1903-1930.* Quezon City: Ateneo de Manila University Press.

Fernandez, Perfecto V.
1970 *The Philippines. (Bibliographical introduction to legal history and ethnology).* J. Gilissen, ed., Section F/22. Brussels: Université Libre de Bruxelles, Institut de Sociologie.

Foronda, Marcelino A.
1976 *Kutibeng: Philippine poetry in Iloko, 1621-1971.* Manila: La Salle University.
1978 *Dallang: an introduction to Philippine literature in Ilokano and other essays.* Honolulu: University of Hawaii. (Philippine Studies Program, Occasional Papers, 2).

Fox, Robert B.
1979 "The Philippines during the first millenium BC" In R. B. Smith and W. Watson, eds. *Essays in archaeology, history and historical geography.* New York: Oxford University Press, pp. 227-241.

Francisco, Juan R.
1973 *Philippine palaeography.* Quezon City: Linguistic Society of the Philippines. (Special monograph issue of *Philippine Journal of Linguistics*, 3).

Galdon, Joseph A. (ed.)
1979 *Essays on the Philippine novel in English.* Quezon City: Ateneo de Manila University Press.
1980 *Salimbibig: Philippine vernacular literature.* Quezon City: Council for Living Traditions.

Gonzalez, A.B.
1980 *Language and nationalism: the Philippine experience thus far.* Manila: Ateneo de Manila Press.

Gowing, Peter G., and Robert D. Mcamis (eds.)
1974 *The Muslim Filipinos.* Manila: Solidaridad.

Hart, Donn V.
1964 *Riddles in Filipino folklore: an anthropological analysis.* Syracuse, N.Y.: Syracuse University Press.

Hart, Donn V. (ed.)
1978 *Philippine studies: history, sociology, mass media and bibliography.* DeKalb: Northern Illinois University. (Center for Southeast Asian Studies, Occasional Papers, 6).
1981 *Philipine studies: political science, economics, and linguistics.* DeKalb: Northern Illinois University. (Center for Southeast Asian Studies, Occasional Papers, 8).

Haskins, Jim (gen. ed.)
1982 *The Filipino nation.*
Vol. 1 *A concise history of the Philippines.* By Helen R. Tubagui, et. al.
Vol. 2 *The Philippines: lands and peoples, a cultural geography.* By Eric S. Casino.
Vol. 3 *Philippine art and literature.* By Felipe M. de Leon, Jr. (s.l.). Grolier International Inc., Philippines. (US Printed).

Hernandez, Thomas Capatan.
1976 *The emergence of modern drama in the Philippines, 1898-1912.* Honolulu: University of Hawaii, Philippine Studies. (Philippine Studies Working Paper, 1).

South-East Asia

Hosillos, Lucila.
1984 *Originality as vengeance in Philippine literature.* Quezon City: New Day.

Ileto, Reynaldo Clemena.
1979 *Pasyon and revolution: popular movements in the Philippines, 1840-1910.* Quezon City: Ateneo de Manila University Press.

Jesus, Emilinda V. de
1976 *Mass communications in the Philippines: an annotated bibliography.* Singapore: Asian Mass Communication Research and Information Center. (Asian Mass Communication Bibliography Series 4).

Jocano, F. Landa
1975 *Philippine pre-history: an anthropological overview of the beginnings of Filipino society and culture.* Diliman, Q.C.: Philippine Center for Advanced Studies, Universities of the Philippines System.
1983 *Filipino Muslims: their social institutions and cultural achievements.* Diliman, Q.C.: Asian Center, University of the Philippines.

Johnson, Dora E., et al.
1976 *A survey of materials for the study of uncommonly taught languages: pt. 7 Southeast Asia and the Pacific.* Arlington, Va.: Center for Applied Linguistics.

Larkin, John A. (ed.)
1979 *Perspectives on Philippine historiography: a symposium.* New Haven: Yale University South East Asian Studies. (Yale University Southeast Asia Studies Monograph Series, 21).

LeBar, Frank M. (ed.)
1975 *Ethnic groups of insular Southeast Asia. Vol. 2: Philippines and Formosa.* New Haven: HRAF Press.

Lent, John A.
1971 *Philippine mass communications: before 1811 after 1966.* (Manila) Philippine Press Institute.
1975 *Asian mass communication: a comprehensive bibliography.* (s.l.): Temple University, Philippines: pp.332-496.

Lent, John A (ed.)
1982 *Newspapers in Asia: contemporary trends and problems.* Hong Kong: Heinemann Asia. Philippines: pp. 267-280.

Llamzon, Teodoro A.
1976 *Modern Tagalog: a functional-structural description.* The Hague: Mouton.
1978 *Handbook of Philippine language groups.* Quezon City: Ateno de Manila University Press (for UNESCO).

Loofs, H. H. E.
1978 *Archäologie der Philippinen*. Leiden: Brill. *(Handbuch der Orientalistik.* 7. Abteilung *Kunst und Archäologie*, 6 Bd, 6 Abschnitt).

Lopez, Cecilio.
1944 "Foreign influences in Tagalog." *Philippine Review* 2,2: 43 -49.

Luangco, Gregorio C. (ed.)
1982 *Kandabao: essays on Waray language, literature and culture*. Tacloban City; Divine Word University Publications.

Lumbera, Bienvenido L.
1968 "Assimilation and synthesis, 1700-1800: Tagalog poetry in the eighteenth century." *Philippine Studies* 16: 622-62.
1969 "Consolidation of tradition in nineteenth century Tagolog poetry." *Philippine Studies* 17: 377-411.
1982 *Philippine literature: a history and anthology*. Manila: National Book Store.
1984 *Revaluation: essays on Philippine literature, cinema and popular culture*. (Manila): Index Press.

McFarland, Curtis D.
1981 *A linguistic atlas of the Philippines*. (Manila): De la Salle University and the Linguistic Society of the Philippines.

Mahajani, Usha.
1971 *Philippine nationalism: external challenge and Filipino response, 1565-1946*. St Lucia: University of Queensland Press.

Makarenko, Vladamir A.
1981 *A preliminary annotated bibliography of Filipino linguistics, 1604-1976*. Andrew Gonzalez and Carolina Nemenzo Sacris, eds. Manila: De la Salle University Libraries and Linguistic Society of the Philippines. (De la Salle University Libraries Bibliography Series, 3).

Manuel, E. Arsenio.
1958 *The maiden of the Buhong sky: a complete song from the Bagobo folk epic Tuwaang*. Quezon City: University of Philippines Press.
1969 *Agyu: the Ilianon epic of Mindano*. Manila: University of Santo Tomas.
1975 *Tuwaang attends a wedding*. Quezon Cituy: Ateneo de Manila University Press

Manuud, Antonio G. (ed.)
1967 *Brown heritage: essays on Philippine cultural tradition and literature*. Quezon City: Ateneo de Manila University Press.

Maquiso, Elena G.
1977 *Ulahingan: an epic of the Southern Philippines*. Dumaguete City: Siliman University.

Mashur bin Ghalib Jundam
1983 "Bibliography of Filipino Muslims." In F.L. Jocano, ed. *Filipino Muslims*. Diliman: Asian Center, University of the Philippines, pp. 147-196.

May, Glenn Anthony
1987 *A past recovered*. Quezon City: New Day.

Medina, B. S.
1981 "Pagbabago: the conscious commitment." In Tham Seong Chee, ed. *Essays on literature and society in Southeast Asia*. Singapore: Singapore University Press, pp. 125-144.

Mintz, Malcom, W. and J. del Rosario Britanico
1985 *Bicol - English dictionary: Diksionaryong Bikol - Ingles*. Quezon City: New Day.

Mojares, Resil B.
1975 *Cebuano literature: a survey and bio-bibliography*. Cebu City: University of San Carlos. (San Carlos Publications, Series A, no.10).
1983 *The origins and rise of the Filipino novel: a generic study of the novel until 1940* Quezon City: University of the Philippines Press.

Motus, Cecile B.
1971 *Hiligaynon dictionary*. Honolulu: University of Hawaii Press. (PALI language texts; Philippines.

Panganiban, Jose Villa.
1965-66 *Tesauro diksyunaryo Ingles - Pilipino*. San Juan, Rizal: Limbagan Pilipino. (Reprinted 1971).
1973 *Disyunaryo-tesauro Pilipino - Ingles*. Quezon City: Manlapaz.

Pfeiffer, William R.
1975 *Music in the Philippines, indigenous, folk, modern: an introductory survey*. (s.l.): Siliman Music Foundation.

Phelan, John Leddy.
1959 *The hispanization of the Philippines: Spanish aims and Filipino responses, 1565-1700*. Madison: University of Wisconsin Press.

Ramos, Terestia V. and Videa de Guzman
1971 *Tagalog for beginners*. Honolulu: University of Hawaii Press (PALI language text: Philippines).

Realubit, Marial Lilia F.
1983 *Bikol of the Philippines (: history, literature and general list of literary works)*. Naga City: AMS Press.

Reid, Lawrence A.
1981 "Philippine linguistics: the state of the art, 1970-80." In Donn V. Hart, ed. *Philippine studies: political science, economics and linguistics.* DeKalb: Northern Illinois University. (Center for Southeast Asia Studies Occasional Paper, 8).

Reyes, S.S.
1982 *Nobelang Tagalog, 1905-75: tradisyon et modernismo.* Manila: Ateneo de Manila University Press.

Saito, Shiro.
1972 *Philippine ethnography: a critically selected and annotated bibliography.* Honolulu: University Press of Hawaii. (East-West bibliographic series, 2).

Saito, Shiro and Alice W. Mak
Philippine newspapers: an international union list. Honolulu: University of Hawaii, Philippine Studies Program. (Philippine Studies Occasional Paper, 7).

San Juan, Epifanio (ed.)
1974 *Introduction to modern Pilipino literature.* New York: Twayne.

Schachter, P. and F. Otanes
1972 *Tagalog reference grammer.* Los Angeles: University of California Press.

Scott, William Henry.
1982 *Cracks in the parchment curtain and other essays on Philippine history.* Quezon City: New Day.
1984 *Prehispanic source material for the study of Philippine history.* Rev. edn. Manila: New Day. 1st edn. pub 1968).

Sitoy, T. Valentino
1985 *A history of Christianity in the Philippines, Vol 1: the initial encounter.* Quezon City: New Day.

Stanley, Peter W. (ed.)
1984 *Reappraising an empire: new perspectives on Philippine - American history.* Cambridge Mass.; London Committee on American - East Asian Relations of the Dept. of History in collaboration with the Council on East Asian Studies, Harvard University. (Harvard Studies in American - East Asian Relations, 10).

Steinberg, David J.
1982 *The Philippines: a singular and a plural place.* Boulder: Westview Press.

Taylor, Carson.
1927 *History of the Philippine press.* Manila: (n.p.).

Tiamson, Alfredo T.
1979 *The Muslim Filipinos: an annotated bibliography.* Manila: Filipinas Foundation.

Tiongson, Nicanor G.
1972 "Pasyon." In M. A. and A. Foronda, eds. *Samtoy: essays on Iloko history and culture.* Manila: United Pub. Co.

Veloro, A. T., S. R. Enriquez, and R. Alejandro
1973 *A study of the types of Philippine literature with special emphasis on the novel.* Manila: Philippine Book Company.

Villamor, Ignacio
1922 *La antigua escritura Filipina.* Manila: Tip. Pontifica del Colegio del Santo Thomas.

Wolfenden, Elmer P.
1971 *Hiligaynon reference grammer.* Honolulu: University of Hawaii Press. (PALI Language text: Philippines.

Wolff, John U.
1972 *A dictionary of Cebuano Visayana.* 2 vols. Ithaca: Cornell University, Southeast Asia Program. (Linguistic Series VI, Data Paper 87).
1976 "Malay borrowings in Tagalog." In C. D. Cowan and O. W. Wolters, eds. *Southeast Asian history and historiography: essays presented to D.G.E. Hall.* Ithaca; London: Cornell University Press, pp. 345-367.

Yap, Elsa Paula
1971 *Cebuano-Visayan dictionary.* Honolulu: University of Hawaii Press. (PALI language texts: Philippines).

Zapanta-Manlapaz, Edna.
1981 *Kapampangan literature: a historical survey and anthology.* Quezon City: Ateneo de Manila University Press.

Zorc, R. David Paul.
1979- *Core etymological dictionary of Filipino.* Batchelor (N.T.): Darwin Community College. Fasc 1-3 pub; in progress.

Overseas Chinese

There have been Chinese communities in all the countries of South-East Asia for many years and in some parts of the region for centuries. They have become integrated and acculturated into their host societies in varying degrees, quite substantially in a few cases where inter-marriage and adoption of the local language, religion and culture has occurred (most notably among the Thai elite in the 19th and 20th centuries). In other cases the Chinese until recently remained entirely separate, keeping to their original languages and customs.

The earliest accounts of more or less permanent Chinese communities in South-East Asia relate to Cambodia in the 13th century, where numerous Chinese lived and married, and Palembang (Sumatra) in the 14th century. Many Chinese settled in Java in the 17th century after the Dutch established their base at Batavia and thousands of Chinese gold miners settled in West Kalimantan and the Malay Peninsula in the late 18th century. The strongest stimulation to Chinese immigration occurred after about 1870 when there was a great demand for labour on the plantations and in the mines of colonial Malaya and Indonesia as well as in railroad-building in Thailand. The southern Chinese provinces of Fukien and later Kwangtung were the main sources of migrants: virtually none came from the north. Although large numbers of migrants returned home in due course, many stayed and by 1970 there were nearly 15 million Chinese in South-East Asia. Malaysia, Thailand and Indonesia each have populations of more than 3 million. In 1970 some 40% of Malaysians were Chinese. As a proportion of the total population, they formed in Thailand about 10%; Vietnam 3.5%; Philippines 1.4%; Laos 2%; Cambodia 6.4%; Indonesia 2.6% and Burma 1.6%. The Chinese proportion was largest in Singapore where it constituted 74.5% of the total.

The standard work on the Chinese in South-East Asia, providing information and bibliographical references on the history of the Chinese in each South-East Asian country is **Purcell** (1965). Other useful studies are **Somers-Heidhues** (1974), **Wang Gungwu** (1959, 1978) and **Yong** (1981). **Gosling** and **Lim** (1983) is a multi-disciplinary collection of recent case studies of the Chinese in contemporary South-East Asia. Among the works dealing with the Chinese in a particular country are: on the Chinese in Thailand, **Coughlin** (1960), **Skinner** (1957); in Cambodia, **Wilmott** (1967); in Sarawak, **Chin** (1981); in Indonesia, **Coppell** (1983), **Mackie** (1976), **Suryadinata** (1978a/b, 1979); in the Philippines, **Felix** (1966), **Wickberg** (1965), **Weightman** (1959).

Further sources for bibliographical references are **Clammer** (1981a), **Hendrati** (1975), **Lau Teik Soon** (1976), **Mackie** (1976), **Nagelkerke** (1982), **Nevadomsky** and **Li** (1970), **Parichart Sukhum** (1976), **See Chinben** (1972) and **Uchida** (1960).

Dating Systems

The vast majority of Chinese publications employ the Christian era dating system. For Chinese dating systems, see **Philips** (1963).

Printing and Development of the Press

The first Chinese presses in South-East Asia appear to have been established by missionaries with the help of printers procured from China. In 1815 the *Ch'ai shih-su mei-yueh t'ung-chi-ch'uan* (Chinese Monthly Magazine), edited by William Milne (1785-1822) of the London Missionary Society, was started in Malacca (Melaka). The magazine, which was not merely concerned with missionary matters, was sent to many Chinese settlements in the archipelago and mainland South-East Asia. Milne's Anglo-Chinese Press (also called the Anglo-Chinese College Press) primarily used wood-block printing for its publications in Chinese.

It was not until the late 1870s that Chinese businessmen apparently started to launch their own printing works. The oldest which has been traced is the Koh Yew Hean Press founded in Singapore in about 1877. Little is known about its owner, Lin Heng-nan, a native of the islet of Chin-men, in the province of Fukien. He was not an ordinary merchant since he wrote at least two works which were printed by means of xylographs in his own printing shop. The first book is a manual for Chinese to learn Malay. It appeared in 1877 and was reprinted in 1883 with a preface from the Ch'ing consul Tso Tsu-hsing. The Koh Yoh Hean Press also printed works in Malay (in Arabic as well as Latin scripts) and in English. Lithography was generally used for printing Chinese until the introduction of movable types from China at the beginning of the 20th century. In the Dutch East Indies the first Chinese printers appeared in the early 1880s. They obtained their printing presses from the Dutch and until the beginning of the 20th century exclusively published books and newspapers in romanized Malay.

Lat Pau, published in Singapore from 1881, was the first Chinese-run, Chinese language newspaper in South-East Asia. *Lat Pau* was modelled on Chinese papers in Hong Kong and Shanghai, although it was only as recently as 1872 that the earliest Chinese newspaper had been established in China. Its editor-in-chief Yeh Chi-yun was a scholar from the province of An-hui who had previously worked in Hong Kong for the *Chung Ngoi San Po*. In the Philippines, in 1888, the *Hua Pao* was begun but lasted only a short time. Numerous other Chinese newspapers succeeded it during the following years. In the 1890s short-lived papers also appeared in Penang, Kuala Lumpur and Rangoon.

It was mainly at the turn of the century, however, that a proliferation of Chinese publishing occurred in connection with the arrival of Chinese political refugees: reformers like K'ang Yu-wei and revolutionaries like Sun Yat Sen. Both groups were in search of the financial support of the South Seas Chinese communities. They launched newspapers owned by local capitalists but run by journalists from China. Their aim was to plead their respective political causes and serious battles were waged on paper between the rival newspapers. In Thailand the *Mei-nan Jih-pao*, a paper favourable to the cause of revolution, was established in 1905 and was succeeded by *Hua-hsien Jih-pao* in 1907. In Surabaya a revolutionary paper *Szu-pin Jih-pao* is reported to have commenced in 1903, but only lasted a short time.

Hua To Pao was started in Batavia under the auspices of the newly-created Chinese Reading Club in 1909. It was banned by the Dutch authorities. The main bases of the political protagonists were Singapore, Penang and Rangoon. Only a few of these pioneering newspapers have been preserved in various collections that still need to be systematically catalogued.

Between the wars Chinese newspapers flourished in some parts of South-East Asia. In Thailand, for instance, they had a brief florescence in 1925-9 and later fluctuated according to the political climate, in particular the prevailing government restrictions.

Other Chinese publishing occurred in the first half of the 20th century in such places as Saigon and Hanoi. Printing works existed also in smaller provincial centres such as Ipoh and Penang in Malaysia and Makassar, Medan, Semarang and Surabaya in Indonesia. Chinese daily newpapers were published in all these places.

During the post-World War II period noteworthy features of Chinese publishing have been the increasing number of Chinese dailies and periodicals all over South-East Asia, the rivalry between Communist and Nationalist (Kuomintang) papers and the survival of a rather neutral press. Thus, in Thailand, the *Hua-ch'iao Jih-pao* (founded in 1928) became in 1950 increasingly pro-communist, but folded the following year; the *Hsing-hsien Jih-pao* of the newspaper chain of Aw Boon Haw (the Tiger Balm 'King') was for a short time pro-communist before developing a neutral trend. In Jakarta *Sheng-huo pao* represented the most left-wing view in the 1950s while *Tien-sheng Jih-pao* was the organ of the Kuomintang and *Sin Po* the advocate of a neutral attitude.

Suspicion of Chinese language newspapers led to their suppression in the 1960s and the 1970s in many parts of South-East Asia. Their demise was especially dramatic in Indonesia where the abortive Communist Gestapu coup of 1965 ended the already shaky career of the Chinese press in the Republic. After this time only a government-sponsored Chinese paper remained. Even in Singapore the government compelled the *Nan-yang Siang-pau* (founded in 1923 by Tan Kah Kee) and the *Sin Chew Jit Poh* (founded 1929) — the former two big rivals — to merge in 1983.

In Malaysia, *Nan-yang Siang-Pau*, the largest Chinese language publisher, came under the sway of the governing political party during the 1970s. Furthermore, the government trading corporation, PERNAS, owns the large Chinese dailies *Sin Chew Jit Poh* and *Sing Pin*. In Thailand the leading Chinese-language daily is *Hsing-hsien Jin pao*, which commenced publication in 1950.

On early missionary publishing, see **Byrd** (1970), **Ibrahim** (1982) and **O'Sullivan** (1980). **Tan Yok Song** (1958) discusses *Lat Pau* and its editor; see also **Ho Soo Miang** (1979). Information on the development and state of Chinese publishing in different South-East Asian countries may be found in **Asia Library Services** (1977), **Blaker** (1965), **Chen Mong Hock** (1967), **Ho Soo Miang** (1979), **Hsieh Yu Yong** (1964), **Lent** (1982), **Liem Thian Joe** (1939), **Liu Tzu-Cheng** (1966), **Lu Wei Lin** (1967), **Salmon** (1981), **Skinner** (1951), **Suryadinata** (1971), **Tan** (1972), **Tay** (1973), **Wilmott** (1960) and **Yanjong Jareeyapas** (1976).

Literature

Although the Chinese form a significant segment of the populations of many South-East Asian countries, western scholars have given surprisingly little attention to their writings. For this reason it is impossible to present more than a rudimentary introduction to Chinese language materials. Although this section is concerned with Chinese language writing it should be noted that the Chinese often wrote in the indigenous languages of South-East Asia. Even Chinese language newspapers have sometimes had supplements in local languages. Increasingly scholars are appreciating that the Chinese have made significant contributions to the indigenous literature of South-East Asia. Popular Chinese fiction as well as cloak-and-dagger stories have been translated into the various local languages and serialized in the press and even published in book form from the 1860s onwards (first in Thailand and later in Indonesia, Malaysia and Vietnam). Sometimes these translations were only in manuscript form, as is the case with Cambodian, Javanese and Makassarese versions. Modern fiction from China is also published in South-East Asian languages: Lu Hsun's works, for example, were printed in Indonesian and in Burmese. Simultaneously, Chinese writers also contributed to the development of South-East Asian literatures by writing in the local languages.

Chinese language literature in South-East Asia has been overlooked by Western scholars. The only studies devoted to this significant development have been carried out by researchers based within the area and are mostly written in Chinese. They mainly focus on the literature in colloquial Chinese (called *Ma-hua wenhsueh*) that emerged and developed in Malaysia and Singapore since 1919 following migration of Chinese intellectuals towards the South Seas. Very little is known about the literary production of the Chinese of Thailand, Philippines, Burma, Vietnam and Cambodia. It is therefore possible only to indicate the variety of categories of Chinese writing and say something brief about their contents.

Newspapers are the most common form for Chinese writing in South-East Asia. They are usually concerned with both local and international news and some, such as the *Fookien Times* (*Hsien-Min Jih-pao*) published in the Philippines, take a general interest in the overseas Chinese community in South-East Asia. Since the early 1920s a number of newspapers have given considerable space to literary matters ranging from essays and poetry to serialized novels. Some even have literary supplements. In the late 1920s, compared to Thailand where the newspapers merely reprinted literary works taken from newspapers published in China, those of Singapore and Malaysia printed much literature emanating from writers based in the South Seas. The first literary works printed in book form appeared in 1924. But until World War II the great majority of the literary output was published in newspapers. Many books have been published in Singapore and Malaysia since the late 1940s. But in other countries, Cambodia for example, the press which commenced just before World War II remained the main forum for literary production. Up to the present, Hong Kong and Taiwan still remain the publishing centres which attract overseas Chinese writers, especially those of Thailand, the Philippines and Indonesia.

The literature produced in the South Seas from the early 1920s up to World War II cannot be separated from the successive trends that emerged in China during this period. Writers were concerned with the political situation in the motherland and, above all, with Japanese aggression which gave rise to a literature of resistance. However, very early in the 1920s, the Chinese writers based in the South Seas became conscious of the need for a literature that was influenced by the South-East Asian environment and suited to local readers. A theory for the development of a literature taking its roots in the host countries and consequently called *Nan-yang wen-hsueh* (or 'Literature of the South Seas') arose. This literature was of a rather political character — often anti-feudal and anti-imperialist — and developed in Malaysia and Singapore between the wars. Many works focused on two themes: the vision of the Chinese businessman (the *Taoke*) and the fate of the Chinese coolie.

Poetry, both classical and modern, also attracted many writers. At the end of the last century, a poetry club was established in Singapore and later also in Thailand and Burma. The Chinese poetry of Vietnam, in particular, is said to have achieved a particularly high standard.

As regards non-fiction, Chinese language books have been published on many topics. Those dealing with the South-East Asian Chinese community itself fall into two groups. Firstly, those emanating from private persons and associations which are of a rather commemorative character, but nevertheless contain a lot of valuable information; they are in the form of souvenir magazines of professional associations, high schools, daily newspapers and regional associations. In this group-biographies of eminent leaders as well as autobiographies can also be included. Secondly, researches in the social sciences emanating from scholars mostly based in Singapore and Malaysia that focus on a wide range of topics. These include: the history of the first Chinese settlements in the area traced through epigraphical documents (tombstones, commemorative inscriptions kept in temples and other collective buildings); the history of the first relations between China and the South Seas up to the establishment of the first Manchu consulate in Singapore; the social structure of local Chinese communities; the political life of the Chinese diaspora since the end of the last century; Chinese culture and education; economic activities of the Chinese diaspora and temples, and religious life of the Chinese.

Among the studies on mainland China published in the region or in Hong Kong are diaries of Nanyang Chinese who have visited their homeland. Numerous Chinese language books and articles focus on the host countries of South-East Asia. There exist, for instance, travel notes, histories of individual countries, geographies and language books (dictionaries and grammars of South-East Asian languages) and translations of local fiction. Finally, some of the text books for Chinese schools which have been published in South-East Asia are translations of Western-language works.

A pioneering discussion and bibliography of Chinese writings in romanized Malay is found in **Salmon** (1977). In addition, **Salmon** (1981) provides an account of the development of this literature and an extensively annotated bibliography in the case of Indonesia. See also **Clammer** (1981b) writing on the Straits Chinese literature, **Ding Choo Ming** (1978) and **Kwee** (1977) on Peranakan Chinese literature of Indonesia. **Salmon** and **Lombard** (1974) discuss the translation of Chinese novels into Malay, together with some information and references on translations into Javanese. On *dondang sayanag* (sung poetry), see **Thomas** (1986).

On recent studies on the literature of the Chinese in Malaysia and Singapore, see **Salmon** (1983a). On Chinese writing in some other South-East Asian countries, see **Lee Ju-Lin** (1970). **Yang Sungnian** and **Chou Weichieh** (1980) discuss the literary supplements of Chinese newspapers. **Chao Jung** (1979) and **Goh Thean Chye** (1975) identify Chinese literary publications in Singapore and Malaysia. **Lim Buan Chay** (1978) and **Wong Seng Tong** (1978, 1980) examine the influence of China's literary movements. On the literature of the inter-war period, see **Fang Hsiu** (1977) and **Miao Hsui** (1966). **Salmon** (1983b) provides a recent discussion of novels and short stories from Indonesia, Malaysia and Thailand. On the overseas Chinese poetry, see **Ho Khai-Leong** (1980), **Ho Kuang-Chung** (1967) and **I Chun-Tso** (1956, 1977). Other information and references on Chinese literature may also be found in **Chao Jung** (1979), **Fang Hsiu** (1972), **Ly Singko** (1967), **Miao Hsui** (n.d.), **Wang Gungwu** (1964), **Wong Seng Tong** (1978) and **Yu Wang-Luen** (1967, 1982). On commemorative, non-fictional Chinese publications, see **Tay Lian Soo** and **Gwee Yee Hean** (1975); also **De Beer-Luong** (1982). On epigraphical sources, see **Salmon** (1974); **Yong** (1977) writes on the social structure of the Chinese communities and **Tay Lian Soon** (1982) and **Wu Hua** (1976) deal with Chinese culture and education; **Lin Hsia Sheng** (1975) discusses tombs and the religious life of the overseas Chinese. Finally, an impression of the range of Chinese publications from South-East Asia can be obtained from **Chao Jung** (1979), **Goh Thean Chye** (1975), **Hsu Yun-Ts'iao** (1959, 1965), **Oey** (1953) and **Shu** and **Wan** (1968). Also, the Nanyang University in Singapore has produced an *Index to Chinese periodical literature on Southeast Asia, 1905-66.*

Bibliography

Asia Library Services
1977 *A guide to research materials on Thailand and Laos.* Auburn, New York: Asia Library Services.

Blaker, J. R.
1965 "The Chinese newspapers in the Philippines: toward the definition of a tool." *Asian Studies* (Manila) 3, 2: 243-261.

Byrd, C. K.
1970 *Early printing in the Straits Settlements 1806-1858.* Singapore: Singapore National Library.

Chao Jung
1979 *Singapore-Malaysia Chinese literature dictionary.* Singapore: Educational Publications Bureau. (In Chinese).

Chen Mong Hock
1967 *Early Chinese newspapers in Singapore 1881-1912.* Singapore: Singapore National Library.

Chen Su-Ching
1945 *China and Southeastern Asia.* Chungking.

Chin, John M.
1981 *The Sarawak Chinese.* Kuala Lumpur: Oxford University Press.

Chui Kwei Chiang
1963 "Malayan Chinese newspapers and the Chinese civil war." *Journal of the South Seas Society* 38, 1-2: 1-60.

Clammer, John R.
1981a "French studies on the Chinese in Indochina; a bibliographical survey." *JSEAS* 12,1: 15-26.
1981b "Straits Chinese literature: a minority literature as a vehicle of identity." In Tham Song Cheee, ed. *Essays on literature and society in Southeast Asia.* Singapore: Singapore University Press, pp. 287-302.

Coppell, Charles A.
1983 *Indonesian Chinese in crisis.* Kuala Lumpur: Oxford University Press.

Coughlin, R. J.
1960 *Double identity: the Chinese in modern Thailand.* Hong Kong: Hong Kong University Press.

De Beer-Luong, B.
1982 "Les tribulations d'un journaliste chinois dans les mers du sud." *Archipel* 23: 109-118.

Ding Choo Ming
1978 "An introduction to the Indonesian Peranakan Chinese literature in the Library of the Universiti Kebangsaan." *JMBRAS* 51, 1: 54-61.

Fang Hsiu (ed.)
1972 *Ma-hua hsin-wen-hsueh ta-hsi.* (Compendium of Malayan Chinese literature) Singapore: Shih-Chieh shu-chü, 10 vol.

Fang Hsui
1977 *Notes on the history of Malayan Chinese new literature 1920-1940.* Tokyo: The Centre for East Asian Cultural Studies. (East Asian Cultural Studies Series, No.18). (Abridged translation by Angus W. Macdonald of the original 3 vol. work published in Singapore, 1962-64).

Felix, Alfonso (ed.)
1966 *The Chinese in the Philippines 1550-1770.* Manila: Solidaridad.

Go Thean Chye
1975 *Modern Chinese literature in Malaysia and Singapore: a classified bibliography of books in Chinese.* Kuala Lumpur: Jabatan Pengajian Tionghoa Universiti Malaya. (In Chinese).

Gosling, L. A., Peter and Linda Y. C. Lim (eds.)
1983 *The Chinese in Southeast Asia.* 2 vols. Singapore: Maruzen Asia.

Hendrati, P. R
1975 *Daftar kepustakaan selekif tentang golongan etnis Tionghoa di Indonesia sejak 1945: laporan.* Jakarta: Lembaga Ekonomi dan Kemasyarakatan Nasional.

Ho Khai-Leong
1980 "Modern Chinese poetry in Malaysia." *Archipel* 19: 199-206.

South-East Asia

Ho Kuang-Chung
1967 "Chinese literature in South-East Asia." In F. S. Drake, ed. *Symposium on historical, archaeological and linguistic studies on Southern China, South-East Asia and Hong Kong region.* Hong Kong: Hong Kong University Press, pp. 300-305.

Ho Soo Miang
1979 "The earliest Chinese newspaper of Singapore — the Lat Pau (1881-1932)." *Journal of the South Seas Society* 34, 1-2: 1-100.

Hsieh Yu Yong
1964 *Tai-hua pao-yeh shih* (A short history of Thai-Chinese press). Bangkok: Tai-wei-hsin yin-wu-chü.

Hsü Yün-Ts'aio
1959 "Preliminary bibliography of Southeast Asian studies." *The Bulletin of the Institute of Southeast Asia.* Singapore: Nanyang University, vol.1. (In Chinese).
1965 "Supplement to the preliminary bibliography of Southeast Asian Studies." *Journal of Southeast Asian Researches*, vol.1. (In Chinese).

I Chün-Tso
1956 *Hua-ch'iao shih-hua* (Overseas Chinese poetry). Hong Kong.
1977 *Ssu-hai shih-hsin.* Taiwan: Chang-wu yin-chü.

Ibrahim bin Ismail
1982 "Missionary printing in Malacca 1815-1843." *Libri* 32, 3: 177-206.

Kwee, John B.
1977 *Chinese Malay literature of the Peranakan Chinese in Indonesia, 1880-1942.* Ph.D thesis, University of Auckland.

Lau Teik Soon
1976 "A bibliography on the Malaysian-Singapore Chinese." *Philippine Sociological Review* 24, 1-4: 81-91.

Lee Ju-Lin
1970 "A plea for the study of Nanyang Literature." *Journal of the South Seas Society* 25, 1: 54-68. (In Chinese).

Lent, J. A. (ed.)
1982 *Newspapers in Southeast Asia: contemporary trends and problems.* Hong Kong: Heinemann.

Liem Thian Joe
1939 "Soerat kabar hoeroef Tionghoa di Java." (Chinese newspapers in Java). *Sin Po weekly* 17, 847-49: 21-24; 8-10, 15-16.

Lim Buan Chay
1978 *Chung-kuo tso-chia tsai hsin-chia-p'o chi chi'i Yin hsiang 1927-1948* (Impact of Chinese writers during their stay in Singapore for the period 1927-1948). Singapore: Wan-li Shu-chü.

Lin Hsia-Sheng, et al.
1975   *Selat ku-chi* (Ancient remains of Singapore). Singapore: South Seas Society Monograph no. 13. (In Chinese).

Liu Tzu-Cheng
1966   "Publishing activities in Sarawak." *Journal of the South Seas Society* 20, 1-2: 1—12. (In Chinese).

Lu Wei Lin
1967   "Chinese education and press in Laos." *Journal of Southeast Asian Researches* 3: 40-42. (In Chinese).

Ly Singko
1967   *An anthology of modern Malaysian Chinese stories.* Singapore: Heinemann Educational Books.

Mackie, J. A. C. (ed.)
1976   *The Chinese in Indonesia.* Melbourne: Nelson.

Miao Hsiu
1966   *Ma-hua wen-hsueh shih-hua* (History of Malayan Chinese literature). Singapore: Ch'ing-nien ch'u-pan-she.

Miao Hsiu et al. (ed.)
n.d.   *Hsin-ma hua-wen wen-hsueh ta-hsi* (Compendium of new Malayan Chinese literature). Singapore: Chiao-yü chu-pan-she. 8 vols.

Nagelkerke, Gerald A.
1982   *The Chinese in Indonesia: a bibliography, 18th century-1981.* Leiden: Library of the Royal Institute of Linguistics and Anthropology.

Nevadomsky, J. J. and A. Li
1970   *The Chinese in Southeast Asia: a selected and annotated bibliography of publications in Western languages* 1960-1970. Berkeley: Center for South and Southeast Asian Studies, University of California (Occasional Paper, no. 6).

Oey, Giok Po
1953   *Survey of Chinese language materials on Southeast Asia in the Hoover Institute and Library.* Ithaca: Southeast Asia Program, Cornell University.

O'Sullivan, Leonora.
1984   "The London missionary society: a written record of missionaries and printing presses in the Straits Settlements 1815-1847." *JMBRS* 57, 2: 61-104.

Parichart Sukhum
1976   "The Chinese in Thailand: an annotated bibliography." *Philippine Sociological Review* 24, 1-4: 63-71.

Philips, C. H. (ed.)
1963 *Handbook of oriental history*. London: Royal Historical Society.

Purcell, V.
1965 *The Chinese in Southeast Asia*. London: Oxford University Press. 2nd rev. edn. (Reprinted 1980, Oxford in Asia).

Salmon, C. and D. Lombard
1974 "Les traductions de romans chinois en malais (1880-1930)." In P. B. Lafont and D. Lombard, eds. *Littératures contemporaines de l'Asie du Sud-est. (Colloque du XXIXe Congrès des Orientalistes.* Paris; Asiathèque, pp. 183-202.

Salmon, C.
1974 "Récentes études sur l'épigraphie chinoise en Asie du Sud-est." *Archipel* 8: 213-223.
1977 "Writings in romanized Malay by the Chinese of Malaya: a preliminary enquiry." *Kertas-Kertas penggian Tionghoa: Papers in Chinese Studies.* University of Malaya 1: 69-95.
1981 *Literature in Malay by the Chinese of Indonesia: a provisional annotated bibliography.* Paris: Editions de la Maison des Sciences de l'Homme. (Etudes Insulindiennes-Archipel, 3).
1983a "Recent studies on the literature in Chinese in Malaysia and Singapore." *Archipel* 25: 231-33.
1983b "Taoke or coolies? Chinese visions of the Chinese diaspora." *Archipel* 26: 179-210.

See Chinben
1972 *A bibliography of the Chinese in the Philippines.* Manila: Research division of the Pagkakaisa sa Pag-Unlad.

Shu, A. C. W. and W. W. L. Wan
1968 *Twentieth century Chinese works on Southeast Asia: a bibliography.* Honolulu: East-West Center.

Skinner, G. W.
1951 *Report on the Chinese in Southeast Asia.* Ithaca: Cornell University Southeast Asia Program.
1957 *Chinese society in Thailand: an analytical history.* Ithaca: Cornell University Press.

Somers-Heidues, M. F.
1974 *Southeast Asia's Chinese minorities.* Hawthorn, Victoria: Longmans.

Surydinata, Leo
1971 *The pre-World War II peranakan Chinese press of Java: a preliminary survey.* Athens, Ohio: Ohio University Center for International Studies.
1978a *Pribumi Indonesians, the Chinese minority and China: a study of perceptions and policies.* Kuala Lumpur: Heinemann Educational Books.

1978b *The Chinese minority in Indonesia: seven papers.* Singapore: Chopman Enterprises.

Surydinata, Leo (ed.)
1979 *Political thinking of the Indonesian Chinese 1900-1977.* Singapore: Singapore University Press (for Institute of Southeast Asian Studies).

Tan, A. S.
1972 *The Chinese in the Philippines, 1898-1935: a study of their national awakening.* Quezon City: Garcia Publishing Company.

Tan Yok Song
1958 *Nanyang ti-i pao-jen* (The first journalist of the South Seas). Singapore: Shih-chieh shu-chu.

Tay, B. H.
1973 *History of Chinese newspapers in Singapore 1881-1972.* Singapore: Hsin-ma ch'u-pan-she. (In Chinese).

Tay Lian Soo and Gwee Yee Hean
1975 *Chinese high school souvenir magazines of Malaysia and Singapore.* Kuala Lumpur: Jabatan Pengajian Tionghoa. (In Chinese).

Tay Lian Soo
1982 *Chinese culture in Malaysia and Singapore.* Singapore: South Seas Society Monograph No. 24 (vol. 1).

Thomas, Phillip L.
1986 *Like tigers around a piece of meat: the Baba style of dondang sayanag.* Singapore: ISEAS.

Uchida, N.
1960 *The overseas Chinese: a bibliographical essay based on the resources of the Hoover Institute.* Stanford: Hoover Institute.

Wang Gungwu
1959 *A short history of the nanyang Chinese.* Singapore: Eastern University Press.
1964 "A short introduction to Chinese writings in Malaya." In Wignesan, ed., *Bunga Emas: an anthology of contemporary Malaysian literature 1930-1963.* Kuala Lumpur, Rayirath Raybooks, pp. 249-56.
1978 *The Chinese minority in Southeast Asia.* Singapore: Chopman Enterprises. (Southeast Asia Research Paper, Nanyang University, Singapore Series 1).
1981 *Community and nation: essays on Southeast Asia and the Chinese.* Sydney: Allen and Unwin; Singapore: Heinemann.

South-East Asia

Weightman, G. H.
1959   *The Philippine Chinese: a cultural history of a marginal trading community*. Ithaca: PhD. thesis, Cornell University.

Wickberg, E.
1965   *The Chinese in Philippine life 1850-1898*. New Haven: Yale University Press.

Willmott, W. E.
1960   *The Chinese of Semarang: a changing minority community in Indonesia*. Ithaca: Cornell University Press.
1967   *The Chinese in Cambodia*. Vancouver: University of British Columbia.

Wong Seng Tong
1978   *The impact of China's literary movements on Malaya's vernacular Chinese literature from 1919 to 1941*. Madison: PhD thesis. University of Wisconsin.
1980   "The influence of China's literary movements on Malaysia's vernacular literature in the 1930's." *Tamkang Review* 10, 3-4: 517-34.

Wu Hua
1976   *Hsin-chia-p'o hua-wen chung-hsueh shi-lüeh*. (A brief history of Chinese secondary schools in Singapore). Singapore: Chiao-yü chu-pan-she.

Yang Sungnian and Chou Weichieh
1980   *Hsin-chai-p'o tsao-ch'i hua-wen pao-chang wen-i fu-k'an yen-chiu 1927-1930*. (Study of the literary supplements of the Chinese press in Singapore for the period 1927-1930). Singapore: Chiao-yü ch'u-pan-she.

Yangyong Jareeyapas
1976   "History of Chinese newspapers in Thailand." In *Chinese language newspapers and journals published in Thailand: history and bibliography*. Bangkok: National Library of Thailand. (In Thai).

Yong, C. F.
1977   *Chinese community structure and leadership in pre-war Singapore*. Singapore: South Seas Society Monograph no. 19. (In Chinese).

Yong, C. F. (ed.)
1981   "Ethnic Chinese in Southeast Asia." *Journal of Southeast Asian Studies*, special issue.

Yü Wang-Luen
1967   *Ma-hua wen-hsueh ti-hsing-ch'eng yü fa-chan* (The development of Malayan Chinese literature). Kuala Lumpur: M.A. thesis, Universiti Malaya.
1982   "Women writers of Malaysian Chinese literature." *Archipel* 24: 205-234.